The Rise of AI User Applications

Svetlana Bialkova

The Rise of AI User Applications

Chatbots Integration Foundations and Trends

 Springer

Svetlana Bialkova
Liverpool Business School
Liverpool John Moores University
Liverpool, UK

ISBN 978-3-031-56470-3   ISBN 978-3-031-56471-0 (eBook)
https://doi.org/10.1007/978-3-031-56471-0

This Springer imprint is published by the registered company Springer Nature Switzerland AG
The registered company address is: Gewerbestrasse 11, 6330 Cham, Switzerland

Paper in this product is recyclable.

To my mother Stanka
for her love, support, and inspiration

Preface

With the rise of artificial intelligence (AI) user applications, a gap emerges between algorithmic explanations and actionable understanding. This gap increased the demand to create AI agents demonstrating particular behaviour patterns and ecology, rather than just being engineering artefacts. To fill this shortage, the current book offers the very needed remediation of existing theories, a new read on how to build better AI systems to appropriately meet user needs and market demand.

Although AI is very attractive and popular as a topic, there is a literature gap and lack of practical guidelines on key drivers of agent efficiency and chatbot capacity. Furthermore, there is a caveat between algorithmic explanations and actionable understanding, despite the acknowledged importance of inherently human-centric property.

- How to design intelligent systems?
- How to face the limitations in human-AI design?
- How to augment the system intelligence?
- How to evaluate the (algorithmic) model fit?
- How to measure the system's efficiency and impact?

These queries are only part of the burning questions seeking appropriate answers. Serious industry investments and academic attention are dedicated to investigating AI behaviour and its impact on society and everyday life. Many researchers from various domains ranging from AI, UX, robotics, computer, and cognitive science to psychology, consumer, and marketing experts are looking for solutions. However, there is a need to understand the mechanisms underlying AI agency and to use this knowledge to propose designs that appropriately meet the demand for efficient systems.

The current book suggests a foundational conceptual work on agency efficiency, considering chatbots currently available on the market. Our work aims to organise in a systematic, data-driven approach the core parameters, and factors emerging from the literature. We further address AI system evaluation, a challenging issue requiring the development of suitable metrics and scales. Establishing a broad understanding, we provide the much-needed insight into the tendencies in paradigm shifts. Classifying existing theories in a taxonomy, we offer a novel view on their implementation and a framework of chatbot efficiency.

Literature audits are dispersed, either only in computers, robotics, engineering, and UX or in psychology, consumer, and marketing research. For the first time, hereby, the book offers an in-depth audit of all these domains. We consider this to be crucial for better understanding of AI systems. This overview is especially relevant because high precision lab studies often forget the human nature and users' needs. On the other hand, marketing practices may lack the cutting-edge AI techniques needed to face the increasing user demand for efficiently working systems and algorithmic architectures. Despite the technological advancement, the implementation of artificial intelligence in branding, advertising, and commerce is challenging. Part of the challenge reflects the efficiency of the systems created, although they enrich the collection of algorithms and techniques. While the majority of AI work focuses on ML models, a gap is emerging in terms of actual user needs and experience. Consumers are resistant to adoption and use of AI systems, such as chatbots, e-agents, and voice assistants. This gap requires a better understanding of consumers' needs and demands in regard to the design and implementation of appropriate chatbot technologies.

Put differently, technology development places the consumer at the heart of experience, i.e., a user-centred approach is not an AI algorithmic problem but rather a design challenge. Therefore, there is a need to find the right balance for AI systems between providing a human versus a machine interface. This is an emergent call to better understand the human-AI interface in order to design efficient AI applications.

AI systems are usually created to fulfil specific tasks within a particular domain. Regardless of the method used, the aim of AI is to achieve optimal performance in mimicking human behaviour. Not surprisingly, then, human behaviour is the core of developing new intelligent systems that mirror people's thoughts and feelings. Scientists try to translate these to machines, focusing on mathematical equations and algorithms. Individual AI behaviour considers the "cognitive" attributes of algorithms as well as the utility of using techniques from psychology in the study of machine behaviour. Naturally, engineers call for designing bot-specific characteristics inspired by human behaviour and user impact. Explainable AI (XAI) addressing the above aims at understanding the system and providing the very needed solutions.

Despite the call for a broad view necessary to explain in a holistic framework the system and the processing underlying its behaviours, the research is fragmented. Often addressed in various studies in a wide array of disciplines, experts lack the connections, speak different tech languages, and thus miss the core elements that may supply solutions for designing chatbots and AI agents that are well desired and thus accepted by the end user.

The current book embraces the above challenges in an attempt to provide the needed understanding of user demands, by defining the key drivers of chatbot efficiency and agency capacity. We address several gaps, by offering a distinctive combination of content, theory, practice evaluation, and a holistic framework that could be implemented in the design of intelligent systems to appropriately meet user needs and market demand. We offer a comprehensive view and recommendation to experts from the entire spectrum of academia busy with AI to join efforts in creating humanised AI applications to appropriately meet the user demand for adequate systems. The current book will benefit AI explanations and AI explanation user studies.

The work will cover the following three parts:

- **Evolution of Theory**
  A perspective from HCI, usability, computer science, cognitive science, psychology, and marketing will be provided, summing up the core terms in a taxonomy (Chaps. 1–3).

- **Key Drivers of Chatbot Efficiency—A Holistic Framework**
  We focus on the strengths and potential of the framework for designing AI systems to appropriately meet user demand for functional and enjoyable interaction (Chaps. 4–7).

- **Implementing New Generation Systems**
  Avenues for AI to transform business and life are discussed through the implementation of new generation of AI systems (Chaps. 8 and 9). XAI challenges, solutions, and future perspectives are presented as well (Chaps. 10–12).

The book is structured as follows:

Part I, *Evolution of Theory* builds the fundamentals with the theoretical background based on a detailed literature review that was conducted to determine potential factors that might play a role in AI agency performance and chatbot evaluation. We first performed a profound literature audit, providing an overview of classical theories (from HCI, UX, cognitive sciences, psychology, marketing, and consumer behaviour) and recent HCI-AI research, with the hope that the book will engage experts in an interdisciplinary endeavour.

Chapter 1, "Introduction to Chatbot AI Applications" presents the state of the art concerning the rise of AI applications and how this has changed the marketing landscape and everyday life in general. Chapter 2, "Audit of Literature on Chatbot Applications" offers an extensive exploration, summarising the core concepts and terms emerging from relevant previous research in a taxonomy. Chapter 3, "Core Theories Applied in Chatbot Context" enhances the theoretical foundation, providing a solid base to build around our conceptual framework.

The conceptual framework is presented in detail in PART II, *Key Drivers of Chatbot Efficiency—A Holistic Framework*. The factors emerging from the literature as key drivers of chatbot efficiency and agent performance have been tested in empirical work encompassing consumers who have actually used chatbots before.

Chapter 4, "Shaping Chatbot Efficiency—How to Build Better Systems?" explores the core parameters emerging as key drivers of chatbot efficiency. These parameters are examined in an empirical study in Chap. 5, "Chatbot Efficiency—Model Testing". To address our research goal, we invited a wide range of consumers to provide their opinion after the actual use of chatbots currently available on the

market. We looked at factors predetermining satisfaction, (positive) attitude formation, and thus the potential use and recommendation of a chatbot. The results from
a survey including consumers who have used chatbots in their daily life showed
that enhanced functionality and interactivity are pivotal factors leading to better
evaluation of chatbot quality and ease of use. Enjoyment also emerged to interplay
with quality evaluation and ease of use perception. The more positive the attitudes
toward the chatbot were, the higher was the intention to use and to recommend the
chatbot. Note that previous work often looked at cognitive and affective components
in isolation, while current research offers a holistic view, which is one of the core
contributions.

In Chap. 6, "Anthropomorphism—What Is Crucial?" we further zoom-in into the
factors that actually load on functionality and enjoyment. In particular, anthropomorphic and social aspects are highlighted. Chapter 7, "Chatbot Agency—Model
Testing" addresses the core parameters hypothesised to determine chatbot agency
in an empirical study investigating the opinions of consumers who have used a
chatbot at least once in their daily life. Based on the outcomes of the empirical
studies conducted, a holistic framework encompassing the parameters under investigation, i.e., cognitive, emotional, and social is suggested. The framework provides a
structure through which various relationships between constructs can be evaluated.
The framework could be implemented to design innovative AI systems that enhance
the consumer experience and transform businesses. The part concludes with toolkit
boxes that could be applied to measure AI performance and how it is perceived
by the end users. Implementing the toolkit at the prototyping stage and before the
launch of (new) chatbots to the market is expected to help AI system developers
and UX experts to anticipate pitfalls in design, and to elaborate better systems that
appropriately meet the user demand for functional and enjoyable chatbot AI agency.

PART III. *Implementing New Generation Systems* offers an overview of how
the implementation of new generation systems opens avenues for AI transformation. Chapter 8, "AI Connecting Business and Consumers" enumerates key channel
deployment and integration. It further explores the possibilities for AI agency
enhancement and autonomy. Note, however, that new AI system implementation
comes with some challenges. These are discussed in Chap. 9, "AI Transforming
the Business and Everyday Life". As emerging from the literature audit, as well
as confirmed by the empirical studies hereby, consumers who have used chatbots
currently available on the market but have not been satisfied with the agent's performance were resistant to future use. Current findings are a warning call to develop
appropriate AI technologies that may enhance the potential of chatbot implementation through improved functionality, interactivity, and lifted enjoyment. The book
provides the needed understanding and transparently communicates the priorities to
stakeholders on how to achieve such a desired design. Recommendations on how to
overcome consumer resistance toward AI systems and advice for policy measures
concerning risks regarding the AI boost are offered.

Chapter 10, "Data Management" conducts a deep dive into the core aspects and techniques in order to provide managerial solutions, especially given the enormous amount of data, variability, and lack of interpretability. Harmful behaviours in algorithmic systems are also discussed, and guidelines on how to possibly face the increasing demand for system transparency is suggested.

Chapter 11, "Explainable AI (XAI)" provides a classification of XAI properties and goals. We also discuss governing AI vs. AI governance, emerging as a serious issue, especially given the fast development of new-generation AI systems. Chapter 12, "Conclusion and Future Perspectives" summarises the final remarks, as well as offers further food for thoughts on what the future brings, recognising the current human-AI design and the long journey we embark on to make it better.

It is hoped that the current work will provide a clear and comprehensive picture of what was missing and where the most relevant research gaps are. We offer a holistic and structured framework that clearly maps out the extant literature in relation to the drivers and outcomes of chatbot adoption and usage. More emotionally intelligent bots, providing adaptive and smoother interactions with humans are required. Expected to replace human–human interactions in various everyday situations, they have to deliver a pleasant and valuable experience, to satisfy user needs, and to meet market demand. Filling these gaps, we elaborate on research from diverse disciplines to create a conceptual framework of chatbot agency in the context of AI-enabled marketing applications. The book could be seen as a manifesto to experts from HCI, AI, UX, computer and cognitive sciences, psychology, consumer, and marketing disciplines who want to work together in designing collaborative human-AI systems.

Liverpool, UK   Dr. Svetlana Bialkova

Contents

About the Author

Svetlana Bialkova is an internationally recognised expert, global professor, author, and speaker. She holds a Ph.D., Radboud University, The Netherlands, and a JSPS fellowship, BSI RIKEN, Japan. She received several awards and secured funding, including PI role. She taught various academic courses and has worked on numerous projects in top international labs in The Netherlands, Belgium, Germany, Denmark, Switzerland, UK, and Japan.

She explores the joint interaction between human, media, and technology, and how this influences the multisensory experience. Translating fundamental knowledge into practice, she realised several industry-related initiatives and projects with huge societal relevance. She also participated in various consortia advising policy implementation at EU level and across the globe.

List of Figures

List of Tables

Part I
Evolution of Theory

Chapter 1
Introduction to Chatbot AI Applications

Abstract Artificial intelligence (AI) applications are expected to revolutionise the traditional marketing space, tremendously changing business, and social life. Chatbots as one of these applications are forecasted to generate significant profit by substituting the manpower and thus are being increasingly implemented to speed up various business operations, to facilitate service provided, sales activities, and processes. Despite the recognised benefits and market profit, consumer resistance toward AI systems questions the ability of chatbots to justify the term intelligence. This is a challenging question inviting further investigation. The current chapter embraces this challenge providing an overview of how AI, and in particular chatbots change the marketing landscape. Defining the state of the art, we look at parameters characterising chatbot intelligence and efficiency. We zoom-in into potential factors determining consumers resistance toward chatbots currently available on the market. Our investigation reports an emergent demand to understand, create, and communicate in the way humans do, i.e., consumers still prefer a human agent front of chatbots. Such outcome is a warning call for human–computer interaction (HCI) research and User experience (UX) design to join efforts with psychology, consumer, and marketing expertise, in order to design and implement AI systems going beyond algorithmic explanation. Efficient AI systems are needed that appropriately meet the user request for high-quality chatbots satisfying their demand for enjoyable and functional interaction, offering an enhanced consumer journey.

1.1 The Rise of AI User Applications

Artificial intelligence commonly defined as the intelligence of machines or software, as opposed to the intelligence of humans attracted attention since centuries. Rigorous academic research is dated back in 1950s (e.g., Turing, 1950; McCarthy et al., 1955). In the last decade, AI enjoys massive attention and uprising. Predicted to change everyday life, the way business is done, society and the environment as a whole, AI uprise has been supported with great investments from various industries climbing from \$12 to \$97 billion in only 5 years (Statista, 2023).

Forecasted to add value to the global economy up to $4.4 trillion annually (McKinzey, 2023), AI applications are expected to revolutionise the traditional marketing, sales activities, and processes. With the prediction of doubled customer service interactions to be handled completely by chatbots, various AI systems are being continuously implemented and improved. Only in Europe, the Digital Decade target requires that more than 75% of EU companies adopt AI technologies by 2030 (DESI, 2022).

The high market and societal demand have led to observed increasing importance of human–computer interaction (HCI) research and User experience (UX) design. Having the potential to analyse big customer data in a timely and efficient manner, AI needs to demonstrate sufficient capabilities to justify the term intelligence. Making machines learn and think like humans was pointed out as a long-term goal of AI, a while ago (Zheng et al., 2017). Still, there is even an increasing demand to understand, create, and communicate in the way humans do. AI should be considered a tool allowing humans and machines to work better together (Li & Hilliges, 2021; Russell, 2019). Thus, the authors recommend that AI focus to be placed on mathematical equations, algorithms, and models to achieve the desired optimality.

From one side, exploring AI behaviour will help us understand how human behaviour will be shaped by the introduction of intelligent machines into everyday scenarios. In particular, it is vital to investigate how humans perceive the use of AI systems in various contexts, and thus whether and how the use of algorithms and machines is accepted. The degree to which human-like AI may produce or reduce discomfort in humans needs to also be taken into account.

From other side, we have to point out that humans are currently creating the AI systems. Therefore, engineering human-like AI mirrors the actual behaviour of people, and training AI systems based on direct data outcomes or passive observation of human performance is obvious. It is a human decision which algorithms to be selected and what feedback to be provided to the specific algorithms and mathematical models used. Hens, feedback loops between human influence on AI behaviour and the influence of AI on human behaviour need to be studied, especially in natural settings where algorithms are increasingly employed in decision making and in system training.

Generative AI, for example can learn from existing artefacts to generate new, realistic artefacts that reflect the characteristics of the training data without repeating it. Proven to produce a variety of novel content, in the form of images, video, text, speech, music, software code, and product designs, Gen AI is largely adopted by different industries, in various context applications (see Table 1.1. for an overview of Generative AI application). Due to the close nature and the training mode, however, GenAI is less understood than the conventional black box predictive models. Gen AI has more variety than predictions. There is built-in randomness. This is a serious challenge as it is difficult to create identical situation and translate/mirror analogical examples and scenarios.

Note, that the majority of AI systems operate, coexist, and interact with humans in hybrid and complex dynamic manners, and thus interchangeably machines shape human behaviour and vice versa. In this respect, a note of caution is needed. It is

Table 1.1 AI applications overview

AI gen	Text generation	Image generation	3D-object generation	Voice generation	Video generation
Applications	Chatbots	Art	Gaming	Text-to-speech	VR
	Content creation	Design	Architecture	Virtual assistant	AR
	Translation	Gaming	Design	Audiobook	Gaming
	Summary-Condense	Text-to-image	Medicine	Voice cloning	Entertainment
	Knowledge management	Data-augmentation			Education and training
		Ads and media			Advertising

still a challenge to directly examine how the interactions between various intelligent systems may vary their behaviour, as a function of the parameters altered during the engineering process. The interaction between AI systems may have subsequent impact on human behaviour in natural settings, and on society as a whole. Hence, the long-run dynamics of these hybrid entities should be examined, focusing on (human) social interactions and how these interactions are modified as a result of the implementation of intelligent systems.

Therefore, we could say that the rise of AI applications is of great interest for many stakeholders affected by algorithmic decisions, i.e., from business managers to end users through experts in different domains. The development of meaningful systems and explainable AI (XAI) based on user-centric design inspired not only UX experts, developers, annotators, and engineers, but also data science teams and human operator of the system, as well as involved consumer, marketing researchers, and regulatory bodies.

1.2   State of the Art

AI agents which use complex and simple algorithms for decision makings, we believe, cannot be well understood without exploring the behavioural context in which any action occurs, a largely ignored fact by researchers in computer science and robotics. The everyday and social environment in which any algorithm operates needs to also be studied, especially given that the technological development leads to a shift in paradigms and the reshaping of human–human/human-AI interactions, and thus the formation of relationships that alter the environment, society, and life itself. Considering the complexity of human-AI interactions, several challenges have emerged, which at the same time open the most intriguing area of study.

To construct effective AI systems, practitioners need to understand the design from a human perspective. Furthermore, a historical overview can provide path dependence, explaining otherwise puzzling behaviour. At each step, aspects of the algorithms are reused in new scenarios, facilitating performance, shaping behaviour, and opening avenues for future innovations. Algorithms may embody certain features and ignore others depending on the success rate the AI applications demonstrate. As a result, of quality and robustness, particular machine behaviour may spread across applications and contexts.

Flexibility in algorithms and the purpose they are created will further determine how their inheritance system is changing. Therefore, a wide array of research has focused on developing new algorithms that possess both performance advantages and interpretable properties (for an overview see Arrieta et al., 2020; but see also Guidotti et al., 2018; Liao and Varshney, 2021). The large number of explainable AI (XAI) and AI explanation user studies demonstrate the desire of scientists to understand and to build better systems. See Fig. 1.1 for AI approach pyramid, summing up the core methods currently used.

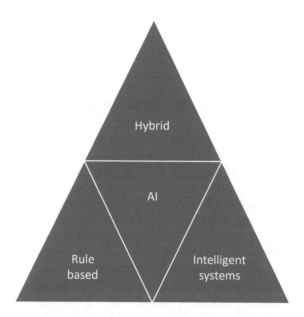

Fig. 1.1 AI approach pyramid

Furthermore, there is a move to develop systems that can learn new things without requiring explicit programming, having ambitions to match and exceed every aspect of human intelligence. These tendencies are very much inspired by the need for verification and improvement of the AI systems, learning from these systems, as well as to comply with legislation. Contestability, empowerment and redressing information asymmetries, control over system performance, evaluation of individual algorithmic results, and public administration transparency are only part of the purpose of XAI. Resulting from legal requirements, as suggested in a recent report (Maxwell & Dumas, 2023) on combining legal and human–computer interaction (HCI) approaches, the need to achieve meaningful algorithmic explainability was acknowledged.

XAI studies started to address the above issues in an attempt to understand the system's underlying mechanisms, as well as to provide the very needed solutions. However, experts should join efforts to face the open challenges for AI systems. For example, training processes with neural networks may result in deviation due to impaired parameters, or damaged values that are difficult to correlate with correct results. Furthermore, small changes in data sets might reflect a dramatic change in interpretation, thus leading the system to mismatch information and to generate wrong decision with fatal subsequences, i.e., in autonomous driving, finance market loss, and health care. System evasion (adversary) attacks may also lead to such vulnerability, which calls emergent exploration and thus to advising measures on how to preclude possible harmful, unexpected, and undesired AI behaviour. Methods involving XAI research are vital not only for explaining the system's behaviour to users, but also for suggesting reliable technology and encouraging the development of guidelines, including at the policy level how to best employ AI.

1.3 How AI Changes the Marketing Landscape

The benefit for companies of reducing labour and spending has fostered the implementation of Artificial Intelligence (AI) by many organisations across the globe (International Federation of Robotics, 2020). Chatbots being one of these software applications are used to conduct online chat conversations via text or text-to-speech (e.g., Kramer et al., 2009). AI-based chatbots vary depending on the approaches employed, i.e., rule-based, ML-based, or hybrid AI.

AI can reflect various aspects of the chatbot context by incorporating different techniques and data processing methods. For example, a script might be written by humans to aid chatbot(s) in what they should say and provide solutions following an algorithm. Chatbots could also react in a more natural way, having the "freedom" to track conversation, selecting from vocabulary and responding accordingly (for an overview, see Miao et al., 2022). Currently, chatbots are mainly text-based and are sometimes mixed with graphical user interface (GUI) components, such as buttons and informational elements. By combining advanced technologies that include natural language processing (NLP), machine learning, cloud computing, and biometrics, this new generation of AI is a frontline service provider different from human customer service as well as self-service technology (SST). Most importantly, collecting and handling large amounts of consumer data, AI-based systems are supposed to boost market intelligence, customer journey, and business impact.

Known also as e-service (e.g., Chen et al., 2022) conversational agents (for a review see Lim et al., 2022; Mariani et al., 2023), they are often involved in substituting the direct contact with a live human agent (e.g., Chung et al., 2020; Lee & Choi, 2017), to provide information to buyers (e.g., Qiu & Benbasat, 2009), and to facilitate the customer services (e.g., Lou et al., 2022).

Chatbots are increasingly adopted by various organisations in different industries and contexts, ranging from banking (Belanche et al., 2019; Fares et al., 2022; Hari et al., 2022; Trivedi, 2019), telecommunications (Nupoor & Cata, 2021), media and entertainment (Lee & Choi, 2017; Sajjadi et al., 2019; Zarouali et al., 2018), retail and shopping (Chung et al., 2020; De Cicco et al., 2020; Kannan et al., 2023; Ma & Sun, 2020), travel, tourism, and hospitality (Bigné, 2023; Buhalis, 2020; Jiménez-Barreto, et al., 2021, 2022), to education (Mayer et al., 2003; Keiper et al., 2023), and health care (Laranjo et al., 2018).

The tasks or activities also cover a large variety, e.g., from credit score algorithms driving loan decisions; online price-shaping algorithms that navigate consumers toward specific products and offers; social media bots influencing opinions; VR agents advising children in the learning process, or agents helping elderly people and providing healthcare assistance, to home bots performing regular household

Table 1.2 Key industries, relevant academic papers, and examples from marketing practices (branded applications)

Industry	References (academic)	Branded Applications
Automotive	Medeiros et al. (2023)	Hey, Mercedes voice commander Fiat Chrysler (Amazon Echo) NVIDIA drive concierge Harley Davidson
Banking, finance, stock market	Belanche et al. (2019), Fares et al. (2022), Hari et al. (2022), Trivedi (2019)	MasterCard KAI MasterCard chatbot Credit score algorithms
Education	Mayer et al. (2003), Keiper et al. (2023)	AJE Editing Service Duolingo Grapheme Keeko robot teaching at kindergarten (China case)
Cosmetics and beauty	Whang et al. (2022)	L'Oréal using AI for social listening HelloAva Sephora
Fashion	Chung et al. (2020), Landim et al. (2022)	Burberry Emma (FB messenger in Zalando) Louis Vuitton ZARA carruseles Sephora Virtual artist
Food and beverage	De Cicco et al. (2020)	Domino Pizza Deep Brew McCormick foods using IBM Watson ManyChat Nestlé nutrition assistant Starbuck's Whole Foods Market Uber eats-optimise delivery
Health care	Laranjo et al. (2018), Huang and Ki (2023),	Atlas Babylon Health IBM Watson for medical diagnosis
Media and entertainment	Lee and Choi (2017), Sajjadi et al. (2019), Zarouali et al. (2018),	Cinebot (ticket reservation) Disney + Netflix content personalisation Spotify-Discover weekly

(continued)

Table 1.2 (continued)

Industry	References (academic)	Branded Applications
Retail and shopping real-time sales tracker personalisation	Chung et al. (2020), De Cicco et al. (2020), Kannan et al. (2023), Ma and Sun (2020)	Google Dialogflow Walmart IKEA eBay Amazon
Sport and leisure	Keiper et al. (2023)	Google AlphaGo NBA Score
Telecommunication	Nupoor and Cata (2021)	IZZI—Odido **Magenta**—Deutsche Telekom Verizon
Tourism and hospitality	Bigné (2023), Bigné et al. (2021), Bialkova (2023d), Buhalis (2020), Buhalis and Cheng (2020), Pereira et al. (2022), Pillai and Sivathanu (2020)	TripAdvisor Airbnb Booking.com TUI
Transport and travel	Jiménez-Barreto et al. (2021, 2022)	AIR NZ-Oscar Google Kayak KLM SnapTravel

tasks and machines mapping our everyday life. See Table 1.2 for a summary of key industries with relevant academic references, and leading marketing applications.

1.4   The Chatbots Breakthrough

We have to point out hereby that chatbots have been recognised as a promising marketing communication tool decades ago (Holzwarth et al., 2006). Surprisingly, however, the technology is still in its infancy, encountering several challenges (Bialkova, 2021, 2022a, 2022b).

Research investigating chatbot efficiency is also challenging, because it aims to more concisely and accurately measure the actual use. One may argue that chatbots are known to be highly efficient. However, this does not mean that chatbot applications created by high precision labs and operating with superspeed and with great intelligence are functional, useful, efficient, and able to satisfy user needs and market demand. Chatbot AI agency has emerged as a substantial research area, calling for investigation into user experience, design, and implications.

Although explanation was acknowledged to be rooted in inherently human-centric property, and the field is starting to embrace human-centred approaches (Liao & Varshney, 2021; Steels, 2022; Xu et al., 2021), there is a caveat between algorithmic explanations and actionable understanding. A clear, holistic, and comprehensive picture, however, is missing on what has been researched and where the most relevant research gaps are.

Current work addresses the above challenges by identifying actionable solutions. To provide a much-needed understanding on key drivers of chatbot efficiency, we closely inspect parameters hypothesised to reflect, respectively, consumer satisfaction, attitudes, future use, and recommendations of chatbots. Another important contribution is that we perform a detailed study about the actual use of and interactions with chatbots, which is very rare. Note that in prior research, mostly lab studies were performed to test mock-ups, and thus lacked the actual user experience. Therefore, to operationalise the human-centred perspectives in AI algorithms, there is a need to include assessment methods that better account for the user evaluation, real needs, and actual demand when interacting in different downstream usage contexts. Hereby, we present such a comprehensive methodology based on data from real market applications.

We take into account that the evolution of AI-based machine behaviour mirrors the user demand and the human behaviour itself. Naturally, some of the most intriguing questions concern the ways in which the introduction of intelligent systems into social systems can alter human beliefs and behaviours. Not surprisingly, then, various studies have started to look at attitudes toward these new technologies.

1.4.1 Attitudes Toward Chatbots

Attitudes toward technology have been recognised to predetermine the intention to use and the actual system use, a long time ago by the Technology Acceptance Model, TAM (Davis et al., 1989). However, understanding why users accept or reject a technology has proven to be one of the most challenging issues. Part of the challenge reflects the wide array of various attitudes and satisfaction metrics that have been employed, often lacking adequate justification. A further challenge is to determine the factors loading on attitudes formation and change in regard to chatbots.

Current investigation is especially relevant because, from the service marketing literature, it is acknowledged that customers who are satisfied with the service agent performance form positive attitudes (Zeithaml et al., 1996), they are returning and are very likely to recommend the service, brand, or company (Bettencourt, 1997). In the same vein, in the retailing literature it has been well documented that when a salesperson meets the customer expectations, this reflects customer satisfaction and the consequent behaviour (Ramsey & Sohi, 1997) in terms of favourable purchase intentions and positive word of mouth (Reynolds & Arnold, 2000; Reynolds & Beatty, 1999). From human–computer interaction literature, however, was reported that when a chatbot reacts differently than the user expects, this can be considered as an error (Chaves & Gerosa, 2021), changing the user perspective and thus possibly precluding chatbot acceptance (de Sa Siqueira et al., 2023).

Therefore, the question hereby is whether chatbots currently available on the market provide a satisfactory experience, leading to positive attitudes and thus acceptance.

1.5 Why Consumers Are Resistant?

Chatbots have not been necessarily accepted by the end users (Choi, 2021; Ben Mimoun et al., 2017), despite their increasing integration and enhanced AI incorporation in marketing. Such resistance to chatbots acceptance is an emergent call to better understand consumers' needs and demands when it comes to the development and implementation of appropriate technologies for assembling machine learning, natural language processing, and reasoning. Providing such understanding is crucial for the way practices evaluate the outputs of various AI algorithms, and thus, may be a game-changer in shaping the field's progressive future.

Although recent papers have highlighted the urgency of studying how quality is shaped when customer services are provided by chatbots, the outcomes are not consistent (Lou et al., 2022). The system readiness has also been questioned in a few studies (Flavián et al., 2021; Huang & Rust, 2018). Furthermore, a disclosure of chatbot identity before the machine–customer conversation was reported to even reduce purchase rates by more than 79% (Luo et al., 2019). Despite the recognised benefit that AI-driven agents might improve customer relationship management (Libai et al., 2020), the quality of consumer choice (Xiao & Benbasat, 2007) and engagement (Yang et al., 2022) through personalised recommendation, consumers are resistant toward these new technologies. Launching good quality chatbots, satisfying consumer needs and demands turns to be a challenge (Bialkova, 2021, 2023a).

How communication quality modulates customer services expected to be provided by chatbots (Chung et al., 2020), and how service quality determines chatbot adoption (Flavián et al., 2021) were addressed recently in laboratory studies, reporting positive outcomes. Although there is no doubt that e-service quality must be smooth, satisfying, timely, effective, and accurate (Zeithaml et al., 2002), in reality, such communication might not necessary be the case. Some studies questioning the chatbot quality perception have expressed controversial views (Chen et al., 2022; Lou et al., 2022). Other researchers even have not been able to show a direct effect of involvement on recommendation quality, defined as the extent to which recommended products fit the wishes and desires of consumers, and the perceived usefulness of the agent as productivity outputs (Ben Mimoun et al., 2017). The above findings invite further investigations into chatbot efficiency and future use.

There is a need for a structured framework that clearly maps out extant literature in relation to the drivers and outcomes of chatbot adoption and usage. More emotionally intelligent bots, providing adaptive and smoother interactions with humans are required (Bialkova, 2023b, 2023c). Expected to replace human–human interactions in various everyday situations, they have to deliver a pleasant and valuable experience to satisfy user needs and to meet market demand. Filling these gaps, we elaborate on the research from diverse disciplines to create a conceptual framework of chatbot agency in the context of AI-enabled marketing applications.

To understand how to build better systems, we first look at the literature, enrolling a profound audit of existing papers and relevant work. The theoretical notions are the fundaments to build our conceptual framework on chatbot efficiency and agent capacity. This framework we test in empirical studies, exploring the opinion of consumers who have used a chatbot at least once in their daily life. With this approach, we believe it is crucial to shed light on chatbot efficiency currently available on the market, and therefore, to develop well-informed solutions on the factors shaping quality and ease of use, emerging from the literature audit as key drivers of attitudes toward chatbot(s) and the intention to use them in future.

The theoretical background is provided in the next Chap. 2 (Bialkova 2024), and the empirical framework is addressed in Part II of the current book.

References

Arrieta, A. B., Díaz-Rodríguez, N., del Ser, J., Bennetot, A., et al. (2020). Explainable Artificial Intelligence (XAI): Concepts, taxonomies, opportunities and challenges toward responsible AI. *Information Fusion, 58,* 82–115.

Belanche, D., Casaló, L. V., & Flavián, C. (2019). Artificial Intelligence in FinTech: Understanding robo-advisors adoption among customers. *Industrial Management & Data Systems, 119*(7), 1411–1430.

Ben Mimoun, M. S., Poncin, I., & Garnier, M. (2017). Animated conversational agents and e-consumer productivity: The roles of agents and individual characteristics. *Information & Management, 54*(5), 545–559. 43.

Bettencourt, L. A. (1997). Customer voluntary performance: Customers as partners in service delivery. *Journal of Retailing, 73*(3), 383–406.

Bialkova, S. (2021). Would you talk to me? The role of chatbots in marketing. In *ICORIA2021,* June 26–28, in Bordeaux, France.

Bialkova, S. (2022a). How may I help you? Chatbots implementation in marketing. In *European marketing academy conference, EMAC2022,* May 24–27, in Budapest, Hungary.

Bialkova, S. (2022b). *Interacting with Chatbot: How to enhance functionality and enjoyment?* AEMARK2022, 7–10 September 2022. Valencia, Spain.

Bialkova, S. (2023a). I want to talk to you: Chatbot marketing integration. *Advances in Advertising Research, (Vol. XII, pp. 23–36),* https://doi.org/10.1007/978-3-658-40429-1_2

Bialkova, S. (2023b). AI-driven customer experience: Factors to consider. In *Philosophy of artificial intelligence and its place in society* (pp. 341–357). IGI Global.

Bialkova, S. (2023c). How to optimise interaction with Chatbots? Key parameters emerging from actual application. *International Journal of Human-Computer Interaction.* https://doi.org/10.1080/10447318.2023.2219963.

Bialkova, S. (2023d). I need your help: Key parameters guiding satisfaction with chatbots. In *European marketing academy conference, EMAC2023*, 23–26 May 2023, Odense, Denmark.

Bialkova, S. (2024). Audit of literature on chatbot applications. In *The rise of AI user applications: Chatbots integration foundations and trends*. (Chap. 2). Springer. https://doi.org/10.1007/978-3-031-56471-0_2.

Bigné, E. (2023). Artificial intelligence in tourism. In Moutinho et al (Eds.), *Philosophy of artificial intelligence and its place in society* (pp. 98–115). IGI Global.

Bigné, E., Nicolau, J. L., & William, E. (2021). Advance booking across channels: The effects on dynamic pricing. *Tourism Management, 86*, 104341.

Buhalis, D. (2020). Technology in tourism-from information communication technologies to eTourism and smart tourism towards ambient intelligence tourism: A perspective article. *Tourism Review, 75*(1), 267–272.

Buhalis, D., & Cheng, E. S. Y. (2020). Exploring the use of Chatbots in hotels: Technology providers' perspective. In J. Neidhardt & W. Wörndl (Eds.), *Information and communication technologies in tourism 2020*. Springer.

Chaves, A. P., & Gerosa, M. A. (2021). How should my chatbot interact? A survey on social characteristics in human-chatbot interaction design. *International Journal of Human-Computer Interaction, 37*(8), 729–758.

Chen, Q., Gong, Y., Lu, Y., & Tang, J. (2022). Classifying and measuring the service quality of AI chatbot in frontline service. *Journal of Business Research, 145*, 552–568.

Choi, Y. (2021). A study of employee acceptance of artificial intelligence technology. *European Journal of Management and Business Economics, 30*, 318–330.

Chung, M., Ko, E., Joung, H., & Kim, S. J. (2020). Chatbot e-service and customer satisfaction regarding luxury brands. *Journal of Business Research, 117*, 587–595.

Davis, F. D., Bagozzi, R. P., & Warshaw, P. R. (1989). User acceptance of computer technology: A comparison of two theoretical models. *Management Science, 5*(8), 982–1003.

De Cicco, R., Silva, S. C., & Alparone, F. R. (2020). Millennials' attitude toward chatbots: An experimental study in a social relationship perspective. *International Journal of Retail & Distribution Management, 48*(11), 1213–1233.

de Sa Siqueira, M., Muller, B. C., & Bosse, T. (2023). When do we accept mistakes from chatbots? The impact of human-like communication on user experience in chatbots that make mistakes. *International Journal of Human–Computer Interaction.*

DESI. (2022). *Digital economy and society index (DESI) 2022 | Shaping Europe's digital future* (europa.eu). Last Accessed January 15, 2024.

Fares, O. H., Butt, I., & Lee, S. H. M. (2022). Utilization of artificial intelligence in the banking sector: A systematic literature review. *Journal of Financial Services Marketing*, 1–18.

Flavián, C., Pérez-Rueda, A., Belanche, D., & Casaló, L. V. (2021). Intention to use analytical artificial intelligence (AI) in services–the effect of technology readiness and awareness. *Journal of Service Management, 33*(2), 293–320.

Guidotti, R., Monreale, A., Ruggieri, S., Turini, F., Giannotti, F., & Pedreschi, D. (2018). A survey of methods for explaining black box models. *ACM Computing Surveys, 51*(5), Article 93.

Hari, H., Iyer, R., & Sampat, B. (2022). Customer brand engagement through Chatbots on bank websites—Examining the antecedents and consequences. *International Journal of Human-Computer Interaction, 38*(13), 1212–1227.

Holzwarth, M., Janiszewski, C., & Neumann, M. M. (2006). The influence of avatars on online consumer shopping behavior. *Journal of Marketing, 70*(4), 19–36.

Huang, M. H., & Rust, R. T. (2018). Artificial intelligence in service. *Journal of Service Research, 21*(2), 155–172.

Huang, M., & Ki, E. J. (2023). Examining the effect of anthropomorphic design cues on healthcare Chatbots acceptance and organization-public relationships: Trust in a warm human Vs. a competent machine. *International Journal of Human–Computer Interaction, Advance online publication*, 1–13.

International Federation of Robotics (2020).

Jiménez-Barreto, J., Rubio, N., Mura, P., Sthapit, E., & Campo, S. (2022). Ask Google assistant where to travel tourists' interactive experiences with smart speakers: An assemblage theory approach. *Journal of Travel Research, 62*(4), 734–752.

Jiménez-Barreto, J., Rubio, N., & Molinillo, S. (2021). Find a flight for me, Oscar! Motivational customer experiences with chatbots. *International Journal of Contemporary Hospitality Management, 33*(11), 3860–3882.

Kannan, P. K., Yang, Y., & Zhang, K. (2023). Unlocking deeper insights into customer engagement through AI-powered analysis of social media. *Data Management and Business Review, 3*(1 & 2).

Keiper, M. C., Fried, G., Lupinek, J. M., & Nordstrom, H. E. (2023). Artificial intelligence in sport management education: Playing the AI game with ChatGPT. *Journal of Hospitality, Leisure, Sport & Tourism Education, 23*, Article 100456.

Kramer, N. C., Bente, G., Eschenburg, F., & Troitzsch, H. (2009). Embodied conversational agents. *Social Psychology, 40*(1), 26–36.

Landim, A. R. D. B., Pereira, A. M., Vieira, T., Costa, E. de B., Moura, J. A. Wanick, B. V., & Bazaki, E. (2022). Chatbot design approaches for fashion E-commerce: An interdisciplinary review. *International Journal of Fashion Design, Technology and Education, 15*(2), 200–210.

Laranjo, L., Dunn, A. G., Tong, H. L., Kocaballi, A. B., Chen, J. A., Bashir, R., Surian, D., Gallego, B., Magrabi, F., Lau, A. Y., & Coiera, E. W. (2018). Conversational agents in healthcare: A systematic review. *Journal of the American Medical Informatics Association: JAMIA, 25*, 1248–1258.

Lee, S., & Choi, J. (2017). Enhancing user experience with conversational agent for movie recommendation: Effects of self-disclosure and reciprocity. *International Journal of Human-Computer Studies, 103*, 95–105.

Li, Y., & Hilliges, O. (2021). *Artificial intelligence for human computer interaction: A modern approach, book preface, Human–Computer interaction series.* Springer.

Liao, Q. V., & Varshney, K. R. (2021). *Human-centered explainable AI (XAI): From algorithms to user experiences.* https://arxiv.org/abs/2110.10790.

Libai, B., Bart, Y., Gensler, S., Hofacker, C. F., Kaplan, A., Kötterheinrich, K., & Kroll, E. B. (2020). Brave new world? On AI and the management of customer relationships. *Journal of Interactive Marketing, 51*, 44–56.

Lim, W. M., Kumar, S., Verma, S., & Chaturvedi, R. (2022). Alexa, what do we know about conversational commerce? Insights from a systematic literature review. *Psychology & Marketing, 39*, 1129–1155.

Lou, C., Kang, H., & Tse, C. H. (2022). Bots vs. humans: How schema congruity, contingency-based interactivity, and sympathy influence consumer perceptions and patronage intentions. *International Journal of Advertising, 41*(4), 655–684.

Luo, X., Tong, S., Fang, Z., & Qu, Z. (2019). Frontiers: Machines vs. humans: The impact of artificial intelligence chatbot disclosure on customer purchases. *Marketing Science, 11*, 1–11.

Ma, L., & Sun, B. (2020). Machine learning and AI in marketing—Connecting computing power to human insights. *International Journal of Research in Marketing, 37*(3), 481–504.

Mariani, M., M., Hashemi, N., & Wirtz, J. (2023). Artificial intelligence empowered conversational agents: A systematic literature review and research agenda. *Journal of Business Research, 161*, 113838.

Mayer, R. E., Sobko, K., & Mautone, P. D. (2003). Social cues in multimedia learning: Role of speaker's voice. *Journal of Educational Psychology, 95*(2), 419–425.

Maxwell, W., & Dumas, B. (2023). *Meaningful XAI based on user-centric design methodology.* Combining Legal and Human-Computer Interaction (HCI_Approaches to Achieve Meaningful Algorithmic Explainability. Centre on Regulation in Europe (CERRE).

Medeiros, T., Medeiros, M., Azevedo, M., Silva, M., Silva, I., & Costa, D. G. (2023). Analysis of language-model-powered Chatbots for query resolution in PDF-based automotive manuals. *Vehicles., 5*(4), 1384–1399.

McCarthy, J., Minsky, M. L., Rochester, N., and Shannon, C. E. (1955). A Proposal for the Dartmouth Summer Research Project on Artificial Intelligence, August 31, Retrieved from https://www-formal.stanford.edu/jmc/history/dartmouth/dartmouth.html.

McKinzey. (2023). https://www.mckinsey.com/mgi/overview/in-the-news/ai-could-increase-cor porate-profits-by-4-trillion-a-year-according-to-new-research Last Accessed January 15, 2024.

Miao, F., Kozlenkova, I. V., Wang, H., Xie, T., & Palmatier, R. W. (2022). An emerging theory of avatar marketing. *Journal of Marketing, 86*(1), 67–90.

Nupoor, R., & Cata, A. (2021). Intelligent algorithms: Evaluating the design of Chatbots and search. *Technical Communication, 68*(2), 22–40.

Pereira, T., Limberger, P. F., Minasi, S. M., & Buhalis, D. (2022). New insights into consumers' intention to continue using Chatbots in the tourism context. *Journal of Quality Assurance in Hospitality & Tourism.*

Pillai, R., & Sivathanu, B. (2020). Adoption of AI-based chatbots for hospitality and tourism. *International Journal of Contemporary Hospitality Management, 32*(10), 3199–3226.

Qiu, L., & Benbasat, I. (2009). Evaluating anthropomorphic product recommendation agents: A social relationship perspective to designing information systems. *Journal of Management Information Systems, 25*(4), 145–181.

Ramsey, R., & Sohi, R. S. (1997). Listening to your customers: The impact of perceived salesperson listening behavior on relationship outcomes. *Journal of the Academy of Marketing Science, 25*, 127–137.

Reynolds, K. E., & Arnold, M. J. (2000). Customer loyalty to the salesperson and the store: Examining relationship customers in an upscale retail context. *Journal of Personal Selling & Sales Management, 20*, 89–98.

Reynolds, K. E., & Beatty, S. E. (1999). Customer benefits and company consequences of customer-salesperson relationships in retailing. *Journal of Retailing, 75*, 11–32.

Russell, S. (2019). *Human compatible: Artificial intelligence and the problem of control.* Viking.

Sajjadi, P., Hoffmann, L., Cimiano, P., & Kopp, S. (2019). A personality-based emotional model for embodied conversational agents: Effects on perceived social presence and game experience of users. *Entertainment Computing, 32*, Article 100313.

Statista. (2023). *Total global AI investment 2015–2022.* Statista. Last Accessed January 15, 2024.

Steels, L. (Ed.). (2022). *Foundations for meaning and understanding in human-centric AI.* Published by Venice International University.

Trivedi, J. (2019). Examining the customer experience of using banking Chatbots and its impact on brand love: The moderating role of perceived risk. *Journal of Internet Commerce, 18*(1), 91–111.

Turing, A. M. (1950). Computing machinery and intelligence. *Mind, 59*(236), 433–460.

Whang, J., Song, J. H., Lee, J., & Choi, B. (2022). Interacting with Chatbots: Message type and consumers' control. *Journal of Business Research, 153*, 309–318.

Xiao, B., & Benbasat, I. (2007). E-commerce product recommendation agents: Use, characteristics, and impact. *MIS Quarterly, 31*(1), 137–209.

Xu, W., Dainoff, M. J., Ge, L., & Gao, Z. (2021). Transitioning to human interaction with AI systems: New challenges and opportunities for HCI professionals to enable human-centered AI. *International Journal of Human-Computer Interaction, 39*, 494–518.

Yang, Y., Zhang, K., & Kannan, P. K. (2022). Identifying market structure: A deep network representation learning of social engagement. *Journal of Marketing, 86*(4), 37–56.

Zarouali, B., Van den Broeck, E., Walrave, M., & Poels, K. (2018). Predicting consumer responses to a Chabot on Facebook. *Cyberpsychology, Behavior, and Social Networking, 21*(8), 491–497.

Zeithaml, V. A., Berry, L. L., & Parasuraman, A. (1996). The behavioral consequences of service quality. *Journal of Marketing, 60*, 31–46.

Zeithaml, V. A., Parasuraman, A., & Malhotra, A. (2002). Service quality delivery through web sites: A critical review of extant knowledge. *Journal of the Academy of Marketing Science, 30*(4), 362–375.

Zheng, N. N., Liu, Z. Y., Ren, P. J., et al. (2017). Hybrid-augmented intelligence: Collaboration and cognition. *Frontiers Information Technology & Electronic Engineering, 18*, 153–179.

Chapter 2
Audit of Literature on Chatbot Applications

Abstract Making sophisticated software applications economically feasible does not necessarily mean that user needs and demands are met in regard to chatbots (Bialkova 2021, 2022a). Creating chatbots that consumers are willing to use is not an easy task. In particular, understanding the key drivers of chatbot efficiency, reflecting in consumer satisfaction, attitudes, use, and recommendation of a chatbot, calls further investigation. The current chapter aims to provide a profound literature audit in order to identify the key drivers of chatbot efficiency. First, the evolution of research on chatbot applications is discussed, in line with different industries and contexts, ranging from banking, telecommunications, retail, travel, and tourism, to education and health care. The main emerging trends are summarised in a thematic map, raising fundaments to build our theoretical framework. The literature audit encompassed research on human–computer interaction and usability, cognitive science and psychology, as well as consumer behaviour and marketing papers. This multidisciplinary approach provides the opportunity to generate an overarching picture that could be used to better understand what are the ingredients needed to build efficient chatbot AI applications. The core theoretical notions are organised around three main pillars: acceptance models, behavioural theories, and social influence theories. Fundamental concepts from cognitive (e.g., quality, functionality), affective (e.g., enjoyment), and social (e.g., personal care, social presence) perspectives are presented in a holistic framework.

2.1 Evolution of Research in Chatbot Marketing Applications

AI end-user applications have attracted significant amount of scholarly attention in AI and HCI (for a review see, Arrieta et al., 2020; Guidotti et al., 2018; Russell & Norvig, 2022), usability (for a review, see Borsci et al., 2022; Ren et al., 2019), and marketing literature (for a review, see Lim et al., 2022; Landim et al., 2022; Loureiro et al., 2021; Mariani et al., 2023; Mustak et al., 2021). In all of these bibliometric

Table 2.1 Thematic map (factors in alphabetical order)

Core components (AI chatbots)			
Utilitarian (cognitive)	Hedonic (emotional)	Social	Effect/Outcome

• Accuracy
• Competence
• (perceived) Control
• Credibility
• Ease of use
• Engagement
• Functionality
• Informativeness
• Interactivity
• Privacy risk/
  concern
• Trust
• Quality
• Usefulness
	• Attractiveness
	• Coolness
	• Cuteness
	• Desire
	• Enjoyment
	• Empathy
	• Pleasure
		• Anthropomorphism
		• Human-likeness
		• Agent disclosure
		  (human/bot)
		• Human voice
		  (human/bot)
		• Parasocial interaction
		• Personal care
		• Self-expressiveness
		• Social cognition
		• Social influence
		• Social norm
		• Social presence
			• Attitudes
			• Acceptance
			• Adoption experience
			• Performance
			  expectancy
			• Purchase intent
			• Satisfaction
			• Recommendation
			• Use (intention/
			  actual)

analyses, it was reported an increased number of articles published over the past decade.

Despite the enormous number of previous papers, there is a lack of systematic reading, a taxonomy of core factors and fundamental theories. Therefore, what is crucial in the current context is to look at the key theories, conceptual models, and parameters that have been explored in previous work. Such a systematic overview will be a cornerstone to build around our theoretical model. Another important note, we hereby focus on the body of literature pertaining to AI-enabled chatbots as a whole and not as a subset. This methodological approach will allow us to consciously avoid reviews encompassing only a subsample, instead of the entire population.

For the purpose of the current book, a detailed auditing of the literature has been performed on AI and chatbots. Three main pillars emerged, i.e., utilitarian (cognitive), hedonic (affective/emotional), and social factors as predictors of the effect of AI on consumer behaviour, see Table 2.1 for a summary.

We have a close look at each of the pillars as described in Table 2.1. Respectively, we start with the key effects as a result of the interaction with chatbots/AI systems. In the following, we provide the details, and a summary is presented in Table 2.2.

2.2   Acceptance and Use (Outcomes Evaluation)

Attitudes were explored in almost all of the studies audited in the current review. Defined as "beliefs about an object/person" evaluated (Expectancy value model), affected the intention to behave and actual behaviour, considered as "individual's feelings about the performed behaviour" (see Theory of Planned Behaviour, TPB, Ajzen, 1991), attitudes are extensively addressed toward technology (Ashfaq et al.,

Table 2.2 Effect on user response

Effect		
Construct	Definition	References
Attitudes toward chatbot	Attitudes defined as "beliefs about an object/person" are evaluated (Expectancy value model), affecting the intention to behave and actual behaviour; "individual's feelings about the performed behaviour" Theory of Planned Behaviour (TPB), see Ajzen (1991)	Ashfaq et al. (2021), Balakrishnan and Dwivedi (2021), Bialkova (2021, 2022b, 2023a, 2023e), Pitardi and Marriott (2021), Poushneh (2021b)
Attitudes toward brand	See above	Roy and Naidoo (2021)
Experience	A multidimensional construct that involves cognitive, emotional, behavioural, sensorial, social components, Schmitt (1999), but see also Lemon and Verhoef (2016)	Bawack et al. (2021), Bialkova (2019, 2022c, 2023d), Fernandes and Oliveira (2021) , Guerreiro and Loureiro (2023)
Satisfaction	Occurs when customers find that products or services meet or exceed their positive expectations	Bialkova (2022b, 2023a, 2023b, 2023e), Chaves and Gerosa (2021), Chung et al. (2020), Chopra (2019), de Sa Siqueira et al. (2023), Gelbrich et al. (2021), Poushneh (2021b)
Acceptance	Acceptance, adoption, and usage of a system, See Technology Acceptance Model, TAM, Davis et al. (1989), Venkatesh (2000)	Ben Mimoun et al. (2017), Choi (2021), Fernandes and Oliveira (2021), Meyer-Waarden et al. (2020), Rese et al. (2020)
Adoption Intention	See above	Kowalczuk (2018), Vimalkumar et al. (2021)
Motivation to use Motivation to adopt and use	Motivation paradigms and Gratification Theory (Katz original work as of 1959; but for overview see Katz et al., 1973)	Chopra (2019), McLean and Osei-Frimpong (2019)
Intention to USE–> actual Use	TAM (Davis et al., 1989)	Blut et al. (2021), Bialkova (2021, 2023a, 2023e), Landim et al. (2022), Moriuchi (2021), Pillai and Sivathanu (2020)

(continued)

Table 2.2 (continued)

Effect

Construct	Definition	References
Actual use	Using system/product/ services	Bialkova (2023a, 2023b, 2023c), Pillai and Sivathanu (2020)
Stickiness	The intention of user to continue using	Pillai and Sivathanu (2020)
Behaviour intent	In terms of adoption	Kowalczuk (2018)
Purchase intent	Intention to purchase product/ service	Roy and Naidoo (2021), Luo et al. (2019)
Recommendation	Spreading positive word of mouth	Bialkova (2021, 2022b, 2023a, 2023e)

2021; Balakrishnan & Dwivedi, 2021; Bialkova, 2023a; Pitardi and Marriot, 2021; Poushneh, 2021b), and toward brand/company (Bialkova & Barr, 2022; Roy & Naidoo, 2021). A positive attitude toward chatbots was a prerequisite for the future use (Bialkova, 2022b, 2023e; Pitardi & Marriott, 2021) and recommendation (Bialkova, 2021, 2023a) of the system used. Attitudes toward chatbots were modulated by various utilitarian (cognition related) and hedonic (emotion related) factors, as enumerated in the next sections. Some studies also noted the role of social factors in shaping attitudes toward chatbots (Bialkova, 2022b, 2023e).

Experience. As part of the core objectives, we are interested in determining what is the experience consumers have with AI and chatbots. Experience is defined as a multi-dimensional construct that involves cognitive, emotional, behavioural, sensorial, and social components (Schmitt, 1999; but see also Lemon & Verhoef, 2016). Although experience is crucial in shaping acceptance, not many studies have explored actual experience with chatbots. Usually, studies address mock-ups and lab experimentation. However, few studies have investigated construct experience in line with prior experience (Bawack et al., 2021; Fernandes & Oliveira, 2021; Guerreiro & Loureiro, 2023). There is also an emerging tendency to look at the experience after actual use of chatbots currently available on the market (Bialkova, 2023a). Experience is closely related to consumer satisfaction.

Satisfaction. Occurs when customers find that products or services meet or exceed their positive expectations and is explored in various domains. From retailing, we know that consumers are satisfied when salespersons meet their expectations (Ramsey & Sohi, 1997). In service marketing, it was noted that consumers who are satisfied with service quality have favourable intentions (e.g., Zeithaml et al., 1996, 2002). Satisfaction is a key predictor of acceptance of technology (e.g., Wixom & Todd, 2005), and acceptance of the system used (e.g., Chaves & Gerosa, 2021). Not surprisingly then, satisfaction has been addressed in numerous studies, with various scales and approaches (e.g., Chopra, 2019; Chung et al., 2020; Gelbrich et al., 2021; Poushneh, 2021b). Nevertheless, when consumer expectations are not met (Chaves & Gerosa, 2021) chatbot acceptance may be precluded (de Sa Siqueira et al., 2023).

This is presumably due to the fact that some of the factors turn into barriers, but this is a warning call to reconsider chatbots currently available on the market (Bialkova, 2023b, 2023c).

Acceptance and Use. Positive attitudes and lifted satisfaction led to the intention to use, the actual use, acceptance, and adoption of technology, as we know from marketing classics. The acceptance, adoption, and usage of a system was addressed in several studies, in various contexts, since the introduction of the Technology Acceptance Model, TAM (Davis et al., 1989). In the chatbot context, the majority of the papers in our literature audit explore acceptance, and the factors predetermining it. Acceptance (or respectively rejection) of the AI system is also important for the future relationship between the customer and the brand, i.e., in terms of product purchases (Luo et al., 2019; Roy & Naidoo, 2021), recommendation, i.e., spreading positive word of mouth (Bialkova, 2021, 2023a), and brand advocacy (Bialkova, 2022c, 2023d). As acknowledged in the marketing literature, any brand wants to maintain a sustainable relationship with its customers. In this respect, AI could play a crucial role.

What is much more interesting hereby is what the factors driving the above effects are. We look at these factors, namely cognitive, emotional, and social, as emerging from the audit of the literature. Details are discussed in the next section, and Fig. 2.1 presents the taxonomy of AI agency, encompassing the classification of core chatbot characteristics and the respective human response.

2.3 Cognitive Evaluation

The utilitarian (mainly in the marketing literature) also referred to as cognitive (mainly in the psychology and HCI literature) components are presented in detail below and summarised in Table 2.3.

Quality reflects the (system) success. In the chatbot context, it was addressed as information and communication quality (measuring semantic success), system quality (measuring technical success), and service quality (measuring organisational impact and effectiveness success), for an overview see Trivedi, 2019 (based on DeLone and McLean, 2003). The quality of the advice from the online agent was also acknowledged as a factor for system adoption (Wang and Benbasat, 2016). Naturally, quality has been addressed in variety of studies (Ashfaq et al., 2020; Bialkova, 2021, 2022a; Chung et al., 2020; Chen et al., 2022; Kowalczuk, 2018; Lou et al., 2022; Xiao & Benbasat, 2007). Although it has been recognised as a core factor in chatbots and AI evaluation (Bialkova, 2023a), the authors noted that in reality, the currently existing marketing applications may lack the quality required and expected by consumers. Moreover, some laboratory studies testing mock-ups have reported that chatbot quality hardly meets consumer demand (Ben Mimoun et al., 2017; Meyer-Waarden et al., 2020; Wirtz et al., 2018). These outcomes call for further investigation into how to improve the quality of chatbot and AI systems.

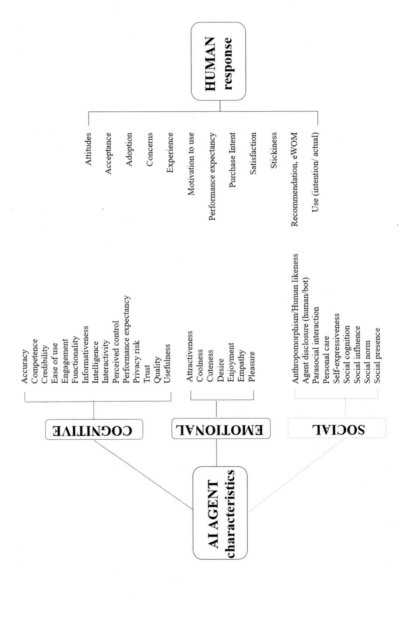

Fig. 2.1 Taxonomy of core agent characteristics and respective human response

Table 2.3 Cognitive determinants as emerging from the literature audit

Cognitive determinants

Factor	Definition	References
Quality	Reflects the (system) success, For an overview in the context of chatbots, see Trivedi (2019), but also DeLone and McLean (2003) for a general overview in information system success	Ashfaq et al. (2020), Bialkova (2021, 2022a, 2023a), Ben Mimoun et al. (2017), Chung et al. (2020), Kowalczuk (2018), Lou et al. (2022), Meyer-Waarden et al. (2020), Xiao and Benbasat (2007), Wang and Benbasat (2016), Wirtz et al. (2018)
Ease of use	Reflecting the degree to which the user expects the tech system to be free of effort (Davis et al., 1989)	Ashfaq et al. (2020), Bialkova (2021, 2023a, 2023b, 2023e), Blut et al. (2021), Balakrishnan and Dwivedi (2021), Chopra (2019), Fernandes and Oliveira (2021), Kowalczuk (2018), Meyer-Waarden et al. (2020), Pitardi and Marriott (2021), Rese et al. (2020)
Functionality	Associated with a correct technical functioning, Parasuraman et al. (2005), but see also Davis et al. (1989)	Ashfaq et al. (2021), Ben Mimoun et al. (2017), Bialkova (2021, 2022b, 2023a, 2023b, 2023c), Chattaraman et al. (2019), Fernandes and Oliveira (2021), Lee and Cho (2020), Pitardi and Marriott (2021)
Competence	Effective in accomplishing what was set out to do, See Spitzberg (2006) for overview on Computer-Mediated Communication Competence	Blut et al. (2021), Bialkova (2023b, 2023c), Chopra (2019), Cheng and Jiang (2021), Chung et al. (2020), Edwards et al. (2014), Meyer-Waarden et al. (2020), Pitardi and Marriott (2021), Roy and Naidoo (2021), Wang and Benbasat (2016)
Accuracy	Precision of the system	Arrieta et al. (2020), Bialkova (2023c), Guidotti et al. (2018), Chung et al. (2018), Cheng and Jiang (2021)
Intelligence Functional intelligence	The ability to acquire and apply knowledge and skills	Pillai and Sivathanu (2020), Poushneh (2021b)
Informativeness	Reflects the quality of information (Delone and McLean, 1992)	Arrieta et al. (2020), Ashfaq et al. (2020), Bialkova (2022b, 2023b, 2023c), Trivedi (2019)
Control	People's perception of the ease or difficulty of performing the behaviour of interest (Ajzen, 1991)	McLean and Osei-Frimpong (2019), Poushneh (2021b), Pillai et al. (2020), Tassiello et al. (2021)

(continued)

Table 2.3 (continued)

Cognitive determinants

Factor	Definition	References
Effort expectancy	The degree of ease associated with the use of the system (Venkatesh et al. 2003)	Moriuchi (2021)
Performance expectation	One's desire to be in control and able to predict his or her surroundings (valid for performance expectation and effort expectation)	Moriuchi (2021), Vimalkumar et al. (2021)
Usefulness	The degree to which a person believes that using a particular system would enhance his or her job performance (Davis et al. 1989) Useful = capable of being used advantageously	Balakrishnan and Dwivedi (2021), Ben Mimoun et al. (2017), Blut et al (2021), Fernandes and Oliveira (2021), Kowalczuk (2018), Meyer-Waarden et al. (2020), Pillai and Sivathanu (2020), Pitardi and Marriott (2021), Rese et al. (2020), Zarouali et al. (2018)
Engagement	Reflects the degree of involvement (Bialkova & van Gisberge 2017) and absorption (Sundar et al. 2016) with technology	Moriuchi (2021), Lin and Wu (2023), Tsai et al. (2021)
Interactivity	Emphasised role of interaction between the user and the system	Ben Mimoun et al. (2017), Bialkova (2023a), Fernandes and Oliveira (2021), Go and Sundar (2019), Holzwarth et al. (2006), Poushneh (2021a, 2021b), Sundar et al. (2016)

Ease of use is one of the core components of the Technology Acceptance Model, TAM (Davis et al., 1989), and not surprisingly then, it was addressed in a large number of papers (Balakrishnan & Dwivedi, 2021; Bialkova, 2023a; Blut et al., 2021; Chopra, 2019; Fernandes & Oliveira, 2021; Kowalczuk, 2018; Pitardi & Marriott, 2021; Rese et al., 2020). Note that some of the researchers have not been able to substantiate the effect of ease of use on satisfaction (e.g., Ashfaq et al., 2020), or on the intention to (re)use chatbots (e.g., Meyer-Waarden et al., 2020). Unfriendly user interfaces and poor cryptic designs were reported to cause even dissatisfaction, which reflected in disappointment, frustration, exhaustion, and annoyance (Pan et al., 2023).

The degree of ease associated with the use of the system (Venkatesh et al., 2003) was separately addressed as **effort expectancy** (Moriuchi, 2021). Effort expectation and performance expectation fulfil the definition of one's desire to be in control and able to predict his or her surroundings. Human performance is guided by two types of control mechanisms: (1) top-down, reflecting executive, goal-directed, endogenous, conscious control; and (2) bottom-up, also defined as automatic, stimulus-driven, exogenous, and subconscious (for an overview see Bialkova, 2008). **Performance expectation** was specifically explored in relation to trust in voice assistance systems (Vimalkumar et al., 2021).

Usefulness derives from the word useful "capable of being used advantageously" and is a core component of the TAM (Davis et al., 1989). Defined as "the degree to which a person believes that using a particular system would enhance his or her job performance" (Davis, 1989), usefulness has been broadly investigated by studies from the literature audit reported hereby (e.g., Balakrishnan & Dwivedi, 2021; Blut et al., 2021; Fernandes & Oliveira, 2021; Kowalczuk, 2018; Pillai and Sivathanu, 2020; Pitardi & Marriott, 2021; Rese et al., 2020; Zarouali et al., 2018, 2021). Note, however, that some works have not been able to confirm the hypothesised relation between quality and the perceived usefulness of the agent (Ben Mimoun et al., 2017), neither relationship between chatbot competence and its usefulness (Meyer-Waarden et al., 2020). In the chatbot context, not surprisingly then, many studies have addressed the possibilities of how to improve the service quality (Chen et al., 2022), usability (de Sa Siqueira et al., 2023), and reliability of the system used (e.g., Araujo, 2018).

Functionality associated with a correct technical functioning (Parasuraman et al., 2005) was suggested to encompass ease and usefulness of the system, functional, and interface characteristics (TAM, Davis et al., 1989). In the context of chatbots, functionality has been extensively explored (Ashfaq et al., 2021; Ben Mimoun et al., 2017; Bialkova, 2023a; Chattaraman et al., 2019; Lee & Cho, 2020; Fernandes & Oliveira, 2021; Pitardi & Marriott, 2021). Enhanced effectiveness and e-consumer productivity were reported during online purchases, when a virtual agent was employed in website communication (Ben Mimoun et al., 2017). A chatbot being functional in resolving client issues immediately is recognised by the consumers, and they are very likely to gravitate toward this technology, as reported in service market scenarios (Moriuchi et al., 2020). Recent studies from our laboratory have also acknowledged the importance of functionality in chatbot end-user evaluation (Bialkova, 2021, 2023a, 2023e).

Competence studied earliest in the context of Computer-Mediated Communication (for an overview see Spitzberg, 2006), logically, was investigated in the robots (Edwards et al., 2014; Yagoda and Gillan (2012); and chatbots applications (Bialkova, 2023b, 2023c; Blut et al., 2021; Chopra, 2019; Chung et al., 2020; Meyer-Waarden et al., 2020; Pitardi & Marriott, 2021; Roy & Naidoo, 2021). The stimulation of positive attitudes and feelings of trust toward technology were acknowledged when competent AI agency was realised by the chatbot in use (Pitardi & Marriott, 2021). Trust in AI (Chopra, 2019) was also reported when the online service agents exhibited accurate and competent communication. Furthermore, competent chatbots lift customer satisfaction (Chung et al., 2020), and thus navigate the customer-brand relationship (Cheng & Jiang, 2022). Competence associated with human-like behaviour was hypothesised to mediate the intention to use the bot (Blut et al., 2021). Surprisingly, however, recent work was not able to statistically substantiate the correlation between chatbot competence and usefulness (Meyer-Waarden et al., 2020).

Accuracy is the trueness and precision of the measurement method and results (ISO 5725). Hereby, we define accuracy as the precision of the system (Bialkova, 2023c). It has been extensively examined in the usability literature. In the AI context, accuracy is associated with the extent to which the model accurately predicts unseen instances (Guidotti et al., 2018) and is measured by the accuracy score, which reflects the number of correct answers divided by the total number of questions (Huysmans et al., 2011). In the context of chatbot end-user applications, it was hypothesised to reflect the precision of the marketing information provided (Cheng & Jiang, 2021). Despite the enormous number of definitions and measuring scales used with respect to the environments/scenarios the accuracy is assessed, ensuring timely and adequate e-agency is a prerequisite for accurate performance. Accuracy was therefore associated with proper agent functioning (Bialkova, 2023c).

Informativeness measures the quality of information. It was associated with the semantic success of the technology (Delone and McLean, 1992).Machine learning (ML) models have been suggested to extract huge amount of information (Arrieta et al., 2020), to provide adequate information and knowledge to the user, in order to sort out particular problem(s). In the context of chatbots, it was assumed that high informativeness impacts the chatbots' capability to provide timely, sufficient, and relevant information (Trivedi, 2019). The authors further noted positive experiences with enriched informativeness. Recent studies have also acknowledged the role of informativeness in modulating functionality (Bialkova, 2023c), and thus, in shaping satisfaction when interacting with chatbots (Bialkova, 2022b, 2023b).

Perceived control was recognised as essential factor to increase consumer confidence (Hoffman & Novak, 1996) in using technology (Dabholkar, 1996; Venkatesh, 2000). In the chatbot and Voice Assistance (VA) context, several authors have explored the role of control (McLean & Osei-Frimpong, 2019; Poushneh, 2021b; Pillai et al., 2020; Tassiello et al., 2021).Yet, the debate is still open and sensitive to what extent the agent could be autonomous or controlled. We dedicate a special discussion on this intriguing question in Chap. 11 (Bialkova, 2024g).

Engagement reflects the degree of involvement (Bialkova & van Gisbergen, 2017) and absorption (Sundar et al., 2016) by technology. The need to maintain engagement, enjoyment, trust, and productivity was recognised a long time ago in the human–computer interaction literature (Bickmore & Picard, 2005). In the context of chatbots, it was studied in line with anthropomorphism (Moriuchi, 2021) and social interaction (Lin & Wu, 2023; Tsai et al., 2021).

Interactivity definitions vary, but almost all of these emphasised the role of interaction between the user and the system (Bialkova, 2023a, 2023b). Interactivity has been addressed in many of the studies included in the current literature audit, since the infancy of chatbot implementation (e.g., Fernandes & Oliveira, 2021; Go & Sundar, 2019; Holzwarth et al., 2006; Ben Mimoun et al., 2017; Poushneh, 2021a, 2021b; Sundar et al., 2016). While some of the papers looked at the human–computer interaction, others especially zoomed-in into the chatbot agency interactivity (e.g., interface, communication characteristics). When individuals interact more easily with a technological system, they will perceive greater efficacy, as reported by the TAM (Davis et al., 1989). Furthermore, enhanced online interaction was claimed to offspring sense of connection between the user and the company offering the chatbot agency (Ben Mimoun et al., 2017). As a result, attitudes and consequent user behaviour were reshaped. Note also, that from psychology, we know that there is an interactional causal structure determining the agency of persons/ humans (Bandura, 1989), i.e., a reciprocal causation determined by action, cognitive, affective, and other personal factors, and environmental events. We discuss in detail human-like behaviour in the section Anthropomorphism.

2.4 Affective Evaluation

Concerning the affective aspects, hedonic known also as emotional components are discussed below (see Table 2.4, for a summary).

Attractiveness is usually associated with having a pleasant visual appearance. In the context of robots, chatbots and AI systems having an attractive voice was also pointed out. Aesthetics (and social appeal) have also been recognised as crucial for lifting attractiveness in human–computer interactions (Sundar et al., 2014), toward new high-tech environments such as AR (Bialkova & Barr, 2022) and VR (Bialkova, 2023b). In the context of chatbots, attractiveness has been addressed in several papers (Ashfaq et al., 2021; de Gennaro et al., 2020; Holzwart et al., 2006; Lou et al., 2022; Miao et al., 2022; McLean & Osei-Frimpong, 2019).

Enjoyment is a core effect (Russell, 2003) reflecting happiness, and is likely the most desirable emotion, often employed by marketers to boost purchases. Linked to pleasurable experience, it was addressed to study attitudes toward technology (Dabholkar & Bagozzi, 2002) and adoption of technology, a long time ago (Davis

Table 2.4 Affective components as emerging from the literature audit

Emotional determinants		
Factor	Definition	References
Attractiveness	Aesthetic and social appeal, Sundar et al. (2014) Having a pleasant visual appearance, an attractive voice	Ashfaq et al. (2021), de Gennaro et al. (2020), Holzwart et al. (2006), Lou et al. (2022), Miao et al. (2022), McLean and Osei-Frimpong (2019),
Enjoyment	Arising from connection or sensory pleasure, and often associated with happiness (Paul Ekman, Atlas of Emotions)	Ashfaq et al. (2020), Bialkova (2021, 2022a, 2022b, 2023a), Kowalczuk (2018), Landim et al. (2022), Lee and Choi (2017), Pillai et al. (2020), Pitardi and Marriott (2021), Rese et al. (2020), Xu et al. (2022), Zarouali et al. (2018),
Empathy	Comprehension of another person's emotions and feelings, Liu and Sundar (2018)	de Gennaro et al. (2020), Liu and Sundar (2018), Liu-Thompkins et al. (2022)

et al., 1989). Enjoyment was claimed to further enhance the ease of use perception (Venkatesh, 2000) and liking of the technology used (Bialkova, 2019, 2022c). Logically then, in the chatbot literature, it was addressed in line with attitudes (Bialkova, 2022a, 2023a; Pitardi & Marriott, 2021), future use intentions (Bialkova, 2022b, 2023e; Lee & Choi, 2017; Rese et al., 2020) and shopping intention in AI-powered retail (Pillai et al., 2020). Pleasurable experiences when interacting with chatbots result in positive attitudes toward the brand (Bialkova, 2022a) and positive attitudes toward the chatbot (Pitardi & Marriott, 2021). Interactional enjoyment was acknowledged to mediate the relationship between user satisfaction and intention to use a chatbot (Lee & Choi, 2017; Rese et al., 2020).

Empathy reflects the comprehension of another person's emotions and feelings (Liu & Sundar, 2018). Demonstrating empathy seems to be favoured over unemotional robots (Liu & Sundar, 2018) and chatbot AI (de Gennaro et al., 2020; Liu-Thompkins et al., 2022) and computational modelling in general (for an extensive review, see Yalçın & DiPaola, 2020).

Note that all of the above components are associated with human emotions. A reasonable question arises hereby whether AI has feelings. A recent study, however, claimed that AI can think but cannot feel (Bakpayev et al., 2022). This is a very interesting issue worth further attention, and possibly research when it comes to XAI (challenges).

2.5 Social Components

Social agency (of AI systems, robots, etc.) has been extensively explored since the earliest research on human–computer interaction (see Table 2.5 for a summary).

Anthropomorphism from the Greek words anthropos (for man) and morphe (form/structure). It is associated with AI system having human-like behaviour, communication style, and interfaces. Although some philosophical views argue that superintelligent AI systems may not necessarily exhibit anthropomorphic motivation and human beliefs (Bostrom, 2012), AI systems, especially chatbot agents are designed and expected to behave in a human-like manner. Therefore, many researchers dedicated investigation on anthropomorphism of chatbots and AI systems (e.g., Blut et al., 2021; Chaves & Gerosa, 2021; Chong et al., 2021; Fernandes & Oliveira, 2021; Grazzini et al., 2023; Guerreiro & Loureiro, 2023; Lim et al., 2022; Liu-Thompkins et al., 2022; Miao et al., 2022; Pillai & Sivathanu, 2020; Qiu & Benbasat, 2009; Tsai et al., 2021).

Personal care reflects the need for personal attention, understanding, and empathy. Adding personal touch to e-services was acknowledged to reflect social presence (Gefen & Straub, 2003). It further shapes consumer satisfaction, as it has been well documented in the service marketing literature (Parasuraman et al., 2005; Zeithaml et al., 2002). The researchers pointed out the need for personalisation, as it may have a beneficial role for the advancement of the service provided.

Table 2.5   Social determinants as emerging from the literature audit

Social determinants

Factor	Definition	References
Anthropomorphism Human-likeness	Having human-like behaviour; Communication style; Interfaces	Adam et al. (2021), Araujo (2018), Balakrishnan and Dwivedi (2021), Bickmore and Picard (2005), Blut et al. (2021), Chaves and Gerosa (2021), Chong et al. (2021), de Sa Siqueira et al. (2023), Fernandes and Oliveira (2021), Go and Sundar (2019), Guerreiro and Loureiro, (2023), Lim et al. (2022), Liu-Thompkins et al. (2022), Liu and Sundar (2018), Lu et al. (2016), Miao et al. (2022), Moriuchi (2021), Munnukka et al. (2022), Pillai and Sivathanu (2020), Poushneh (2021b), Qiu and Benbasat (2009), Roy and Naidoo (2021), Sheehan et al. (2020), Sundar et al. (2016), Tsai et al. (2021), Zarouali et al. (2018, 2021)
Personal care	Requiring human touch, e.g., personal attention, seeking understanding, and empathy, Parasuraman et al., (2005), Zeithaml et al. (2002)	Bickmore and Picard (2005), Bialkova (2022b, 2023c), Cheng and Jiang (2021), Miao et al. (2022)
Social presence	A sense/feeling of being with another in a mediated environment, Biocca et al. (2003)—see for an overview, but see also Lombard and Ditton (1997)	Ben Mimoun et al. (2017), Bialkova (2022b, 2023b), Blut et al. (2021), Fernandes et al. (2021), de Sa Siqueira et al. (2023), Go and Sundar (2019), Gelbrich et al. (2021), Feine et al. (2019), Jain et al. (2022), Landim et al. (2022), Lee et al., (2005, 2006), Liu-Thompkins et al. (2022), Lu et al. (2016), McLean and Osei-Frimpong (2019), Munnukka et al. (2022), Pitardi and Marriott (2021), Qiu and Benbasat (2009), Tsai et al. (2021), Xu et al. (2022)
Social cognition	Social Cognitive Theory Bandura's original work as of 1977 (for details see Bandura, 1989), For details see section Social Cognitive Theory	Chong et al. (2021), Pitardi and Marriott (2021), Mariani et al. (2023)
Social (influence)	Degree to which an individual perceives that important others believe that he or she should use the new system (Venkatesh et al., 2003) (for details see social influence Theory)	Loureiro et al. (2021), Moriuchi (2021), Vimalkumar et al. (2021)

(continued)

Table 2.5 (continued)

Social determinants		
Factor	Definition	References
Subjective social norm	Subjective norm reflects what significant others might think of one's actions (Ajzen, 1991)	Fernandes and Oliveira (2021), McLean and Osei-Frimpong (2019), Wirtz et al. (2018)

Recent work in the AI context has already mentioned that personalisation (Greene & Shmueli, 2023; Lopes & Cavique, 2023) is important for lifting customers social engagement (Yang et al., 2022). In the chatbot context, better interaction, customisation, and thus direct effects on consumer-brand relationships were also reported when the service agent offered to customers individual attention and care (Cheng & Jiang, 2021). Enhanced purchase intent was associated with agent social response (e.g., social presence, personalisation) and enjoyable interaction with an avatar exhibiting anthropomorphic features (Miao et al., 2022).

Social presence was defined as "sense of being with another in a mediated environment" (Biocca et al., 2003). In Biocca's terms, a virtual environment can submerge the perceptual system of the user. Social presence can be achieved through a mediated environment (Tu, 2000; Witmer & Singer, 1998). According to earlier definition, presence is the degree to which the medium facilitates awareness of the other person (Fulk et al., 1987). It refers to the extent to which a medium is perceived as sociable, warm, sensitive, personal, or intimate when it is used to interact with other people (Lombard & Ditton, 1997). Some recent studies in the chatbot context have associated social presence with the degree of salience of the other person in the interaction (Go & Sundar, 2019), presumably due to the nature of the study, namely anthropomorphic, human-like chatbot features. The authors recognised the facilitating role of chat agents when interacting with other people (i.e., social presence) without physical co-presence. Nevertheless, social presence reflects the sense of human contact, warmth, or sociability (Ben Mimoun et al., 2017). Associated with human-like behaviour, social presence was hypothesised to modulate purchase intent Lu et al., 2016), attitudes (Pitardi & Marriott, 2021), trust (Qiu & Benbasat, 2009; Tsai et al., 2021), privacy concerns and use (Xu et al., 2022). In the context of robots, social presence has been addressed in both, cognitive, i.e., functional (Lee et al., 2005), and emotional, i.e., enjoyment (Lee et al., 2006) human-like aspects. In the chatbot context, however, some studies have not been able to demonstrate improved social presence due to human-like features (de Sa Siqueira et al., 2023).

Social cognition postulates a central role of cognitive processes in social interactions. We discussed hereby in detail Social Cognitive Theory (see Chap. 3, Bialkova, 2024a) and in line with the key theories implemented in the chatbot application. In the current context, it has been applied in terms of competence (Pitardi & Marriott, 2021), warmth and effectiveness (Roy & Naidoo, 2021), agency (Chong et al., 2021), social interactions, and experiences (Mariani et al., 2023). Note however, warmth and competence are the two fundamental dimensions of social perception that drive peoples' responses to specific interactions (Fiske et al., 2007). Put differently, we could say that both cognitive (e.g., competence) and affective (e.g., warmth) aspects are reflecting social perception.

Social influence is also discussed hereby in detail (see section Social Influence Theory, Chap. 3, Bialkova, 2024a) in line with the key theories implemented in the chatbot context. In the tech context, it has been defined as the degree to which an individual perceives that important others believe that he or she should use the new system (Venkatesh et al., 2003). In fact, this definition reflects the notion of "subjective norm", as suggested in the Theory of Planned Behaviour, TPB (Ajzen, 1991). Social influences (in terms of subjective norm, voluntariness, and image) have been reported to enhance acceptance of technology (Venkatesh & Davis, 2000) and thus have been addressed in various tech applications. It was reported that despite the awareness that users have that they are interacting with computers, they tend to respond socially, as they would do when interacting with humans (Nass & Moon, 2000). Similarly, this tendency was observed for social robots (Loureiro et al., 2021), chatbots (Moriuchi, 2021), and voice assistants, VA (Vimalkumar et al., 2021).

Subjective social norm reflects the notion of subjective norm, i.e., what significant others might think of one's actions (Ajzen, 1991). It is acknowledged in the literature as **Normative Social Influence** and has utilitarian nature. It was studied in line with the acceptance (Fernandes & Oliveira, 2021) and adoption (McLean & Osei-Frimpong, 2019) of new technologies based on the general assumption that people choose to take action if they know that this is accepted by society and referents, also known as to conformity. People conform to enhance their social status and to make them appear important within their peer groups.

Note, however, that in the HCI context, the direct effect of subjective norm on behavioural intention for system usage was reported to be voluntary (Venkatesh & Davis, 2000). In this respect, we have to point out hereby the need for AI systems to display appropriate behaviour. The demonstration of appropriate actions and "emotions" according to societal norms has already been questioned in the context of robots (Wirtz et al., 2018). This is a very important issue, that is worth attention, especially given the increasing concerns about the risks, privacy, and trust in the AI systems implemented in everyday contexts.

So far, we have seen mostly positive aspects, cognitive, affective, and social. However, the implementation of AI and chatbots is raising several and serious concerns.

2.6 Privacy Concerns

Along with the benefits of using chatbots and AI applications in everyday scenarios, several concerns have emerged. Previous work has dedicated special attention to privacy issues, risks, trust, and credibility of the AI chatbot system (see Table 2.6 for a summary). We discuss these issues in detail below, as well as dedicate a section on further challenges in Chap. 9, Bialkova, 2024f.

Table 2.6 Concerns as emerging from the literature audit

Concerns		
Factor	Definition	References
Privacy (concerns)	Kokolakis (2017) (a) privacy of a person—refers to the protection of a person against undue interference, such as physical search (b) territorial privacy—reflects the physical area surrounding a person (c) **informational privacy**-controlling whether and how personal data can be gathered, stored, processed, and disseminated	Bawack et al. (2021), Pitardi and Marriott (2021), Rese et al. (2020), Vimalkumar et al. (2021)
Trust	Trust reflects the willingness to rely on exchange partners in whom one has confidence, Moorman et al. (1993)	Bawack et al. (2021), Fernandes and Oliveira (2021), Hasan et al. (2021), Huang and Ki (2023), McLean and Osei-Frimpong (2019), Pillai and Sivathanu (2020), Pitardi and Marriott (2021), Poushneh (2021a), Przegalinska et al. (2019), Vimalkumar et al. (2021), Wang and Benbasat (2016)
Credibility of info/content Source/chatbot	Trustworthiness of source, Hovland & Weiss (1951)	Ben Mimoun et al. (2017), Chung et al. (2020), Lee and Choi (2017)
Risk (perceived)	Perceived threat to an individual's privacy	Kowalczuk (2018), Hasan et al. (2021), Jain et al. (2022), McLean and Osei-Frimpong (2019), Moriuchi (2021), Pitardi and Marriott (2021), Rese et al. (2020), Vimalkumar et al. (2021)

Privacy concerns become more and more pronounced with the advance of technology and the implementation of AI in everyday contexts. Information privacy reflecting the control of how personal data are gathered, stored, processed, and disseminated (for an overview, see Kokolakis, 2017) has started to be addressed in various studies, mainly in line with trust (Vimalkumar et al., 2021), attitudes (Pitardi & Marriott, 2021) and ethics (Følstad et al., 2021). Based on the web privacy literature, for AI, it has also been argued that privacy concerns as well as personality types are critical factors impacting trust and the willingness to disclose personal information (Bawack et al., 2021). Privacy is a predictor of behavioural intentions (Rese et al., 2020), and thus of the adoption of AI (Vimalkumar et al., 2021).

Trust assures reliance on the character, or truth of someone or something. Reflecting the willingness to rely on exchange partners in whom one has confidence (for a review, see Moorman et al., 1993), trust has been widely explored in regard to the adoption of new technologies. Trust depends on social interaction and control (Poushneh, 2021a), and loads on attitudes (Pitardi & Marriott, 2021). Trust and privacy have been found to play a central role in the adoption of AI-based voice assistants (e.g., Bawack et al., 2021; Fernandes & Oliveira, 2021; McLean & Osei-Frimpong, 2019; Pitardi & Marriott, 2021; Poushneh, 2021a; Vimalkumar et al., 2021) and chatbots (Pillai & Sivathanu, 2020; Przegalinska et al., 2019). Whether and how users trust an AI system depends on the perceived risks. Trust is dynamic (Siau & Wang, 2018), and may have different levels, ranging from confidence that the algorithmic model will perform well to a mechanistic understanding of more complex models and scenarios (Lipton, 2018).

Credibility reflecting trustworthiness is discussed since the antiquity in relation to effective persuasion of the listeners and has been explored across different domains (for an overview see Rieh & Danielson, 2007). A landmark in academic research focuses on the influence of various characteristics of the informational source on the effectiveness of communication (Hovland & Weiss, 1951). Message and information credibility has been recognised as core aspect in consumer perception, and thus, adoption of technology and response toward a company (Bialkova & te Paske, 2021). Chatbots perceived to be credible influence the interaction with consumers (Chung et al., 2020). Credibility of AI agent navigates attitudes and consequent behaviour (Ben Mimoun et al., 2017), and mediates the connection between customer and company (Lee & Choi, 2017). By contrast, when the system is not perceived to be credible or trustworthy, this may generate some negative feelings and even risks.

Risk is associated with a perceived threat to an individual's privacy. In the chatbot context, it was acknowledged to reflect the increased level of information that technology gathers on individuals beyond the individual's knowledge and sometimes control (McLean & Osei-Frimpong, 2019). Perceived risk predetermines the perceived value of the voice assistant and its continuous use (Jain et al., 2022). Note, however, some studies have reported that risk may reflect in anxiety (Moriuchi, 2021). Such outcome is a serious argument that invites further attention, especially given that risk for consumers mediates brand loyalty (Hasan et al., 2021), and thus could damage the company image. Furthermore, risk may raise privacy concerns (Rese et al., 2020), having a negative impact on trust (Pitardi & Marriott, 2021) and the adoption of AI systems (McLean & Osei-Frimpong, 2019).

In the above paragraph, we already reported that trust is a crucial determinant of willingness to adopt. Put differently, there is a need for reconsideration of privacy measures, and if necessary, to advise new legislation policy at EU and international level to protect consumers' privacy when it comes to AI implementation and the launch of new systems in the mass market. We return to this discussion in Chap. 9 challenges (Bialkova, 2024f) and Chap. 11 AI governance (Bialkova, 2024g).

In the above sections, we highlighted the key concepts as emerging from literature audit concerning chatbots AI agencies. On this base we have derived a taxonomy of AI agency, encompassing classification of core chatbot characteristics and respective human response, see Fig. 2.1. We test possible relationships between hypothesised parameters in Part II of current book, theoretical notions as presented in Chaps. 4 and 6 (Bialkova, 2024b, 2024d), and empirical work as reported in Chaps. 5 and 7, (Bialkova, 2024c, 2024e).

Most of the terms have their roots in classical theories from information technology, computer, and cognitive sciences, HCI, UX, psychology, consumer behaviour, and marketing. In Chap. 3, we present these core theories.

References

Adam, M., Wessel, M., & Benlian, A. (2021). AI-based chatbots in customer service and their effects on user compliance. *Electronic Markets, 31*, 427–445.

Ajzen I. (1991). The theory of planned behavior. *Organizational Behavior and Planned Decision Processes, 50*, 179–211.

Araujo, T. (2018). Living up to the chatbot hype: The influence of anthropomorphic design cues and communicative agency framing on conversational agent and company perceptions. *Computers in Human Behavior, 85*, 183–189.

Arrieta, A. B., Díaz-Rodríguez, N., del Ser, J., Bennetot, A., et al. (2020). Explainable Artificial Intelligence (XAI): Concepts, taxonomies, opportunities and challenges toward responsible AI. *Information Fusion, 58*, 82–115.

Ashfaq, M., Yun, J., & Yu, S. (2021). My smart speaker is cool! Perceived coolness, perceived values, and users' attitude toward smart speakers. *International Journal of Human-Computer Interaction, 37*(6), 560–573.

Bakpayev, M., Baek, T. H., van Esch, P., & Yoon, S. (2022). Programmatic creative: AI can think but it cannot feel. *Australasian Marketing Journal, 30*(1), 90–95.

Balakrishnan, J., & Dwivedi, Y. K. (2021). Conversational commerce: Entering the next stage of AI-powered digital assistants. *Annals of Operations Research*, 1–35.

Bandura, A. (1989). Human agency in social cognitive theory. *American Psychologist, 44*(9), 1175–1184.

Bawack, R. E., Wamba, S. F., & Carillo, K. D. A. (2021). Exploring the role of personality, trust, and privacy in customer experience performance during voice shopping: Evidence from SEM and fuzzy set qualitative comparative analysis. *International Journal of Information Management, 58*, 102309.

Ben Mimoun, M. S., Poncin, I., & Garnier, M. (2017). Animated conversational agents and e-consumer productivity: The roles of agents and individual characteristics. *Information & Management, 54*(5), 545–559. 43.

Bialkova, S. (2008). *Control mechanisms in task switching.* Ipskamp.

Bialkova, S. (2019). Consumers journey enhancement: The VR impact. In *European marketing academy conference, EMAC2019,* May 28–31, in Hamburg, Germany.

Bialkova, S. (2021). Would you talk to me? The role of chatbots in marketing, ICORIA2021, June 26–28, in Bordeaux, France.

Bialkova, S. (2022a). How May I Help You? Chatbots implementation in marketing. In *European marketing academy conference, EMAC2022,* May 24–27, in Budapest, Hungary.

Bialkova, S. (2022b). *Interacting with Chatbot: How to enhance functionality and enjoyment? AEMARK2022, 7–10 September 2022.* Valencia, Spain.

Bialkova, S. (2022c). From attention to action: key drivers to augment VR experience for everyday consumer applications. In *Proceedings of 29th IEEE, conference on virtual reality and 3D user interfaces (VR), 8th workshop on everyday virtual reality,* 12–16 March 2022, in Christchurch, New Zealand.

Bialkova, S. (2023a). I want to talk to you: Chatbot marketing integration. *Advances in Advertising Research,* (Vol. XII, pp. 23–36), https://doi.org/10.1007/978-3-658-40429-1_2.

Bialkova, S. (2023b). AI-driven customer experience: Factors to consider. In *Philosophy of artificial intelligence and its place in society* (pp. 341–357). IGI Global.

Bialkova, S. (2023c). How to Optimise Interaction with Chatbots? Key Parameters Emerging from Actual Application. *International Journal of Human-Computer Interaction.* https://doi.org/10.1080/10447318.2023.2219963

Bialkova, S. (2023d). Enhancing multisensory experience and brand value: Key determinants for extended, augmented, and virtual reality marketing applications. In A. Simeone, B. Weyers, S. Bialkova, & R.W. Lindeman (Eds.), *Everyday virtual and augmented reality* (pp. 181–195). *Human–computer interaction series.* Springer.

Bialkova, S. (2023e). I need your help: Key parameters guiding satisfaction with chatbots. In *European marketing academy conference, EMAC2023*, 23–26 May 2023, in Odense, Denmark.

Bialkova, S. (2024a). Core theories applied in chatbot context. In *The rise of AI user applications: Chatbots integration foundations and trends.* (Chapter 3). Springer. https://doi.org/10.1007/978-3-031-56471-0_3

Bialkova, S. (2024b). Shaping chatbot efficiency-How to build better systems? In *The rise of AI user applications: Chatbots integration foundations and trends.* (Chapter 4). Springer. https://doi.org/10.1007/978-3-031-56471-0_4

Bialkova, S. (2024c). Chatbot efficiency—Model testing. In *The rise of AI user applications: Chatbots integration foundations and trends.* (Chapter 5). Springer. https://doi.org/10.1007/978-3-031-56471-0_5

Bialkova, S. (2024d). Anthropomorphism-What is crucial? In *The rise of AI user applications: Chatbots integration foundations and trends.* (Chapter 6). Springer. https://doi.org/10.1007/978-3-031-56471-0_6

Bialkova, S. (2024e). Chatbot agency—Model testing. In *The rise of AI user applications: Chatbots integration foundations and trends.* (Chapter 7). Springer. https://doi.org/10.1007/978-3-031-56471-0_7

Bialkova, S. (2024f). AI transforming business and everyday life. In *The rise of AI user applications: Chatbots integration foundations and trends.* (Chapter 9). Springer. https://doi.org/10.1007/978-3-031-56471-0_9

Bialkova, S. (2024g). Explainable AI. In *The rise of AI user applications: Chatbots integration foundations and trends.* (Chapter 11). Springer. https://doi.org/10.1007/978-3-031-56471-0_11

Bialkova, S., & Barr, C. (2022). Virtual try-on: How to enhance consumer experience? In *Proceedings of IEEEVR2022, 8th workshop on everyday virtual reality*, March 12–16, 2022, in Chritschurch, New Zealand.

Bialkova, S., & te Paske, S. (2021). Campaign participation, spreading e-WOM, purchase: How to optimise CSR effectiveness via Social media? *European Journal of Management and Business Economics, 30*(1), 108–126.

Bialkova, S., & van Gisbergen, M. S. (2017). When sound modulates vision: VR applications for art and entertainment. In *Proceedings of IEEE VR2017, 3rd workshop on everyday virtual reality*, 18–22 March 2019, Los Angeles, US.

Bickmore, T. W., & Picard, R. W. (2005). Establishing and maintaining long-term human-computer relationships. *ACM Transactions on Computer-Human Interaction, 12*(2), 293–327.

Biocca, F., Harms, C., & Burgoon, J. K. (2003). Toward a more robust theory and measure of social presence: Review and suggested criteria. *Presence: Teleoperators & Virtual Environments, 12*, 456–480.

Blut, M., Wang, C., Wünderlich, N., & Brock, C. (2021). Understanding anthropomorphism in service provision: A meta-analysis of physical robots, chatbots, and other AI. *Journal of the Academy of Marketing Science, 49*, 632–658.

Borsci, S., Malizia, A., Schmettow, M., et al. (2022). The Chatbot usability scale: The design and pilot of a usability scale for interaction with AI-based conversational agents. *Personal Ubiquitous Computing, 26*, 95–119.

Bostrom, N. (2012). The superintelligent will: Motivation and instrumental rationality in advanced artificial agents. *Minds & Machines, 22*, 71–85.

Chattaraman, V., Kwon, W. S., Gilbert, J. E., & Ross, K. (2019). Should AI-Based, conversational digital assistants employ social-or task-oriented interaction style? A task-competency and reciprocity perspective for older adults. *Computers in Human Behavior, 90*, 315–330.

Chaves, A. P., & Gerosa, M. A. (2021). How should my chatbot interact? A survey on social characteristics in human-chatbot interaction design. *International Journal of Human-Computer Interaction, 37*(8), 729–758.

Chen, Q., Gong, Y., Lu, Y., & Tang, J. (2022). Classifying and measuring the service quality of AI chatbot in frontline service. *Journal of Business Research, 145*, 552–568.

Cheng, Y., & Jiang, H. (2022). Customer brand relationship in the era of artificial intelligence: Understanding the role of chatbot marketing efforts. *Journal of Product & Brand Management, 31*(2), 252–264.

Choi, Y. (2021). A study of employee acceptance of artificial intelligence technology. *European Journal of Management and Business Economics, 30*, 318–330.

Chong, T., Yu, T., Keeling, D. I., & de Ruyter, K. (2021). AI-chatbots on the services frontline addressing the challenges and opportunities of agency. *Journal of Retailing and Consumer Services, 63*, 102735.

Chopra, K. (2019). Indian shopper motivation to use artificial intelligence: Generating Vroom's expectancy theory of motivation using grounded theory approach. *International Journal of Retail & Distribution Management, 47*(3), 331–347.

Chung, M., Ko, E., Joung, H., & Kim, S. J. (2020). Chatbot e-service and customer satisfaction regarding luxury brands. *Journal of Business Research, 117*, 587–595.

Dabholkar, P. A. (1996). Consumer evaluations of new technology-based self-service options: An investigation of alternative models of service quality. *International Journal of Research in Marketing, 13*, 29–51.

Dabholkar, P. A., & Bagozzi, R. P. (2002). An attitudinal model of technology-based self-service: Moderating effects of consumer traits and situational factors. *Journal of the Academy of Marketing Science, 30*(3), 184–201.

Davis, F. D. (1989). Perceived usefulness, perceived ease of use, and user acceptance of information technology. *MIS Quarterly, 13*(3), 319–339.

Davis, F. D., Bagozzi, R. P., & Warshaw, P. R. (1989). User acceptance of computer technology: A comparison of two theoretical models. *Management Science, 5*(8), 982–1003.

de Gennaro, M., Krumhuber, E. G., & Lucas, G. (2020). Effectiveness of an empathic chatbot in combating adverse effects of social exclusion on mood. *Frontiers in Psychology, 10*, Article 3061.

DeLone, W. H., & McLean, E. R. (1992). Information systems success: The quest for the dependent variable. *Information System Research, 3*(1), 60–95.

DeLone, W. H., & McLean, E. R. (2003). The DeLone and McLean model of information systems success: A ten-year update. *Journal of Management Information System, 19*(4), 9–30.

de Sa Siqueira, M., Muller, B. C., & Bosse, T. (2023). When do we accept mis-takes from chatbots? The impact of human-like communication on user experience in chatbots that make mistakes. *International Journal of Human–Computer Interaction.*

Edwards, C., Edwards, A., Spence, P. R., & Shelton, A. K. (2014). Is that a bot running the social media feed? Testing the differences in perceptions of communication quality for a human agent and a bot agent on Twitter. *Computers in Human Behavior, 33*, 372–376.

Ekman, P. (2016). *Atlas of emotions.* Retrieved from www.paulekman.com.

Feine, J., Gnewuch, U., Morana, S., & Maedche, A. (2019). A taxonomy of social cues for conversational agents. *International Journal of Human Computer Studies, 132*, 138–161.

Fernandes, T., & Oliveira, E. (2021). Understanding consumers' acceptance of automated technologies in service encounters: Drivers of digital voice assistants adoption. *Journal of Business Research, 122*, 180–191.

Fiske, S. T., Cuddy, A. J., & Glick, P. (2007). Universal dimensions of social cognition: Warmth and competence. *Trends in Cognitive Sciences, 11*(2), 77–83.

Følstad, A., Araujo, T., Law, E. L. C., et al. (2021). Future directions for chatbot research: An interdisciplinary research agenda. *Computing, 103*, 2915–2942.

Fulk, J. W., S. C., Schmitz, J., & Power, G. J. (1987). A social information processing model of media use in organizations. *Communication Research, 14*(5), 520–552.

Gefen, D., & Straub, D. (2003). Managing user trust in B2C e-services. *e-Service Journal, 2*(2), 7–24.

Gelbrich, K., Hagel, J., & Orsingher, C. (2021). Emotional support from a digital assistant in technology-mediated services: Effects on customer satisfaction and behavioral persistence. *International Journal of Research in Marketing, 38*, 176–193.

Go, E., & Sundar, S. S. (2019). Humanizing chatbots: The effects of visual, identity and conversational cues on humanness perceptions. *Computers in Human Behavior, 97*, 304–316.

Grazzini, L., Viglia, G., & Nunan, D. (2023). Dashed expectations in service experiences effects of robots human-likeness on customers' responses. *European Journal of Marketing, 57*(4), 957–986.

Greene, T., & Shmueli, G. (2023). Persons and personalization on digital platforms: A philosophical perspective. In L. Moutinho, L. Cavique, & E. Bigné (Eds.), *Philosophy of artificial intelligence and its place in society* (pp. 214–270). IGI global.

Guerreiro, J., & Loureiro, S. M. C. (2023). I am attracted to my cool smart assistant! Analyzing attachment-aversion in AI-human relationships. *Journal of Business Research, 161*, 113863.

Guidotti, R., Monreale, A., Ruggieri, S., Turini, F., Giannotti, F., & Pedreschi, D. (2018). A survey of methods for explaining black box models. *ACM Computing Surveys, 51*(5), Article 93.

Hasan, R., Shams, R., & Rahman, M. (2021). Consumer trust and perceived risk for voice-controlled artificial intelligence: The case of Siri. *Journal of Business Research, 131*, 591–597.

Hoffman, D. L., & Novak, T. P. (1996). Marketing in hypermedia computer-mediated environments: Conceptual foundations. *Journal of Marketing, 60*, 50–68.

Holzwarth, M., Janiszewski, C., & Neumann, M. M. (2006). The influence of avatars on online consumer shopping behavior. *Journal of Marketing, 70*(4), 19–36.

Hovland, C. I., & Weiss, W. (1951). The influence of source credibility on communication effectiveness. *Public Opinion Quarterly, 15*, 635–650.

Huang, M., & Ki, E. J. (2023). Examining the effect of anthropomorphic design cues on health-care chatbots acceptance and organization-public relationships: Trust in a warm human Vs. a competent machine. *International Journal of Human–Computer Interaction.*

Huysmans, J., Dejaeger, K., Mues, C., Vanthienen, J., & Baesens, B. (2011). An empirical evaluation of the comprehensibility of decision table, tree and rule based predictive models. *Decision Support Systems, 51*, 141–154.

Jain, S., Basu, S., Dwivedi, Y. K., & Kaur, S. (2022). Interactive voice assistants—Does brand credibility assuage privacy risks? *Journal of Business Research, 139*, 701–717.

Katz, E., Haas, H., & Gurevitch, M. (1973). On the use of the mass media for important things. *American Sociological Review, 38*(2), 164–181.

Kokolakis, S. (2017). Privacy attitudes and privacy behaviour: A review of current research on the privacy paradox phenomenon. *Computers & Security, 64*, 122–134.

Kowalczuk, P. (2018). Consumer acceptance of smart speakers: A mixed methods approach. *Journal of Research in Interactive Marketing, 12*(4), 418–431.

Landim, A. R. D. B., Pereira, A. M., Vieira, T., Costa, E. de B., Moura, J. A. Wanick, B. V., & Bazaki, E. (2022). Chatbot design approaches for fashion E-commerce: An interdisciplinary review. *International Journal of Fashion Design, Technology and Education, 15*(2), 200–210.

Lee, H., & Cho, C. H. (2020). Uses and gratifications of smart speakers: Modelling the effectiveness of smart speaker advertising. *International Journal of Advertising, 39*(7), 1150–1171.

Lee, S., & Choi, J. (2017). Enhancing user experience with conversational agent for movie recommendation: Effects of self-disclosure and reciprocity. *International Journal of Human-Computer Studies, 103*, 95–105.

Lee, K. M., Park, N., & Song, H. (2005). Can a robot be perceived as a developing creature? *Human Communication Research, 31*(4), 538–563.

Lee, K. M., Peng, W., Jin, S., & Yan, C. (2006). Can robots manifest personality? An empirical test of personality recognition, social responses, and social presence in human-robot interaction. *Journal of Communication, 56*(4), 754–772.

Lemon, K. N., & Verhoef, P. C. (2016). Understanding customer experience throughout the customer journey. *Journal of Marketing, 80*(6), 69–96.

Lim, W. M., Kumar, S., Verma, S., & Chaturvedi, R. (2022). Alexa, what do we know about conversational commerce? Insights from a systematic literature review. *Psychology & Marketing, 39*, 1129–1155.

Lin, J. S., & Wu, L. (2023). Examining the psychological process of developing consumer-brand relationships through strategic use of social media brand Chatbots. *Computers in Human Behavior, 140*, 107488.

Lipton, Z. C. (2018). The Mythos of Model Interpretability: In machine learning, the concept of interpretability is both important and slippery. *Queue, 16*(3), 31–57.

Liu, B., & Sundar, S. S. (2018). Should machines express sympathy and empathy? Experiments with a health advice chatbot. *Cyberpsychology, Behavior and Social Networking, 21*(10), 625–636.

Liu-Thompkins, Y., Okazaki, S., & Li, H. (2022). Artificial empathy in marketing interactions: Bridging the human AI gap in affective and social customer experience. *Journal of the Academy of Marketing Science, 50*(6), 1198–1218.

Lombard, M., & Ditton, T. (1997). At the heart of it all: The concept of presence. *Journal of Computer Mediated Communication, 3*(2), JCMC321.

Lopes, N. C., & Cavique, L. (2023). Causal machine learning in social impact assessment. In L. Moutinho, L. Cavique, & E. Bigné (Eds.), *Philosophy of artificial intelligence and its place in society* (pp. 214–270). IGI global.

Lou, C., Kang, H., and Tse, C. H. (2022). Bots vs. humans: How schema congruity, contingency-based interactivity, and sympathy influence consumer perceptions and patronage intentions. *International Journal of Advertising, 41*(4), 655–684.

Luo, X., Tong, S., Fang, Z., & Qu, Z. (2019). Frontiers: Machines vs. humans: The impact of artificial intelligence chatbot disclosure on customer purchases. *Marketing Science, 11*, 1–11.

Loureiro, S. M. C., Guerreiro, J., & Tussyadiah, I. (2021). Artificial intelligence in business: State of the art and future research agenda. *Journal of Business Research, 129*, 911–926.

Lu, B., Fan, W., & Zhou, M. (2016). Social presence, trust, and social commerce purchase intention: An empirical research. *Computers in Human Behavior, 56*, 225–237.

Mariani, M. M., Hashemi, N., & Wirtz, J. (2023). Artificial intelligence empowered conversational agents: A systematic literature review and research agenda. *Journal of Business Research, 161*, 113838.

McLean, G., & Osei-Frimpong, K. (2019). Hey Alexa … examine the variables influencing the use of artificial intelligent in-home voice assistants. *Computers in Human Behavior, 99*, 28–37.

Meyer-Waarden, L., Pavone, G., Poocharoentou, T., Prayatsup, P., Ratinaud, M., Tison, A., & Torn, S. (2020). How service quality influences customer acceptance and usage of Chatbots? *Journal of Service Management Research, 4*(1), 35–51.

Miao, F., Kozlenkova, I. V., Wang, H., Xie, T., & Palmatier, R. W. (2022). An emerging theory of avatar marketing. *Journal of Marketing, 86*(1), 67–90.

Moorman, C., Deshpandé, R., & Zaltman, G. (1993). Factors affecting trust in market research relationships. *Journal of Marketing, 57*, 81–101.

Moriuchi, E. (2021). An empirical study on anthropomorphism and engagement with disembodied AIs and consumers' re-use behavior. *Psychology and Marketing, 38*(7), 21–42.

Moriuchi, E., Landers, V. M., Colton, D. A., & Hair, N. (2020). Engagement with chatbots versus augmented reality interactive technology in e-commerce. *Journal of Strategic Marketing, 29*, 375–389.

Munnukka, J., Talvitie-Lamberg, K., & Maity, D. (2022). Anthropomorphism and social presence in Human-Virtual service assistant interactions: The role of dialog length and attitudes. *Computers in Human Behavior, 135*, 107343.

Mustak, M., Salminen, J., Ple, L., & Wirtz, J. (2021). Artificial intelligence in marketing: Topic modeling, scientometric analysis, and research agenda. *Journal of Business Research, 124*, 389–404.

Nass, C., & Moon, Y. (2000). Machines and mindlessness: Social responses to computers. *Journal of Social Issues, 56*(1), 81–103.

Pan, S., Cui, J., & Mou, Y. (2023). Desirable or distasteful? Exploring uncertainty in human-chatbot relationships. *International Journal of Human–Computer Interaction.*

Parasuraman, A., Zeithaml, V. A., & Malhotra, A. (2005). E-S-QUAL a multiple-item scale for assessing electronic service quality. *Journal of Service Research, 7*(3), 213–233.

Rieh, S. Y., & Danielson, D. R. (2007). Credibility: A multidisciplinary framework. *Annuual Review of Information Science and Technology, 41*, 307–364.

Pillai, R., & Sivathanu, B. (2020). Adoption of AI-based chatbots for hospitality and tourism. *International Journal of Contemporary Hospitality Management, 32*(10), 3199–3226.

Pillai, R., Sivathanu, B., & Dwivedi, Y. K. (2020). Shopping intention at AI-powered automated retail stores (AIPARS). *Journal of Retailing and Consumer Services, 57*, 102207.

Pitardi, V., & Marriott, H. R. (2021). Alexa, she's not human but… Unveiling the drivers of consumers' trust in voice-based artificial intelligence. *Psychology & Marketing, 38*, 626–642.

Poushneh, A. (2021a). Impact of auditory sense on trust and brand affect through auditory social interaction and control. *Journal of Retailing and Consumer Services, 58*, 102281.

Poushneh, A. (2021b). Humanizing voice assistant: The impact of voice assistant personality on consumers' attitudes and behaviors. *Journal of Retailing and Consumer Services, 58*, 102283.

Przegalinska, A. K., Ciechanowski, L., Stróz, A., Gloor, P. A., & Mazurek, G. (2019). In bot we trust: A new methodology of chatbot performance measures. *Business Horizons, 62*(6), 785–797.

Qiu, L., & Benbasat, I. (2009). Evaluating anthropomorphic product recommendation agents: A social relationship perspective to designing information systems. *Journal of Management Information Systems, 25*(4), 145–181.

Ramsey, R., & Sohi, R. S. (1997). Listening to your customers: The impact of perceived salesperson listening behavior on relationship outcomes. *Journal of the Academy of Marketing Science, 25*, 127–137.

Ren, R., Castro, J. W., Acuña, S. T., & Lara, J. D. (2019). Evaluation techniques for Chatbot usability: A systematic mapping study. *International Journal of Software Engineering and Knowledge Engineering, 29*(11–12), 1673–1702.

Rese, A., Ganster, L., & Baier, D. (2020). Chatbots in retailers' customer communication: How to measure their acceptance? *Journal of Retailing and Consumer Services, 56*, 102176.

Roy, R., & Naidoo, V. (2021). Enhancing chatbot effectiveness: The role of anthropomorphic conversational styles and time orientation. *Journal of Business Research, 126*, 23–34.

Russell, J. A. (2003). Core affect and the psychological construction of emotion. *Psychological Review, 110*(1), 145–172.

Russell, S., & Norvig, P. (2022). *Artificial intelligence: A modern approach* (4th ed.). Pearson.

Schmitt, B. H. (1999). *Experiential Marketing.* The Free Press.

Sheehan, B., Jin, H. S., & Gottlieb, U. (2020). Customer service chatbots: Anthropomorphism and adoption. *Journal of Business Research, 115*, 14–24.

Siau, K. L., & Wang, W. (2018). Building trust in artificial intelligence, machine learning, and robotics. *Cutter Business Technology Journal, 31*(2), 47–53.

Spitzberg, B. H. (2006). Preliminary development of a model and measure of Computer-mediated communication (CMC) competence. *Journal of Computer-Mediated Communication, 11*(2), 629–666.

Sundar, S. S., Bellur, S., Oh, J., Jia, H., & Kim, H. S. (2016). Theoretical importance of contingency in human-computer interaction: Effects of message interactivity on user engagement. *Communication Research, 43*(5), 595–625.

Sundar, S. S., Tamul, D. J., & Wu, M. (2014). Capturing "cool": Measures for assessing coolness of technological products. *International Journal of Human-Computer Studies, 72*(2), 169–180.

Tassiello, V., Tillotson, J. S., & Rome, A. S. (2021). "Alexa, orderme a pizza!": The mediating role of psychological power in the consumer–voice assistant interaction. *Psyhology & Marketing, 8*(7), 1069–1080.

Trivedi, J. (2019). Examining the customer experience of using banking chatbots and its impact on brand love: The moderating role of perceived risk. *Journal of Internet Commerce, 18*(1), 91–111. 265.

Tsai, W. H. S., Liu, Y., & Chuan, C. H. (2021). How chatbots' social presence communication enhances consumer engagement: The mediating role of parasocial interaction and dialogue. *Journal of Research in Interactive Marketing, 15*(3), 460–482.

Tu, C. (2000). On-line learning migration: From social learning theory to social presence theory in a CMC environment. *Journal of Network and Computer Application, 23*, 27–37.

Venkatesh, V. (2000). Determinants of perceived ease of use: Integrating control, intrinsic motivation, and emotion into the technology acceptance model. *Information Systems Research, 11*(4), 342–365.

Venkatesh, V., & Davis, F. D. (2000). A theoretical extension of the technology acceptance model: Four longitudinal field studies. *Management Science, 46*(2), 186–204.

Venkatesh, V., Morris, M. G., Davis, G. B., & Davis, F. D. (2003). User acceptance of information technology: Toward a unified view. *MIS Quarterly, 27*(3), 425–478.

Vimalkumar, M., Sharma, S. K., Singh, J. B., & Dwivedi, Y. K. (2021). 'Okay Google, what about my privacy?' User's privacy perceptions and acceptance of voice-based digital assistants. *Computers in Human Behavior, 120*, 106763.

Wang, W., & Benbasat, I. (2016). Empirical assessment of alternative designs for enhancing different types of trusting beliefs in online recommendation agents. *Journal of Management Information Systems, 33*, 744–775.

Wirtz, J., Patterson, P. G., Kunz, W. H., Gruber, T., Lu, V. N., Paluch, S., & Martins, A. (2018). Brave new world: Service robots in the frontline. *Journal of Service Management, 29*(5), 907–931.

Witmer, G., & Singer, M. J. (1998). Measuring presence in virtual environments: A presence questionnaire. *Presence: Teleoperators and Virtual Environments, 7*(3), 225–240.

Wixom, B., & Todd, P. (2005). A theoretical integration of user satisfaction and technology acceptance. *Information Systems Research, 16*(1), 85–102.

Xiao, B., & Benbasat, I. (2007). E-commerce product recommendation agents: Use, characteristics, and impact. *MIS Quarterly, 31*(1), 137–209.

Xu, K., Chan-Olmsted, S., & Liu, F. (2022). Smart speakers require smart management: Two routes from user gratifications to privacy settings. *International Journal of Communication, 16*, 192–214.

Yagoda, R., & Gillan, D. (2012). You want me to trust ROBOT? The development of a human-robot interaction trust scale. *International Journal of Social Robotics, 4*(3), 235–248.

Yalçın, Ö., & DiPaola, S. (2020). Modeling empathy: Building a link between affective and cognitive processes. *Artificial Intelligence Review, 53*, 2983–3006.

Yang, Y., Zhang, K., & Kannan, P. K. (2022). Identifying market structure: A deep network representation learning of social engagement. *Journal of Marketing, 86*(4), 37–56.

Zarouali, B., Makhortykh, M., Bastian, M., & Araujo, T. (2021). Overcoming polarization with chatbot news? Investigating the impact of news content containing opposing views on agreement and credibility. *European Journal of Communication, 36*(1), 53–68.

Zarouali, B., Van den Broeck, E., Walrave, M., & Poels, K. (2018). Predicting consumer responses to a chatbot on Facebook. *Cyberpsychology, Behavior, and Social Networking, 21*(8), 491–497.

Zeithaml, V. A., Berry, L. L., & Parasuraman, A. (1996). The behavioral consequences of service quality. *Journal of Marketing, 60*, 31–46.

Zeithaml, V. A., A. Parasuraman, & Malhotra, A. (2002). Service quality delivery through web sites: A critical review of extant knowledge. *Journal of the Academy of Marketing Science, 30*(4), 362–375.

Chapter 3
Core Theories Applied in Chatbot Context

Abstract Despite the enormous effort to understand the factors driving chatbot effectiveness, researchers are not univocal. The profound literature audit we performed demonstrated that various theories have been employed in order to identify the key drivers of chatbot efficiency. Utilitarian (i.e., cognitive related), hedonic (emotion related), and social components emerged to shape the chatbot performance evaluation, as summarised in the thematic map and taxonomy we developed (see Chap. 2). The core theoretical notions are organised around three main pillars: acceptance models, behavioural theories, and social influence theories. The acceptance models included are: TAM, UTAU, Diffusion of Innovation, Gratification theory, and Uncanny Valley theory. Frameworks like the Planned behaviour, Reasoned action, Self-determination, Motivation, and Big five are among the most frequently cited in the papers audited and thus are discussed hereby in detail. In addition to these theories, anthropomorphism, social agency, social presence, social response, parasocial interaction, and CASA theories are brought to the table. Fundamental paradigms, with relevant examples and related papers, are summarised in taxonomy of core theories applied in chatbot context (see Fig. 3.1) and presented in detail below.

3.1   Acceptance Models

3.1.1   Technology Acceptance Model (TAM)

Technology Acceptance Model (TAM) was suggested by Davis et al. (1989) and is one of the most influential models that has been applied in various contexts. It addresses the ability to predict peoples' acceptance of technology, by measuring their intentions, and the ability to explain the intentions in terms of attitudes, subjective norms, perceived usefulness, and perceived ease of use. According to the original model (Davis et al., 1989), perceived **usefulness** explains more than half of the variance in intentions and thus is a strong predictor of peoples' intentions. Perceived **ease of use** had a small, but significant effect on intentions, although this effect softened with time. **Attitudes** only partially mediated the effects of beliefs on **intentions**. In contrast to researchers' expectations, subjective **norms** had no effect on intentions. TAM was a cornerstone for many studies exploring the acceptance of chatbots to build around and address TAM core constructs, as well as, to hypothesise additional constructs. See Table 3.1 for details on studies applying TAM in chatbot AI context.

3.1.2   Unified Theory of Acceptance and Use of Technology (UTAUT)

Unified theory of acceptance and use of technology (UTAUT) suggested by Venkatesh et al. (2003) could be seen as an extension of the TAM. It encompasses four core determinants of intention and usage and up to four moderators of key relationships. The direct determinants of user acceptance and usage behaviour are performance expectancy, effort expectancy, social influence, and facilitating conditions. The moderators were hypothesised in terms of attitudes toward using technology, self-efficacy, and anxiety. UTAUT is also very popular among researchers exploring chatbot acceptance (e.g., Fernandes et al., 2021; Kowalczuk, 2018; Lim et al., 2022; Mariani et al., 2023; McLean & Osei-Frimpong, 2019; Moriuchi, 2021; Pitardi & Marriott, 2021; Vimalkumar et al., 2021).

3.1.3   Consumer Acceptance of Technology (CAT) Model

Consumer Acceptance of Technology (CAT) model is a further extension of UTAUT. According to Kulviwat et al.'s (2007) theoretical notion, attitudes, and thus adoption intentions depend on both cognitive and affective components. The Kulviwat model was tested in the chatbot context by Zarouali et al. (2018). A slightly different perspective was used by Hasan et al. (2021), who claimed that adopter personal characteristics are crucial in accepting AI systems. In particular, psychographics and sociodemographics that explain innovation adoption were addressed. Note, however, that psychographics (e.g., gender, age, and experience) are already moderators in UTAUT. From the consumer adoption literature, we also know that the innovation's perceived attributes and the adopter's characteristics are recognised as important drivers of consumer adoption.

3.1.4   Diffusion of Innovation (DOI)

Diffusion of Innovation (DOI) in the original formulation (Rogers, 1995; but also see the 1st edition as of 1962) encountered for the rate of adoption to depend on the perceived attributes of innovation, type of innovation decision, communication

Table 3.1 Acceptance of technology theories and models as applied in chatbot context

Theory	Origin	CORE concepts/constructs	Application—key references AI
TAM Technology acceptance model	Davis (1989) Davis et al. (1989)	*Usefulness *Ease of use *Attitudes *Intentions *Subjective norm	Balakrishnan and Dwivedi (2021) Bialkova (2021, 2023a) Fernandes and Oliveira (2021) Kowalczuk (2018) Lim et al. (2022) Mariani et al. (2023) McLean and Osei-Frimpong (2019) Moriuchi (2021) Rese et al. (2020) Pillai and Sivathanu (2020) Pitardi and Marriott (2021) Vimalkumar et al. (2021) Zarouali et al. (2018)
UTAUT Unified theory of acceptance and use of technology	Venkatesh et al. (2003)	*Performance expectancy *Effort expectancy *Social influence *Facilitating conditions *Attitude *Self-efficacy *Anxiety	Fernandes and Oliveira (2021) Kowalczuk (2018) Lim et al. (2022) Mariani et al. (2023) McLean and Osei-Frimpong (2019) Moriuchi (2021) Pitardi and Marriott (2021) Vimalkumar et al. (2021)
CAT model Consumer acceptance of technology model	Kulviwat et al. (2007)	*Innovation's attributes *adopter's characteristics *Cognitive/affective components	Hasan et al. (2021) Zarouali et al. (2018)
DOI Diffusion of innovations	Rogers (1995), but see also the original 1st edition as of 1962	*Perception of using, *relative advantage; *perceived characteristics of innovating, PCI (Moore & Benbasat, 1991)	Hasan et al. (2021)

(continued)

Table 3.1 (continued)

Theory	Origin	CORE concepts/ constructs	Application—key references AI
U&GT Gratification theory	Katz et al. (1973), for overview see Ruggiero (2000)	*Satisfy consumers social and psychological needs (e.g., Ruggiero, 2000) *Cognitive *Affective *Personal integrative *Social integrative *Tension-free needs (Mariani et al., 2023)	Jain et al. (2022) Mariani et al. (2023) McLean and Osei-Frimpong, (2019) Rese et al. (2020) Xie et al. (2022)
Uncanny valley theory	Mori (original work from 1970, but see 2012)	A sense of dislike, unease, unpleasantness, or eeriness	Balakrishnan and Dwivedi (2021) Ciechanowski et al. (2019) Gray and Wegner (2012) Hoyer et al. (2020) Kim et al. (2019) Lim et al. (2022) Liu and Sundar (2018) Mariani et al. (2023) Skjuve et al. (2019)

channels, nature of the social system, extent of change, and agent promotion effort. In the 1990s, it was argued that tech innovations diffuse because of the cumulative decisions of individuals to adopt them (e.g., Moore & Benbasat, 1991, 1996). The core components encountered were the perception of use, relative advantage, perceived characteristics of innovating (PCI). In the latter formulation, the relative advantage, ease of use, image, visibility, compatibility, and result demonstrability were considered (Venkatesh et al., 2003). Voluntariness to use was also included (see also Agarwal & Prasad, 1997, 1998).

3.1.5 Gratification Theory (Uses and Gratification Theory, U&GT)

Gratification theory (Uses and Gratification Theory, U&GT) combines the social and psychological attributes of needs. In the mediated environment, individuals are assumed to be goal oriented and to select media that fit their needs (Katz et al., 1973). An extended definition states that media and the types of content that satisfy consumers' social and psychological needs attract and hold audiences (e.g., Ruggiero, 2000). In the chatbot context, it was assumed that audiences make concerted efforts to exploit media content to further satisfy their goals and objectives (Mariani et al.,

2023; McLean & Osei-Frimpong, 2019; Rese et al., 2020). In particular, five categories of needs were recognised, i.e., cognitive, affective, personal integrative, social integrative, and tension-free needs (for a review, see Mariani et al., 2023). Gratification theory was also applied to capture how the perception of different features of the agent (e.g., utility, hedonic, and social) varies among users (Jain et al., 2022).

3.1.6   Uncanny Valley Theory

Uncanny Valley Theory, when earlier applied in the context of robots, assumed that if they become too human-like, they are at risk of inducing an uncanny feeling in users (e.g., Mori, as originally suggested in 1970, however, for details, see Mori et al., 2012). Uncanniness was associated with a sense of dislike, unease, and unpleasantness. Eeriness in the face of entities that almost, but not quite, resemble healthy humans was also argued. Furthermore, how uncanny perceptions may affect the customer experience, and comfort with technology as a dimension of the customer journey has been explored (Hoyer et al., 2020). In the AI and chatbot context, the uncanny valley theory has been addressed by several papers (e.g., Balakrishnan & Dwivedi, 2021; Ciechanowski et al., 2019; Gray & Wegner, 2012; Lim et al., 2022; Liu & Sundar, 2018; Mariani et al., 2023). It was also reported that a human-like chatbot does not elicit uncanny feelings, even when there is uncertainty related to the true nature of the conversational agent (Skjuve et al., 2019). The authors, however, claimed that although there might not be an uncanny valley effect associated with text-based chatbots, an inadequate conversation flow could create an unpleasant user experience.

3.2   Behavioural Theories

3.2.1   Theory of Reasoned Action (TRA)

Theory of Reasoned Action (TRA) is perhaps one of the most influential and widely applied theories of human behaviour. The work of Fishbein and Ajzen in the 1970s (for an overview see 1974) was an extension of Fishbein's Multiattribute attitude model (1967) assuming that consumers' attitudes toward an object depend on the beliefs they have about several of its attributes. The core objective of TRA is to operationalise attitudes toward behaviour, i.e., attitudes toward the act (rather than just attitudes toward the object). It also recognises the role of normative belief, referred to as subjective norm, i.e., the power of other people to influence what an individual does. By implementing TRA in various contexts, it is aimed to measure behavioural intentions, as predicted by attitude toward the act and beliefs people have toward particular act. In the tech context, TRA is a core pillar in the technology acceptance model, TAM (Davis et al., 1989), the unified theory of acceptance and use of technology, UTAUT (Venkatesh et al., 2003), as well as in diffusion of innovations, DOI (Moore & Benbasat, 1991, 1996). In the chatbot context, TRA was applied in several papers (Bawack et al., 2021; Bialkova, 2021, 2023a; Hasan et al., 2021; Lim et al., 2022). Table 3.2 provides overview on core behavioural theories, including relevant papers referred in the AI chatbot context.

3.2.2 Theory of Planned Behaviour (TPB)

Theory of Planned Behavior, TPB (Ajzen, 1991) differs from the theory of reasoned action with its addition of perceived behavioural control. Essentially, the TPB is an extension of the TRA assuming that intentions to perform behaviours of different kinds can be predicted with high accuracy from the following core components: attitudes toward the behaviour, subjective norms, and perceived behavioural control. Together with perceptions of behavioural control, intentions are supposed to explain a considerable variance in actual behaviour.

3.2.3 Expectancy Theory of Motivation

Expectancy Theory of Motivation, as originally introduced by Vroom (1964) states that motivation is a function of expectancy, instrumentality, and valence. Individuals are motivated to select a specific behaviour over other, and thus, they will behave or act in a certain way, because of the expected result of that selected behaviour. Expectancy is associated with the efforts or actions that lead to a desired outcome. Instrumentality reflects performance but can also be seen as a result/or outcome of efforts. Valence has been associated with the outcome of usage. According to the theory, the motivation of the selected behaviour is determined by the desirability of the outcome. It was further argued that subjects rate the expectancy of the predicted variable and the instrumentality and valence of the outcomes of reaching the predicted variable (for an overview, see Van Eerde & Thierry, 1996). In the tech context, expectancy theory has been applied by several researchers. In the unified theory of acceptance and use of technology (UTAUT) discussed above, we already see that performance expectancy and effort expectancy correlate with the perceived ease (Venkatesh et al., 2003). In the AI chatbot context, the *expectancy theory of motivation* has been explicitly described by few papers (Chopra, 2019; Lim et al., 2022). Chopra (2019) addressed in detail motivation, in terms of intrinsic, extrinsic, and force choice motivation. In fact, motivation was extensively explored in line with self-determination.

Table 3.2   Core behavioural theories applied in the AI chatbot context

Theory	Origin	CORE concepts/constructs	Application—key references AI
Theory of reasoned action (TRA)	Fishbein and Ajzen (1974) But also see the work as of 1975 and 1981; extension of the Fishbein's multiattribute attitude model, suggested in 1967	***Attitudes**—"an individual's positive or negative feelings (evaluative affect) about performing the target behaviour" ***Subjective norm**—"the person's perception that most people who are important to him think he should or should not perform the behaviour in question"	Bawack et al. (2021) Bialkova (2023a) Hasan et al. (2021) Lim et al. (2022)
Theory of planned behaviour (TPB)	Ajzen (1991)	***Intentions** to behave in particular manner can be predicted by ***Attitudes** toward the behaviour ***Subjective norms**, and perceived behavioural control *Intentions to behave are mediating the perceived **behavioural control** in explaining the actual behaviour demonstrated	Lim et al. (2022)
Expectancy theory of motivation	Vroom (1964)	Motivation as a force for behavioural-oriented action is a function of three distinct components, i.e. ***Valence** ***Instrumentality** ***Expectancy (VIE model)** For an overview see van Eerde and Thierry (1996). See also Chopra (2019) for details on: • **Intrinsic motivation** • **Extrinsic motivation** • **Force choice motivation**	Chopra (2019) Lim et al. (2022)
Self-determination theory (SDT)	Deci and Ryan (1980) but see also Ryan et al. (1997)—for self-regulation	**Innate psychological needs** are the basis for people's self-motivation and personality integration (Ryan & Deci, 2000) In particular, needs for •**Competence** •**Relatedness** •**Autonomy**	Jiménez-Barreto et al. (2021) Mariani et al. (2023)

(continued)

Table 3.2 (continued)

Theory	Origin	CORE concepts/constructs	Application—key references AI
Flow theory	Csikszentmihalyi (original work as of 1975), but see also Webster et al. (1993), Nakamura and Csikszentmihalyi (2009)	Flow encompasses: *Perceived control *Attention *User's curiosity and his/her interaction to be intrinsically interesting (Webster et al., 1993—HCI)	Lim et al. (2022) Poushneh (2021b)
Big five factors of personality	Goldberg (1990) McCrae and Costa (1987)	(McCrae & Costa, 1987) *Surgency *Agreeableness *Consciousness *Emotional stability *Intelligence (Goldberg, 1990) *Neuroticism *Extraversion *Openness *Agreeableness (vs. antagonism) *Conscientiousness (vs. undirectedness))	Bawack et al. (2021) Lim et al. (2022)

3.2.4   Self-determination Theory (SDT)

Self-determination Theory (SDT) as suggested by the work of Deci and Ryan (1980), and self-regulation theory (Ryan et al., 1997) have often been applied in the context of human–computer interaction. In particular, the basis for human self-motivation and personality integration is investigated in line with people's inherent growth tendencies and innate psychological needs (Ryan & Deci, 2000). The authors identified three such needs—the needs for competence, relatedness, and autonomy. In the chatbot context, self-determination theory has been mentioned by few researchers (see Table 3.2). It was reported that self-determination affects attitudes and satisfaction (Jiménez-Barreto et al., 2021; Mariani et al., 2023).

3.2.5   Flow Theory

Flow theory emerged when studying optimal experiences in everyday scenarios in the desire to understand what intrinsically motivates people (for an overview, see Nakamura & Csikszentmihalyi, 2009). Flow is experienced when perceived challenges and opportunities for action are in balance with the actor's skills. Not surprisingly then, when interacting with technology, *flow theory* was applied to explain consumers' attitudes and behaviour (e.g., Novak et al., 2000). In the context of HCI experience, the flow incorporates the extent to which the user perceives (a) sense of **control** over the computer interaction, (b) **attention** focused on the interaction, (c) **curiosity** aroused during the interaction, and (d) the interaction is intrinsically **interesting** (Webster et al., 1993). A good flow in overjumping challenging activities is characterised by playful interaction, immersion of the user in the action, and having fun. In the AI context, few researchers build upon flow theory their exploration (for a review, see Lim et al., 2022). It was further acknowledged that functional intelligence, sincerity, and creativity empower consumers to take control of their voice interactions with the voice assistant (Poushneh, 2021b).

3.2.6 Big Five Factors of Personality

Big Five factors of personality is a taxonomy widely recognised with the names of McCrae and Costa (1987) and the work of Goldberg (1990). From the taxonomy of McCrae and Costa, surgency, agreeableness, consciousness, emotional stability, and intelligence emerged as crucial personality traits. According to Goldberg's taxonomy, the *big five* encompass neuroticism, extraversion, openness, agreeableness (vs. antagonism), and conscientiousness (vs. undirectedness). In the chatbot context, the taxonomy of Goldberg was applied (e.g., Bawack et al., 2021; Lim et al., 2022). It was reported that the relationship between personality (agreeableness, emotional instability, and conscientiousness) and voice shoppers' perceptions of customer experience performance are mediated by trust and privacy concerns (Bawack et al., 2021).

3.3 Social Influence Theories

3.3.1 Anthropomorphism Theory

Anthropomorphism theory was earlier applied in line with human–computer interaction (HCI) and robot implementation. The core notion reflects the attribution of human characteristics to inanimate objects, animals, and others in order to help the rationalisation of actions. Cognitive and/or emotional states are attributed based on observation. The idea is to rationalise an entity's behaviour in a given social environment. Although a computer is not a person and does not warrant human treatment or attribution (Nass & Moon, 2000), anthropomorphism mirrors the assignment of human traits and characteristics to computers. It was noted, however, individuals differ in their likelihood of anthropomorphising objects, despite the reported positive effects of reported anthropomorphism on technology use (Duffy, 2003). Not surprisingly then, in the chatbot context, it was reported that the higher the consumers need for human interaction, the stronger the level of anthropomorphism is, and thus, the stronger the adoption relationship is (Sheehan et al., 2020). The effects of anthropomorphic design cues, perceived anthropomorphism on social presence, overall attitudes, and emotions were further acknowledged (Araujo, 2018). Anthropomorphism has been extensively applied in chatbot context (e.g., Blut et al., 2021; Mariani et al., 2023; Roy & Naidoo, 2021). See Table 3.3 for an overview on core social influence theories discussed in the AI chatbot context.

3.3.2   Social Agency Theory

Social agency theory was earlier applied in media context (e.g., Mayer et al., 2003). It was argued that social cues in a multimedia message can prime the social conversation schema in the learner. Once the social conversation schema is activated, learners are highly likely to act as if they are in a conversation with another person. In the HCI context, social cues (e.g., modulated intonation, and the human-like appearance of a computer) encouraged people to interpret the interaction with a computer as being social in nature. Translating these notions to the chatbot context, it was hypothesised that the social rules of human-to-human communication come into play, leading people to act as if they were in a conversation with another human (Aeschlimann et al., 2020), presumably due to the interpretation of the interaction as being social. Moreover, an increased number of human-like features attributed to an artificial agent leads to stronger human-like behaviour. The quality of social interaction also increases with the number of social characteristics an artificial agent possesses. This is probably due to the fact that humans tend to interpret the interaction as a social communicative situation, thus stimulating a deeper processing of the information presented by the agent.

3.3.3   Social Cognitive Theory (SCT)

Social Cognitive Theory (SCT) accords a central role to cognitive, vicarious, self-reflective, and self-regulatory processes. Originally suggested by Bandura (self-efficacy theory, 1977), social learning analysis and expectations of personal efficacy are based on four major sources of information: performance accomplishments, vicarious experience, verbal persuasion, and physiological states. Bandura further subscribes to a model emergent interactive agency, rejecting the dichotomous conception of self as agent and self as object (1986). Crucial to point out for SCT is the notion that people draw on their knowledge, cognitive, and behavioural skills to produce desired results, by acting as agents in their environments (Bandura, 1989). Expansion of postulates, i.e., *Social learning theory* claims that people learn by observing others in the context of their social interactions and experiences. Put differently, people's development is influenced by the environment, others' behaviour, and cognition. Furthermore, the theory assumes that agents are influencing themselves as much

Table 3.3 Social theories applied in the AI chatbot context

Theory	Origin	CORE concepts/ constructs	Application—key references AI
Anthropomorphism theory	Duffy (2003) Nass and Moon (2000)	The tendency to attribute human characteristics (cognitive and emotional) to inanimate objects, to rationalise their actions	Araujo (2018) Blut et al. (2021) Mariani et al. (2023) Roy and Naidoo (2021) Sheehan et al. (2020)
Social agency theory (SAT)	Mayer et al. (2003)	Lifted social interaction with increased number of social characteristics possessed by computer (robot/ VA/AI agent)	Aeschlimann et al. (2020) Lim et al. (2022)
Social cognitive theory (SCT)	Bandura (for an overview see 1989 study, as reflecting the work from 1977, 1986, 1989)	*Central role to cognitive, vicarious, self-reflective, and self-regulatory processes *People draw on their knowledge, cognitive, and behavioural skills to produce desired results, acting as agents over their environments *Self-regulating process *Performance *Vicarious experience *Verbal persuasion *Physiological state	Chong et al. (2021) Mariani et al. (2023) See also Venkatesh et al. (2003) for tech context: *Outcome expectations (performance) *Outcome expectations (personal) *Self-efficacy *Affect, and *Anxiety
Social influence theory (SIT)	Kelman (1958)	Three processes of SI include: *Compliance *Internalisation *Identification	Moriuchi (2021) Vimalkumar et al. (2021)
Social presence theory (SPT)	Short et al. (1976) Biocca et al. (2003)	*Awareness *Representation of others *Social interaction capacity *Mediated communication	Bialkova (2022a, 2022b) Mariani et al. (2023) Moriuchi (2021) Qiu and Benbasat (2009)

(continued)

Table 3.3 (continued)

Theory	Origin	CORE concepts/ constructs	Application—key references AI
Social-response theory (SRT)	Nass et al. (1994) Nass and Moon (2000)	Humans apply social rules when they interact with machines/ computers, assuming these are social actors	Adam et al. (2021) Chattaraman et al. (2019) Lim et al. (2022) Liu and Sundar (2018) Mariani et al. (2023) Poushneh (2021a) Xu et al. (2022)
Para-social relationship	Horton and Wohl (1956)	*Mediated interaction *VA–human relationship when a media user engages in with a media persona	Lim et al. (2022) Pitardi and Marriott (2021) Whang and Im (2020) Youn and Jin (2021)
Computers as social actors (CASA)	Nass et al. (1994) Nass and Moon (2000)	*Social rules *Social actors	Gambino et al. (2020) Liew et al. (2021) Liu and Sundar (2018) Ho et al. (2018)

as they are influencing their environment. In acting as agents themselves, people monitor their actions, and assign cognitive guidelines and self-incentives to produce desired personal changes.

Applying SCT in tech acceptance by Venkatesh et al. (2003), the following core components were suggested to account for social cognition, namely, outcome expectations (performance), outcome expectations (personal), self-efficacy, affect, and anxiety. By applying SCT to analyse AI chatbots in service frontlines, a three-level classification of AI chatbot design was suggested that encompasses anthropomorphic role, appearance, and interactivity (Chong et al., 2021).

3.3.4 Social Influence Theory

Social Influence Theory in Kelman's (1958) terms accounts for three processes responsible for attitude change. These include compliance, internalisation, and identification. Compliance is similar to the subjective norm concept, as discussed by Ajzen's (1991) theory of planned behaviour. Internalisation occurs when an individual accepts the social influence because of the similarity between their thought (process, actions, values) and those of the other members of the social group. Identification is associated with the acknowledgement of social influence and acceptance of this influence by an individual, in order to establish and maintain a satisfying self-defining relationship with another person and/or group. Social influence emerged as a strong predictor of behavioural intentions across different technologies. In the chatbot context, such a relationship has also been confirmed (e.g., Vimalkumar et al., 2021). It was further reported that social influence has a positive impact on voice assistance (VA) usage experience (Moriuchi, 2021).

3.3.5 Social Presence Theory (SPT)

Social Presence Theory (SPT), in terms of salience degree of the other person in the interaction was earliest applied in the context of media by Short and colleagues in the 1970s. It was assumed that media outlets with a high degree of social presence are judged as warm, personal, sensitive, and sociable. The work of Biocca et al. (2003) defined social presence as the sense of being with another. It encounters for awareness of and the representation of the other, the medium's capacity for social interaction, and the presence (or absence) of verbal or non-verbal cues in mediated communication. Although SPT is very popular in mediated environments, in the context of AI agency, only a few studies explicitly mention SPT (Mariani et al., 2023; Qiu & Benbasa, 2009). Social presence was also discussed in line with realistic presence (Moriuchi, 2021), enjoyment (Bialkova, 2022b, 2023b), and functionality (Bialkova, 2023c). The notion of social presence itself was addressed in several studies in the chatbot context (see also Chap. 2, Bialkova, 2024a).

3.3.6 Social Response Theory (SRT)

Social Response Theory (SRT) essentially argues that humans apply social rules when they interact with machines and computers, assuming that computers are social actors (Nass et al., 1994). Such social responses to computers are commonplace and easy to generate. The researchers, however, noted that social responses to computers are not the result of conscious beliefs that computers are human or human-like. It was further claimed that individuals apply social response mindlessly (Lombard & Ditton, 1997; Nass & Moon, 2000). Although humans interact with computers mindlessly, they employ social rules similarly in what they do in human–human interaction such as politeness, self-disclosure, and trust. Such behaviour is a response to social cues in conversation, interaction, and social roles recognised with computers (Nass & Moon, 2000; Reeves & Nass, 1996).

Recent studies in the AI context have also acknowledged the notion that human–computer interaction is fundamentally social (Adam et al., 2021) and thus assigns social actors' roles (e.g., Lim et al., 2022; Liu & Sundar, 2018; Xu et al., 2022).

Mindless responses were further noted (Chattaraman et al. (2019), as humans apply social rules to anthropomorphically designed computers. In other words, individuals are automatically and unconsciously biased toward perceiving computers as social actors (Adam et al., 2021).

3.3.7   Para-Social Relationship

Para-Social Relationship accounts for the mediated interaction. It originates from media communication theories arguing for the illusion of face-to-face relationship with the performer (Horton & Wohl, 1956). In the AI context, Virtual assistant VA–human relationships are assumed when a media user engages with a media persona, in an illusionary mediated experience. Several papers have addressed parasocial behaviour in the chatbot context (Lim et al., 2022; Pitardi & Marriott, 2021; Whang & Im, 2020; Youn & Jin, 2021).

3.3.8   Computers as Social Actors (CASA)

Computers as Social Actors (CASA) paradigm was introduced a while ago (Nass et al., 1994) and has received a good attention in the chatbot context (Gambino et al., 2020; Ho et al., 2018; Liew et al., 2021; Liu & Sundar, 2018). According to the CASA paradigm, users interact with computers applying social rules, although they are aware that computers are inanimate. Such behaviour is generated subconsciously as a natural response to social situations. Despite the fact that computers do not warrant human treatment and attribution, users tend to react socially, expressing politeness and reciprocity toward the agent (Nass & Moon, 2000). A revisit of the CASA paradigm suggested that instead of mindlessly applying human–human action toward the agent, it would be beneficial to explicitly generate such social scripts to be applied in the human–machine interaction (Gambino et al., 2020). As a result of an agent being considered a social actor, it was also argued that the expression of sympathy and empathy is favoured over the unemotional provision of advice (Liu & Sundar, 2018). Moreover, agents perceived to act socially encouraged trust in the system and elevated the purchase intention (Liew et al., 2021).

Figure 3.1 summarises the theoretical notions discussed thus far in a classification of key theories applied in the chatbot context. As seen from the profound literature review and the highlights of fundamental theories, chatbot AI agencies have emerged as a substantial research area, calling for investigation into user experience, design, and implementation. In subsequent Chaps. 4 and 5 (Bialkova, 2024b, 2024c) we perform such an investigation, providing suggestions on how to build better systems.

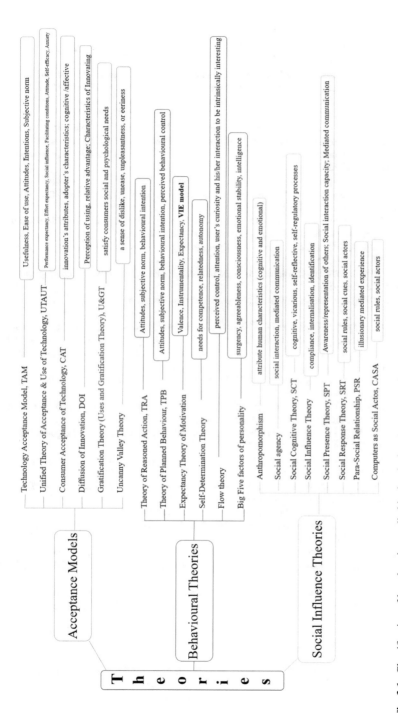

Fig. 3.1 Classification of key theories applied in the chatbot context

References

Adam, M., Wessel, M., & Benlian, A. (2021). AI-based chatbots in customer service and their effects on user compliance. *Electronic Markets, 31*, 427–445.

Aeschlimann, S., Bleiker, M., Wechner, M., & Gampe, A. (2020). Communicative and social consequences of interactions with voice assistants. *Computers in Human Behavior, 112*, 106466.

Agarwal, R., & Prasad, J. (1997). The role of innovation characteristics and perceived voluntariness in the acceptance of information technologies. *Decision Science, 28*(3), 557–582.

Agarwal, R., & Prasad, J. (1998). A conceptual and operational definition of personal innovativeness in the domain of information technology. *Information Systems Research, 9*(2), 204–215.

Ajzen, I. (1991). The theory of planned behavior. *Organizational Behavior and Planned Decision Processes, 50*, 179–211.

Araujo, T. (2018). Living up to the chatbot hype: The influence of anthropomorphic design cues and communicative agency framing on conversational agent and company perceptions. *Computers in Human Behavior, 85*, 183–189.

Balakrishnan J, & Dwivedi, Y. K. (2021). Conversational commerce: Entering the next stage of AI-powered digital assistants. *Annals of Operations Research*, 1–35.

Bandura A. (1977). Self-efficacy: toward a unifying theory of behavioral change. *Psychological Review, 84*(2), 191–215.

Bandura, A. (1986). *Social foundations of thought and action: A social cognitive theory*. Englewood Cliffs, NJ: Prentice-Hall.

Bandura, A. (1989). Human agency in social cognitive theory. *American Psychologist, 44*(9), 1175–1184.

Bawack, R. E., Wamba, S. F., & Carillo, K. D. A. (2021). Exploring the role of personality, trust, and privacy in customer experience performance during voice shopping: Evidence from SEM and fuzzy set qualitative comparative analysis. *International Journal of Information Management, 58*, 102309.

Bialkova, S. (2021). Would you talk to me? The role of chatbots in marketing. In *ICORIA 2021*, June 26–28, Bordeaux, France.

Bialkova, S. (2022a). How may I help you? Chatbots implementation in marketing. In *European Marketing Academy Conference, EMAC 2022*, May 24–27, Budapest, Hungary.

Bialkova, S. (2022b). Interacting with Chatbot: How to enhance functionality and enjoyment? In *AEMARK 2022*, September 7–10, 2022, Valencia, Spain.

Bialkova, S. (2023a). I want to talk to you: Chatbot marketing integration. In *Advances in Advertising Research* (Vol. XII, pp. 23–36). https://doi.org/10.1007/978-3-658-40429-1_2

Bialkova, S. (2023b). AI-driven customer experience: factors to consider. In *Philosophy of artificial intelligence and its place in society* (pp. 341–357). IGI Global.

Bialkova, S. (2023c). How to optimise interaction with chatbots? Key parameters emerging from actual application. *International Journal of Human–Computer Interaction*. https://doi.org/10.1080/10447318.2023.2219963

Bialkova, S. (2024a). Audit of literature on chatbot applications. In *The rise of AI user applications: Chatbots integration foundations and trends*. (Chap. 2). Springer. https://doi.org/10.1007/978-3-031-56471-0_2

Bialkova, S. (2024b). Shaping chatbot efficiency—How to build better systems? In *The rise of AI user applications: Chatbots integration foundations and trends*. (Chap. 4). Springer. https://doi.org/10.1007/978-3-031-56471-0_4

Bialkova, S. (2024c). Chatbot efficiency—Model testing. In *The rise of AI user applications: Chatbots integration foundations and trends*. (Chap. 5). Springer. https://doi.org/10.1007/978-3-031-56471-0_5

Biocca, F., Harms, C., & Burgoon, J. K. (2003). Toward a more robust theory and measure of social presence: Review and suggested criteria. *Presence: Teleoperators & Virtual Environments, 12*, 456–480.

Blut, M., Wang, C., Wünderlich, N., & Brock, C. (2021). Understanding anthropomorphism in service provision: A meta-analysis of physical robots, chatbots, and other AI. *Journal of the Academy of Marketing Science, 49*, 632–658.

Chattaraman, V., Kwon, W. S., Gilbert, J. E., & Ross, K. (2019). Should AI-based, conversational digital assistants employ social-or task-oriented interaction style? A task-competency and reciprocity perspective for older adults. *Computers in Human Behavior, 90*, 315–330.

Chong, T., Yu, T., Keeling, D. I., & de Ruyter, K. (2021). AI-chatbots on the services frontline addressing the challenges and opportunities of agency. *Journal of Retailing and Consumer Services, 63*, 102735.

Chopra, K. (2019). Indian shopper motivation to use artificial intelligence: Generating Vroom's expectancy theory of motivation using grounded theory approach. *International Journal of Retail & Distribution Management, 47*(3), 331–347.

Ciechanowski, L., Przegalinska, A., Magnuski, M., & Gloor, P. (2019). In the shades of the uncanny valley: An experimental study of human–chatbot interaction. *Future Generation Computer Systems, 92*, 539–548.

Davis, F. D. (1989). Perceived usefulness, perceived ease of use, and user acceptance of information technology. *MIS Quarterly, 13*(3), 319–339.

Davis, F. D., Bagozzi, R. P., & Warshaw, P. R. (1989). User acceptance of computer technology: A comparison of two theoretical models. *Management Science, 5*(8), 982–1003.

Deci, E. L., & Ryan, R. M. (1980). Self-determination theory: When mind mediates behavior. *The Journal of Mind and Behavior, 1*(1), 33–43.

Duffy, B. R. (2003). Anthropomorphism and the social robot. *Robotics and Autonomous Systems, 42*(3–4), 177–190.

Fernandes, T., & Oliveira, E. (2021). Understanding consumers' acceptance of automated technologies in service encounters: Drivers of digital voice assistants adoption. *Journal of Business Research, 122*, 180–191.

Fishbein, M., & Ajzen, I. (1974). Attitudes towards objects as predictors of single and multiple behavioral criteria. *Psychological Review, 81*(1), 59–74.

Gambino, A., Fox, J., & Ratan, R. A. (2020). Building a stronger CASA: Extending the computers are social actors paradigm. *Human-Machine Communication, 1*, 71–85.

Goldberg, L. R. (1990). An alternative "description of personality": The big-five factor structure. *Journal of Personality and Social Psychology, 59*(6), 1216–1229.

Gray, K., & Wegner, D. M. (2012). Feeling robots and human zombies: Mind perception and the uncanny valley. *Cognition, 125*, 125–130.

Hasan, R., Shams, R., & Rahman, M. (2021). Consumer trust and perceived risk for voice-controlled artificial intelligence: The case of Siri. *Journal of Business Research, 131*, 591–597.

Ho, A. S., Hancock, J., & Miner, A. S. (2018). Psychological, relational, and emotional effects of self-disclosure after conversations with a chatbot. *The Journal of Communication, 68*, 712–733.

Horton, D., & Wohl, R. (1956). Mass communication and para-social interaction: Observations on intimacy at a distance. *Psychiatry, 19*, 215–229.

Hoyer, W. D., Kroschke, M., Schmitt, B., Kraume, K., & Shankar, V. (2020). Transforming the customer experience through new technologies. *Journal of Interactive Marketing, 51*(1), 57–71.

Jain, S., Basu, S., Dwivedi, Y. K., & Kaur, S. (2022). Interactive voice assistants—Does brand credibility assuage privacy risks? *Journal of Business Research, 139*, 701–717.

Jiménez-Barreto, J., Rubio, N., & Molinillo, S. (2021). Find a flight for me, Oscar! Motivational customer experiences with chatbots. *International Journal of Contemporary Hospitality Management, 33*(11), 3860–3882.

Katz, E., Haas, H., & Gurevitch, M. (1973). On the use of the mass media for important things. *American Sociological Review, 38*(2), 164–181.

Kelman, H. C. (1958). Compliance, identification, and internalization: Three processes of attitude change. *Journal of Conflict Resolution, 2*(1), 51–60.

Kim, S. Y., Schmitt, B., & Thalmann, N. (2019). Eliza in the uncanny valley: Anthropomorphizing consumer robots increases their perceived warmth but decreases liking. *Marketing Letters, 30*(1), 1–12.

Kowalczuk, P. (2018). Consumer acceptance of smart speakers: A mixed methods approach. *Journal of Research in Interactive Marketing, 12*(4), 418–431.

Kulviwat, S., Bruner, G. C., Kumar, A., Nasco, S., & Clark, T. (2007). Toward a unified theory of consumer acceptance technology. *Psychology & Marketing, 24*, 1059–1084.

Liew, T. W., Tan, S.-M., Tee, J., & Gan Goh, G. G. (2021). The effects of designing conversational commerce chatbots with expertise cues. In *2021 14th International Conference on Human System Interaction (HSI)* (pp. 1–6), Gdańsk, Poland.

Lim, W. M., Kumar, S., Verma, S., & Chaturvedi, R. (2022). Alexa, what do we know about conversational commerce? Insights from a systematic literature review. *Psychology & Marketing, 39*, 1129–1155.

Liu, B., & Sundar, S. S. (2018). Should machines express sympathy and empathy? Experiments with a health advice chatbot. *Cyberpsychology, Behavior and Social Networking, 21*(10), 625–636.

Lombard, M., & Ditton, T. (1997). At the heart of it all: The concept of presence. *Journal of Computer Mediated Communication, 3*(2), JCMC321.

Mariani, M. M., Hashemi, N., & Wirtz, J. (2023). Artificial intelligence empowered conversational agents: A systematic literature review and research agenda. *Journal of Business Research, 161*, 113838.

Mayer, R. E., Sobko, K., & Mautone, P. D. (2003). Social cues in multimedia learning: Role of speaker's voice. *Journal of Educational Psychology, 95*(2), 419–425.

McCrae, R. R., & Costa, P. T., Jr. (1987). Validation of the five-factor model of personality across instruments and observers. *Journal of Personality and Social Psychology, 52*, 81–90.

McLean, G., & Osei-Frimpong, K. (2019). Hey Alexa … examine the variables influencing the use of artificial intelligent in-home voice assistants. *Computers in Human Behavior, 99*, 28–37.

Moore, G. C., & Benbasat, I. (1991). Development of an instrument to measure the perceptions of adopting an information technology innovation. *Information Systems Research, 2*, 192–222.

Moore, G. C., & Benbasat, I. (1996). Integrating diffusion of innovations and theory of reasoned action models to predict utilization of information technology by end-users. In K. Kautz, et al. (eds.), *Diffusion and adoption of information technology* (pp.132–146).

Mori, M., Macdorman, K. F., & Kageki, N. (2012). The uncanny valley. *IEEE Robotics & Automation Magazine, 19*(2), 98–100.

Moriuchi, E. (2021). An empirical study on anthropomorphism and engagement with disembodied AIs and consumers' re-use behavior. *Psychology and Marketing, 38*(7), 21–42.

Nakamura, J., & Csikszentmihalyi, M. (2009). Flow theory and research. *Oxford handbook of positive psychology* (pp. 195–206). Oxford University Press.

Nass, C., & Moon, Y. (2000). Machines and mindlessness: Social responses to computers. *Journal of Social Issues, 56*(1), 81–103.

Nass, C., Steuer, J., & Tauber, E. R. (1994). Computers are social actors. In *Proceedings of the SIGCHI Conference on Human Factors in Computing Systems* (pp. 72–28), April 24–28, 1994, Boston, USA.

Novak, T. P., Hoffman, D. L., & Yung, Y. F. (2000). Measuring the customer experience in online environments: A structural modeling approach. *Marketing Science, 19*(1), 22–42.

Pillai, R., & Sivathanu, B. (2020). Adoption of AI-based chatbots for hospitality and tourism. *International Journal of Contemporary Hospitality Management, 32*(10), 3199–3226.

Pitardi, V., & Marriott, H. R. (2021). Alexa, she's not human but… unveiling the drivers of consumers' trust in voice-based artificial intelligence. *Psychology & Marketing, 38*, 626–642.

Poushneh, A. (2021a). Impact of auditory sense on trust and brand affect through auditory social interaction and control. *Journal of Retailing and Consumer Services, 58*, 102281.

Poushneh, A. (2021b). Humanizing voice assistant: The impact of voice assistant personality on consumers' attitudes and behaviors. *Journal of Retailing and Consumer Services, 58*, 102283.

Qiu, L., & Benbasat, I. (2009). Evaluating anthropomorphic product recommendation agents: A social relationship perspective to designing information systems. *Journal of Management Information Systems, 25*(4), 145–181.

Reeves, B., & Nass, C. I. (1996). *The media equation: How people treat computers, television, and new media like real people and places.* Cambridge University Press.

Rese, A., Ganster, L., & Baier, D. (2020). Chatbots in retailers' customer communication: How to measure their acceptance? *Journal of Retailing and Consumer Services, 56*, 102176.

Rogers, E. M. (1995). *Diffusion of innovations* (4th ed.). Free Press.

Roy, R., & Naidoo, V. (2021). Enhancing chatbot effectiveness: The role of anthropomorphic conversational styles and time orientation. *Journal of Business Research, 126*, 23–34.

Ruggiero, T. E. (2000). Uses and gratifications theory in the 21st century. *Mass Communication and Society, 3*(1), 3–37.

Ryan, R. M., & Deci, E. L. (2000). Self-determination theory and the facilitation of intrinsic motivation, social development, and well-being. *American Psychologist, 55*(1), 68–78.

Ryan, R. M., Kuhl, J., & Deci, E. L. (1997). Nature and autonomy: Organizational view of social and neurobiological aspects of self-regulation in behavior and development. *Development and Psychopathology, 9*, 701–728.

Sheehan, B., Jin, H. S., & Gottlieb, U. (2020). Customer service chatbots: Anthropomorphism and adoption. *Journal of Business Research, 115*, 14–24.

Short, J., Williams, E., & Christie, B. (1976). *The social psychology of telecommunications.* Wiley.

Skjuve, M., Haugstveit, I. M., Følstad, A., & Brandtzaeg, P. B. (2019). Help! Is my chatbot falling into the uncanny valley? An empirical study of user experience in human chatbot interaction. *Human Technology, 15*(1), 30–54.

van Eerde, W., & Thierry, H. (1996). Vroom's expectancy models and work-related criteria: A meta-analysis. *Journal of Applied Psychology, 81*(5), 575–586.

Venkatesh, V., Morris, M. G., Davis, G. B., & Davis, F. D. (2003). User acceptance of information technology: Toward a unified view. *MIS Quarterly, 27*(3), 425–478.

Vimalkumar, M., Sharma, S. K., Singh, J. B., & Dwivedi, Y. K. (2021). 'Okay Google, what about my privacy?' User's privacy perceptions and acceptance of voice-based digital assistants. *Computers in Human Behavior, 120*, 106763.

Vroom, V. H. (1964). *Work and motivation.* Wiley.

Webster, J., Treviño, L. K., & Ryan, L. (1993). The dimensionality and correlates of flow in human-computer interactions. *Computers in Human Behavior, 9*, 411–426.

Whang, C. H., & Im, H. (2020). "I Like Your Suggestion!" The role of human likeness and parasocial relationship on the website versus voice shopper's perception of recommendations. *Psychology & Marketing, 38*(4), 581–595.

Xie, C., Wang, Y., & Cheng, Y. (2022). Does artificial intelligence satisfy you? A meta-analysis of user gratification and user satisfaction with AI-powered chatbots. *International Journal of Human–Computer Interaction.*

Xu, K., Chan-Olmsted, S., & Liu, F. (2022). Smart speakers require smart management: Two routes from user gratifications to privacy settings. *International Journal of Communication, 16*, 192–214.

Youn, S., & Jin, S. V. (2021). "In A.I. we trust?" The effects of parasocial interaction and technopian versus luddite ideological views on chatbot-based customer relationship management in the emerging 'feeling economy'. *Computers in Human Behavior, 119*, 106721.

Zarouali, B., Van den Broeck, E., Walrave, M., & Poels, K. (2018). Predicting consumer responses to a chatbot on Facebook. *Cyberpsychology, Behavior, and Social Networking, 21*(8), 491–497.

Part II
Key Drivers of Chatbot Efficiency—A Holistic Framework

Chapter 4
Shaping Chatbot Efficiency—How to Build Better Systems?

Abstract Various types of AI systems are distinguished based on the algorithms deployed, the technical features, and the devices integrated into different applications. The puzzling question hereby is whether these systems provide the desired experience and satisfaction to the user in regard to efficiency of chatbots currently available on the market. As seen from the marketing examples and the profound literature audit reported in the previous chapter, chatbot efficiency perception and thus system adoption and use are very sensitive to user needs and demand for a satisfactory experience. As is well known from the behaviour theories, satisfactory experience fosters positive attitudes and thus great willingness to use a product. From UX, we are also well informed that satisfaction is crucial for inspiring new computational and design frameworks for AI. Therefore, challenging fundamental assumptions on the factors driving attitudes and satisfaction, we aim to provide the much-needed understanding of how to build better systems for AI chatbot implementation. In particular, quality and ease of use are discussed as core parameters loading on the way chatbot efficiency is evaluated. We further look at the factors shaping interactivity. Both cognition and emotion turn to play a role. As functionality (cognitive) and enjoyment (emotional components) have emerged as the most frequently explored in various HCI, UX, and marketing studies, we focus on these parameters and their antecedents. While in previous research abovementioned issues have been addressed in separate studies, often in isolation, hereby we combine cognitive and affective components in a conceptual model that will be tested in empirical studies, as described in detail below.

4.1 Factors Determining Attitudes

Despite the fact that researchers are not univocal on the nature of the factors determining chatbot efficiency (for details, see Chaps. 2 and 3, Bialkova, 2024a, 2024b), ease of use (for overview, see Davis et al., 1989) and communication quality (for overview, see Chung et al., 2020) emerged to be essential for consumer satisfaction and for forming attitudes toward technology. Therefore, we argue that ease of use and quality perception shape the chatbot performance evaluation (see Table 4.1, for a summary on core parameters, and Fig. 4.1, for a summary of the hypotheses tested).

Ease of use, reflecting the degree to which the user expects the tech system to be free of effort (Davis et al., 1989), has been addressed in the chatbot context via various scales (e.g., Ashfaq et al., 2020; Bialkova, 2023a, 2023b; Blut et al., 2021; Fernandes & Oliveira, 2021; Kowalczuk, 2018; Pitardi & Marriott, 2021; Rese et al., 2020). Although ease of use seems to be a must, if not provided at the level required by customers, it turned into a barrier (Wirtz et al., 2018). Note that a recent study was not able to show an effect of perceived ease of use on the intention to reuse a chatbot (Meyer-Waarden et al., 2020). Such an outcome questions the ease of use of chatbots and calls for a new exploration of their effect.

Quality impact was also explored in different studies, and with various scales (e.g., Ashfaq et al., 2020; Ben Mimoun et al., 2017; Bialkova, 2023a; Chung et al., 2020; Kowalczuk, 2018; Lou et al., 2022; Meyer-Waarden et al., 2020; Xiao & Benbasat, 2007). In the context of chatbots, the most commonly used scales reflect the information and communication quality (measuring semantic success), the system quality (measuring technical success), and the service quality (measuring organisational impact and effectiveness success)—for an overview, see Trivedi, 2019 (based on DeLone & McLean, 2003). It was noted that a higher system quality is expected to lead to greater user satisfaction and use (DeLone & McLean, 2003).

However, creating high-quality chatbots that meet consumer demands and foster positive attitudes turns to be a challenging task (Bialkova, 2021, 2023a). Understanding the factors loading on chatbot efficiency, therefore, is crucial to provide a concise and accurate picture of the problems at stake. Translating the above knowledge in the current setting, we therefore predict the following:

H1. The greater the ease of use and the quality are perceived to be:
H1a. the higher the satisfaction will be
H1b. the more positive the attitudes toward chatbot(s) will be.

As a consequence, we assume the following:

H2. The greater the satisfaction and the more positive the attitudes are, the higher the intention to use a chatbot in future will be.
H3. The greater the satisfaction and the more positive the attitudes are, the higher the willingness to recommend chatbots will be.

The more intriguing hereby is: which are the factors that predetermine the ease of use and quality perception, and thus drive chatbot efficiency?

In the following, we elaborate on potential factors emerging from the literature as key drivers of chatbot efficiency, namely functionality, interactivity, and enjoyment.

Table 4.1 Core parameters in chatbot efficiency evaluation

Parameter	Definition	References
Ease of use	The degree to which the user expects the tech system to be free of effort (Davis et al., 1989)	Ashfaq et al. (2020) Bialkova (2023a, 2023b) Blut et al. (2021) Fernandes and Oliveira (2021) Kowalczuk (2018) Meyer-Waarden et al. (2020) Pitardi and Marriott (2021) Rese et al. (2020)
Quality	Information, technical, and overall service success (Trivedi, 2019, based on DeLone & McLean, 2003)	Ashfaq et al. (2020) Bialkova (2021, 2022a, 2023a) Ben Mimoun et al. (2017) Chung et al. (2020) Kowalczuk (2018) Lou et al. (2022) Meyer-Waarden et al. (2020) Xiao and Benbasat (2007) Wirtz et al. (2018)
Functionality	Reflects a correct technical functioning (Parasuraman et al., 2005)	Ashfaq et al. (2021) Ben Mimoun et al. (2017) Bialkova (2023a, 2023b) Chattaraman et al. (2019) Fernandes and Oliveira (2021) Lee and Cho (2020) Pitardi and Marriott (2021)
Interactivity	Extent to which users can manipulate technology (Bialkova & Barr, 2022) and/or control device; emphasised role of interaction between the user and the system	Ben Mimoun et al. (2017) Bialkova (2023a, 2023c) Fernandes and Oliveira (2021) Go and Sundar (2019) Holzwarth et al. (2006) Lou et al. (2022) Poushneh (2021) Tsai et al. (2021)
Enjoyment	Core affect (Russell, 1980), typically arising from connection or sensory pleasure, interchanged with happiness (Ekman, Atlas of Emotions)	Ashfaq et al. (2020) Bialkova (2022b, 2023b) Kowalczuk (2018) Lee and Choi (2017) Pillai et al. (2020) Pitardi and Marriott (2021) Rese et al. (2020) Xu et al. (2022) Zarouali et al. (2018)
Satisfaction	Occurs when customers find that products or services meet or exceed their positive expectations (Chung et al., 2020; Zeithaml et al., 1996)	Bialkova (2023a, 2023b) Chaves and Gerosa (2021) Chung et al. (2020) Gelbrich et al. (2021)

(continued)

Table 4.1 (continued)

Parameter	Definition	References
Attitudes	Beliefs about an object/person are evaluated, affecting intention to behave and actual behaviour (theory of planned behaviour, TPB; Ajzen, 1991)	Ashfaq et al. (2021) Bialkova (2021, 2023a) Pitardi and Marriott (2021)
Intention to use	Willingness to use the system, in this case chatbot	Bialkova (2022b, 2023b) Blut et al. (2021) Moriuchi et al. (2021)
Recommendation	Advocating to friends, family, significant others	Bialkova (2022a; 2023a)

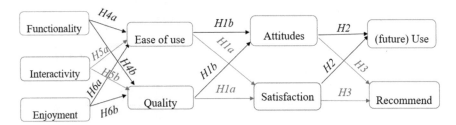

Fig. 4.1 Summary of the hypotheses tested

4.2 Factors Determining Ease of Use and Quality Perception

Considering that intelligent systems' behaviour may vary across contexts and/or as a function of the environmental inputs, one may expect different degrees of the way the agency performance is perceived, i.e., various factors to shape quality and ease of use perception. In this respect, it is worth exploring AI behaviour in different environments and scenarios.

For example, functional and enjoyable interaction enhanced the experience and thus attitude formation (Bialkova, 2023b). Note, however, that these results were valid only for consumers reporting high satisfaction. By contrast, consumers reporting low satisfaction have not enjoyed the experience with the AI system. They found the interaction to be unpleasant and the system to be useless. Similarly, another study from our laboratory exploring the chatbot efficiency of actual applications in the tourism sector (Bialkova, 2023e) pointed out that only satisfied consumers found the system used to be functional. These outcomes should be considered as a warning call to further investigate the factors navigating user experience with AI systems.

4.3 Functionality

Functionality was explored during the implementation of almost any tech device and/or application from mobile to augmented (AR) and virtual reality (VR). However, the need to explore functionality in the chatbot context has been acknowledged (Lee & Cho, 2020). If we adopt the definition that functionality is associated with a correct technical functioning (Parasuraman et al., 2005), we might argue that this definition reflects the ability to function well, in line with the user expectations.

We have to note, however, that functional and interface characteristics have been suggested in end-user systems evaluation a while ago (Davis et al., 1989). From marketing literature, it is also well known that functionality is recognised as a benefit when interacting with a salesperson and leads to time savings, ease of purchase, pleasure gained through interactions, feelings and possibly loyalty toward the company (e.g., Homburg et al., 2011; Xiao & Benbasat, 2007). In e-retailing, website navigation and communication functionality were acknowledged as crucial for visit duration and purchase likelihood (Mallapragada et al., 2016).

A link was assumed between the use of a virtual agent on a website and e-consumer productivity, in the form of efficiency and effectiveness, during online purchases (Ben Mimoun et al., 2017). In the e-service, it was further reported that when a chatbot is able to resolve issues immediately, then consumers are likely to gravitate toward such a technology (Moriuchi et al., 2021). Naturally then, various studies looked at the chatbot functionality and how to enhance it (Ashfaq et al., 2021; Bialkova, 2023a, 2023b; Chattaraman et al., 2019; Fernandes & Oliveira, 2021; Lee & Cho, 2020; Pitardi & Marriott, 2021).

We assume that advanced technology incorporating AI may possibly provide better functionality, and thus, we argue, could enhance the e-agency. For example, by increasing the efficiency of customer time use, providing good and desired solutions, we envisage that the chatbot functionality could boost quality perception and customer satisfaction. Therefore, we hypothesise:

H4. The higher the functionality of a chatbot is perceived to be:
H4a. the greater the ease of use
H4b. the higher the quality will be.

4.4 Enhancing Interaction

Interactivity has been extensively studied in the context of e-agency (Ben Mimoun et al., 2017; Bialkova, 2023a, 2023c; Fernandes & Oliveira, 2021; Go & Sundar, 2019; Lou et al., 2022; Poushneh, 2021; Tsai et al., 2021), since the earliest applications in online shopping (e.g., Holzwarth et al., 2006). It was shown that enhanced online interaction fosters a sense of connection between a customer and a company and therefore shapes attitudes and consequent behaviour (Ben Mimoun et al., 2017). In the same vein, the level of interactivity was positively associated with product attitudes and the intention to return (Bialkova, 2019, 2021). It was further reported that high interactivity not only provides more product information but also creates the necessary flow to enhance user involvement with the product (Bialkova & Barr, 2022).

Although there are different definitions of interactivity, almost all of these emphasise the role of interaction between the user and the system (Bialkova, 2023a). In this respect, it is very important to note hereby, that when individuals interact more easily with a technological system, they will perceive greater efficacy (Davis et al., 1989).

Moreover, the quality of any customer interaction has been reported to be pivotal in the service quality evaluation (Parasuraman et al., 2005) and has been extensively explored since the infancy of service marketing research (Parasuraman et al., 1988) in various online and offline contexts. Note, however, that while in the offline context, the users may directly interact with the service providers, in the online environment this interaction is mediated by the technology.

Recent studies exploring user opinion concerning high-tech AR/VR platforms recognised that interactivity and involvement with technology are crucial for the way experience is evaluated and thus liked (Bialkova & Barr, 2022; Bialkova, 2019, 2023d). The authors reported that better interactivity leads to greater likability (Bialkova, 2019, 2023d) and satisfaction (Bialkova & Barr, 2022).

Translating this in the current context, we could argue that chatbot interactivity may enhance the overall experience and quality perception. Thus, we propose the following hypothesis:

H5. The better the interactivity is perceived to be:
H5a. the greater the ease of use
H5b. the higher the quality will be evaluated.

Furthermore, the interaction with service agents and/or salespersons was pointed out as pivotal for consumer satisfaction and for forming attitudes toward the company, decades ago (Ramsey & Sohi, 1997; Reynolds & Arnold, 2000). In the tech context, interaction is characterised by the level of interactivity, reflecting the extent to which users can manipulate the system technology (Bialkova & Barr, 2022).

It is important to point out hereby that interactivity perception seems to depend on consumers' need for interaction. People with a low need for interaction do not appear to find it fun or amusing to interact with an artificial human, while those with an average or high need for interaction perceive it as pleasant and playful (Ben Mimoun et al., 2017). Product involvement might also shape the interaction perception and consequent behaviour. It was shown that avatars lead to positive attitudes toward the product and enhance the purchase intention, but these effects are moderated by the product involvement (e.g., Holzwarth et al., 2006) and avatar attractiveness (Miao et al., 2022). Furthermore, interactions involving human-like communication style lifted the enjoyment when chatbots have been employed (de Sa Siqueira et al., 2023). Based on the abovementioned findings, we might argue that not only cognitive characteristics (e.g., in terms of functionality and interactivity) but also affective components (e.g., attractiveness, enjoyment) could play a role in the way consumers perceive the chatbot efficiency.

Attractiveness characterised in human–computer interaction with aesthetics (e.g., Sundar et al., 2014), i.e., a pleasant visual appearance and an attractive voice can lead users to perceive the AI agents as cool (Ashfaq et al., 2021; de Gennaro et al., 2020; Guerreiro & Loureiro, 2023). Interestingly, however, a study exploring interactivity and empathy when comparing human and chatbot services has shown that for the same online customer service of a brand, participants rated the human employee to be more competent and warmer than a chatbot (Lou et al., 2022). In the same study, when a human agent expressed sympathy toward the customer during the conversation, participants considered his/her competence to be higher. Note that such a pattern was not observed with the e-service agent. This is a puzzling outcome calling for an investigation on whether and how core affects interplay with chatbot evaluation.

Affective response was acknowledged to be a complex phenomenon, inviting further research when it comes to the interaction with chatbots (Chong et al., 2021). Such exploration is especially relevant, as core effects underlining human emotions (Russell, 1980, 2003) are often used by brands to enhance the advertising appeal (Bialkova, 2019) and thus to twist the consumer mind (Bialkova, 2023d).

4.5 Enjoyment

Enjoyment is probably the most desirable emotion. It typically arises from connection or sensory pleasure and is often associated with happiness (Ekman, Atlas of Emotions). Enjoyable shopping experience is the key to boosting purchase intention and brand advocacy, as is well known from marketing classics. Increased spending and unplanned purchasing were reported in very early studies on offline shopping (Babin et al., 1994), but also in contemporary papers on online shopping (Mallapragada et al., 2016). Similar results are reported from articles in service marketing (Zeithaml et al., 1996), i.e., customer emotional experience with customer services is related to the satisfaction with the firm/brand and determines the consequent behaviour. If customers enjoy the service and experience, they are satisfied, highly evaluate the quality provided, and are very likely to return and to spread positive word of mouth, WOM (Bigné et al., 2020; Stojanovic et al., 2018).

Enjoying the use of technologies was also reported to determine attitudes toward technology-based services (Dabholkar & Bagozzi, 2002). Classified as an intrinsic motivation (Ryan & Deci, 2000) for adopting technology (Davis et al., 1992), enjoyment was shown to induce perceptions of ease of use (Venkatesh, 2000). It was acknowledged to positively influence user attitudes online (Bialkova, 2021), and to foster shoppers purchase intention (Bialkova, 2022a).

Studies of new technologies like augmented reality (AR), virtual reality (VR), and extended reality (XR) applications were able to show that enjoyment loads on

Table 4.2 Summary of the hypotheses tested

	Hypotheses tested
H1	The greater the ease of use and the quality are perceived to be: H1a. the higher the satisfaction will be H1b. the more positive the attitudes toward chatbot(s) will be
H2	The greater the satisfaction and the more positive the attitudes are, the higher the intention to use a chatbot in future will be
H3	The greater the satisfaction and the more positive the attitudes are, the higher the willingness to recommend chatbots will be
H4	The higher the functionality of a chatbot is perceived to be: H4a. the greater the ease of use H4b. the higher the quality will be
H5	The better the interactivity is perceived to be: H5a. the greater the ease of use H5b. the higher the quality will be evaluated
H6	The greater the enjoyment with chatbot interaction is: H6a. the greater the ease of use H6b. the higher the quality will be perceived

consumer experience evaluation, and thus, on brand recommendation (Bialkova, 2019) and purchase intention (Bialkova & Barr, 2022).

Interactional enjoyment was found to be a mediator in the relationship between user satisfaction and intention to use a chatbot (Lee & Choi, 2017; Rese et al., 2020). Pleasurable experience with the chatbot reflected attitudes toward the brand (Bialkova, 2022a) and attitudes toward the bot itself (Pitardi & Marriott, 2021). Enjoyment enhanced the intention of bot future use and recommendation (Bialkova, 2022b, 2023a), as well as the shopping intention at AI-powered retail (Pillai et al., 2020).

Translating these findings to the current context, we could argue that enjoyment is a crucial factor in chatbot perception. Therefore, based on the abovementioned results, we predict the following:

H6. The greater the enjoyment with chatbot interaction is:
H6a. the greater the ease of use
H6b. the higher the quality will be perceived.

4.6 Conceptual Model of Chatbot Efficiency

The above hypotheses are summarised in a conceptual model as shown in Fig. 4.1 (see also Table 4.2, presenting an overview of the hypotheses tested). The conceptual model aims at providing the much-needed understanding on chatbot efficiency evaluation. It is tested in an empirical study as described in detail in Chap. 5 (Bialkova, 2024c).

References

Ajzen, I. (1991). The theory of planned behavior. *Organizational Behavior and Planned Decision Processes, 50*, 179–211.

Ashfaq, M., Yun, J., & Yu, S. (2021). My smart speaker is cool! Perceived coolness, perceived values, and users' attitude toward smart speakers. *International Journal of Human–Computer Interaction, 37*(6), 560–573.

Ashfaq, M., Yun, J., Yu, S., & Loureiro, S. (2020). I, Chatbot: Modeling the determinants of users' satisfaction and continuance intention of AI-powered service agents. *Telematics and Informatics, 54*, 101473.

Babin, B. J., Darden, W. R., & Griffin, M. (1994). Work and/or fun: Measuring hedonic and utilitarian shopping value. *Journal of Consumer Research, 20*, 644–656.

Ben Mimoun, M. S., Poncin, I., & Garnier, M. (2017). Animated conversational agents and e-consumer productivity: The roles of agents and individual characteristics. *Information & Management, 54*(5), 545–559, 43.

Bialkova, S. (2019). Consumers journey enhancement: The VR impact. In *European Marketing Academy Conference, EMAC2019*, May 28–31, Hamburg, Germany.

Bialkova, S. (2021). Would you talk to me? The role of chatbots in marketing. In *ICORIA 2021*, June 26–28, Bordeaux, France.

Bialkova, S. (2022a). How may I help you? Chatbots implementation in marketing. In *European Marketing Academy Conference, EMAC2022*, May 24–27, Budapest, Hungary.

Bialkova, S. (2022b). Interacting with chatbot: How to enhance functionality and enjoyment? In *AEMARK 2022*, September 7–10, 2022, Valencia, Spain.

Bialkova, S. (2023a). I want to talk to you: Chatbot marketing integration. In *Advances in advertising research* (Vol. XII, pp. 23–36). https://doi.org/10.1007/978-3-658-40429-1_2

Bialkova, S. (2023b). AI-driven customer experience: Factors to consider. In *Philosophy of artificial intelligence and its place in society* (pp. 341–357). IGI Global.

Bialkova, S. (2023c). How to optimise interaction with chatbots? Key parameters emerging from actual application. *International Journal of Human–Computer Interaction*. https://doi.org/10.1080/10447318.2023.2219963

Bialkova, S. (2023d). Enhancing multisensory experience and brand value: Key determinants for extended, augmented, and virtual reality marketing applications. In A. Simeone, B. Weyers, S. Bialkova, & R. W. Lindeman (Eds.), *Everyday virtual and augmented reality. Human–Computer Interaction Series* (pp. 181–195). Springer.

Bialkova, S. (2023e). I need your help: Key parameters guiding satisfaction with chatbots. In *European Marketing Academy Conference, EMAC 2023*, May 23–26, 2023, Odense, Denmark.

Bialkova, S. (2024a). Audit of literature on chatbot applications. In *The rise of AI user applications: Chatbots integration foundations and trends*. (Chap. 2). Springer. https://doi.org/10.1007/978-3-031-56471-0_2

Bialkova, S. (2024b). Core theories applied in chatbot context. In *The rise of AI user applications: Chatbots integration foundations and trends*. (Chap. 3). Springer. https://doi.org/10.1007/978-3-031-56471-0_3

Bialkova, S. (2024c). Chatbot efficiency—Model testing. In *The rise of AI user applications: Chatbots integration foundations and trends*. (Chap. 5). Springer. https://doi.org/10.1007/978-3-031-56471-0_5

Bialkova, S., & Barr, C. (2022). Virtual try-on: How to enhance consumer experience? In *Proceedings of IEEEVR2022, 8th Workshop on Everyday Virtual Reality*, March 12–16, 2022, Christchurch, New Zealand.

Bigné, E., Andreu, L., Perez, C., & Ruiz, C. (2020). Brand love is all around: Loyalty behaviour active and passive social media users. *Current Issues in Tourism, 23*(13), 1613–1630.

Blut, M., Wang, C., Wünderlich, N., & Brock, C. (2021). Understanding anthropomorphism in service provision: A meta-analysis of physical robots, chatbots, and other AI. *Journal of the Academy of Marketing Science, 49*, 632–658.

Chattaraman, V., Kwon, W. S., Gilbert, J. E., & Ross, K. (2019). Should AI-based, conversational digital assistants employ social-or task-oriented interaction style? A task-competency and reciprocity perspective for older adults. *Computers in Human Behavior, 90*, 315–330.

Chaves, A. P., & Gerosa, M. A. (2021). How should my chatbot interact? A survey on social characteristics in human-chatbot interaction design. *International Journal of Human-Computer Interaction, 37*(8), 729–758.

Chong, T., Yu, T., Keeling, D. I., & de Ruyter, K. (2021). AI-chatbots on the services frontline addressing the challenges and opportunities of agency. *Journal of Retailing and Consumer Services, 63*, 102735.

Chung, M., Ko, E., Joung, H., & Kim, S. J. (2020). Chatbot e-service and customer satisfaction regarding luxury brands. *Journal of Business Research, 117*, 587–595.

Dabholkar, P. A., & Bagozzi, R. P. (2002). An attitudinal model of technology-based self-service: Moderating effects of consumer traits and situational factors. *Journal of the Academy of Marketing Science, 30*(3), 184–201.

Davis, F. D., Bagozzi, R. P., & Warshaw, P. R. (1989). User acceptance of computer technology: A comparison of two theoretical models. *Management Science, 5*(8), 982–1003.

Davis, F. D., Bagozzi, R. P., & Warshaw, P. R. (1992). Extrinsic and intrinsic motivation to use computers in the workplace. *Journal of Applied Social Psychology, 22*(14), 1111–1132.

de Gennaro, M., Krumhuber, E. G., & Lucas, G. (2020). Effectiveness of an empathic chatbot in combating adverse effects of social exclusion on mood. *Frontiers in Psychology, 10*, Article 3061.

DeLone, W. H., & McLean, E. R. (2003). The DeLone and McLean model of information systems success: A ten-year update. *Journal of Management Information System, 19*(4), 9–30.

de Sa Siqueira, M., Muller, B. C., & Bosse, T. (2023). When do we accept mis-takes from chatbots? The impact of human-like communication on user experience in chatbots that make mistakes. *International Journal of Human–Computer Interaction.*

Ekman, P. (2016). *Atlas of emotions.* Retrieved from www.paulekman.com. Last accessed January 15, 2024.

Fernandes, T., & Oliveira, E. (2021). Understanding consumers' acceptance of automated technologies in service encounters: Drivers of digital voice assistants adoption. *Journal of Business Research, 122*, 180–191.

Gelbrich, K., Hagel, J., & Orsingher, C. (2021). Emotional support from a digital assistant in technology-mediated services: Effects on customer satisfaction and behavioral persistence. *International Journal of Research in Marketing, 38*, 176–193.

Go, E., & Sundar, S. S. (2019). Humanizing chatbots: The effects of visual, identity and conversational cues on humanness perceptions. *Computers in Human Behavior, 97*, 304–316.

Guerreiro, J., & Loureiro, S. M. C. (2023). I am attracted to my cool smart assistant! Analyzing attachment-aversion in AI-human relationships. *Journal of Business Research, 161*, 113863.

Holzwarth, M., Janiszewski, C., & Neumann, M. M. (2006). The influence of avatars on online consumer shopping behavior. *Journal of Marketing, 70*(4), 19–36.

Homburg, C., Müller, M., & Klarmann, M. (2011). When does salespeople's customer orientation lead to customer loyalty? The differential effects of relational and functional customer orientation. *Journal of the Academy of Marketing Science, 39*, 795–812.

Kowalczuk, P. (2018). Consumer acceptance of smart speakers: A mixed methods approach. *Journal of Research in Interactive Marketing, 12*(4), 418–431.

Lee, H., & Cho, C. H. (2020). Uses and gratifications of smart speakers: Modelling the effectiveness of smart speaker advertising. *International Journal of Advertising, 39*(7), 1150–1171.

Lee, S., & Choi, J. (2017). Enhancing user experience with conversational agent for movie recommendation: Effects of self-disclosure and reciprocity. *International Journal of Human-Computer Studies, 103*, 95–105.

Lou, C., Kang, H., & Tse, C. H. (2022). Bots vs. humans: How schema congruity, contingency-based interactivity, and sympathy influence consumer perceptions and patronage intentions. *International Journal of Advertising, 41*(4), 655–684.

Mallapragada, G., Chandukala, S., & Liu, Q. (2016). Exploring the effects of "what" (product) and "where" (website) characteristics on online shopping behavior. *Journal of Marketing, 80,* 21–38.

Meyer-Waarden, L., Pavone, G., Poocharoentou, T., Prayatsup, P., Ratinaud, M., Tison, A., & Torn, S. (2020). How service quality influences customer acceptance and usage of chatbots? *Journal of Service Management Research, 4*(1), 35–51.

Miao, F., Kozlenkova, I. V., Wang, H., Xie, T., & Palmatier, R. W. (2022). An emerging theory of avatar marketing. *Journal of Marketing, 86*(1), 67–90.

Moriuchi, E., Landers, V. M., Colton, D. A., & Hair, N. (2021). Engagement with chatbots versus augmented reality interactive technology in e-commerce. *Journal of Strategic Marketing, 29*(5), 375–389.

Parasuraman, A., Zeithaml, V. A., & Berry, L. (1988). SERVQUAL: A multiple-item scale for measuring consumer perceptions of service quality. *Journal of Retailing, 61*(1), 12–40.

Parasuraman, A., Zeithaml, V. A., & Malhotra, A. (2005). E-S-QUAL: A multiple-item scale for assessing electronic service quality. *Journal of Service Research, 7*(3), 213–233.

Pillai, R., Sivathanu, B., & Dwivedi, Y. K. (2020). Shopping intention at AI-powered automated retail stores (AIPARS). *Journal of Retailing and Consumer Services, 57,* 102207.

Pitardi, V., & Marriott, H. R. (2021). Alexa, she's not human but... unveiling the drivers of consumers' trust in voice-based artificial intelligence. *Psychology & Marketing, 38,* 626–642.

Poushneh, A. (2021). Humanizing voice assistant: The impact of voice assistant personality on consumers' attitudes and behaviors. *Journal of Retailing and Consumer Services, 58,* 102283.

Ramsey, R., & Sohi, R. S. (1997). Listening to your customers: The impact of perceived salesperson listening behavior on relationship outcomes. *Journal of the Academy of Marketing Science, 25,* 127–137.

Rese, A., Ganster, L., & Baier, D. (2020). Chatbots in retailers' customer communication: How to measure their acceptance? *Journal of Retailing and Consumer Services, 56,* 102176.

Reynolds, K. E., & Arnold, M. J. (2000). Customer loyalty to the salesperson and the store: Examining relationship customers in an upscale retail context. *Journal of Personal Selling & Sales Management, 20,* 89–98.

Russell, J. A. (1980). A circumplex model of affect. *Journal of Personality and Social Psychology, 39,* 1161–1178.

Russell, J. A. (2003). Core affect and the psychological construction of emotion. *Psychological Review, 110*(1), 145–172.

Ryan, R. M., & Deci, E. L. (2000). Self-determination theory and the facilitation of intrinsic motivation, social development, and well-being. *American Psychologist, 55*(1), 68–78.

Stojanovic, I., Andreu, L., & Curras-Perez, R. (2018). Effects of the intensity of use of social media on brand equity: An empirical study in a tourist destination. *European Journal of Management and Business Economics, 27*(1), 83–100.

Sundar, S. S., Tamul, D. J., & Wu, M. (2014). Capturing "cool": Measures for assessing coolness of technological products. *International Journal of Human-Computer Studies, 72*(2), 169–180.

Trivedi, J. (2019). Examining the customer experience of using banking chatbots and its impact on brand love: The moderating role of perceived risk. *Journal of Internet Commerce, 18*(1), 91–111, 265.

Tsai, W. H. S., Liu, Y., & Chuan, C. H. (2021). How chatbots' social presence communication enhances consumer engagement: The mediating role of parasocial interaction and dialogue. *Journal of Research in Interactive Marketing, 15*(3), 460–482.

Venkatesh, V. (2000). Determinants of perceived ease of use: Integrating control, intrinsic motivation, and emotion into the technology acceptance model. *Information Systems Research, 11*(4), 342–365.

Wirtz, J., Patterson, P. G., Kunz, W. H., Gruber, T., Lu, V. N., Paluch, S., & Martins, A. (2018). Brave new world: Service robots in the frontline. *Journal of Service Management, 29*(5), 907–931.

Xiao, B., & Benbasat, I. (2007). E-commerce product recommendation agents: Use, characteristics, and impact. *MIS Quarterly, 31*(1), 137–209.

Xu, K., Chan-Olmsted, S., & Liu, F. (2022). Smart speakers require smart management: Two routes from user gratifications to privacy settings. *International Journal of Communication, 16*, 192–214.

Zarouali, B., Van den Broeck, E., Walrave, M., & Poels, K. (2018). Predicting consumer responses to a chatbot on Facebook. *Cyberpsychology, Behavior, and Social Networking, 21*(8), 491–497.

Zeithaml, V. A., Berry, L. L., & Parasuraman, A. (1996). The behavioral consequences of service quality. *Journal of Marketing, 60*, 31–46.

Chapter 5
Chatbot Efficiency—Model Testing

Abstract The factors hypothesised in the conceptual model of chatbot efficiency (see Chap. 4, Bialkova, 2024a) were tested in an empirical study. Users who had used a chatbot at least once in their life were invited to complete a survey and to provide their opinion about the experience they had with the chatbot. 90% of our respondents have employed a chatbot to contact the customer service, showing the growing importance of AI systems in substituting human agents at the front service line. The results from the regression modelling clearly show the relationships between the factors hypothesised in our conceptual model. (1) The greater the quality and the ease of use were perceived to be, the higher the satisfaction was and the more positive the attitudes toward chatbots were. (2) The higher the satisfaction was, the greater was the intention to use a chatbot and the higher the willingness to recommend it. The same tendency emerged for attitudes. (3) Enhanced functionality led to a more positive evaluation of chatbot quality and ease of use. (4) Enjoyment also emerged to play a role in perceived quality and ease of use. Note, however, some of the above parameters may turn into barriers. Although the satisfaction level was relatively good, consumers who are not satisfied with a chatbot will not use it in future. Such outcome is a warning call to look for appropriate techniques for assembling machine learning, natural language processing, and reasoning to build better systems, prioritising a human-centred approach.

5.1 Methodology

5.1.1 Participants

A random sample was approached to complete a survey online. Participants were recruited via social media, and/or invitations were sent via emails to potential respondents. There was a condition that people should have used a chatbot at least once in their daily life in order to take part in the study. Participation was anonymous and voluntary. Participants provided an informed consent prior to the study. The study was approved by the ethics board of the home university, accordingly.

60 people (35 women) completed the survey. The youngest participant was 20 years old, and the oldest was 52 years old. 40% of the respondents had a M.Sc. degree. All have experienced a chatbot before: 38% at least once, 32% more than 5 times, and the rest between 3 and 5 times. For 90% of the respondents, the chatbot was used to contact a customer service. 28% of the respondents also experienced chatbots in product purchase, to ask for help, further product info and/or recommendations. The top three industries where a chatbot has been experienced were banking (40% of the respondents), telecommunication (35%), and fashion (32%).

5.1.2   Procedure and Instrument

After a short introduction and a consent form were provided, the survey was presented. Chatbot functionality, interactivity, and enjoyment have been explored, as well as how these factors could influence the perceived ease of use and quality. Attitudes toward chatbots, satisfaction, intention to use in future, and willingness to recommend have been addressed with separate scales. At the end, sociodemographics were collected, e.g., age, gender, highest education completed. Questions about actual use of chatbots were also asked (as reported in the previous section).

Construct **functionality** encompassed 3 items (e.g., chatbots are functional), and **interactivity** scale included 3 items (e.g., I felt I could interact with the chatbot) that were self-developed and validated in the context of chatbots in earlier studies from our lab, see Bialkova (2023a). **Enjoyment** encompassed 5 items (e.g., sad/joyful) based on Russell (2003). The scale was validated for UX in the VR and new tech context (Bialkova, 2019) and pilots from our lab in the chatbot context (Bialkova, 2022b, 2023b). For functionality and interactivity, a 7-point Likert scale (1 = strongly disagree, 7 = strongly agree) was used; and for enjoyment, a 7-point semantic differential scale was used. See Table 5.1 for a summary of the constructs as used in the survey and the results of the reliability check.

The construct **ease of use** included 5 items (e.g., chatbots are easy to use) adapted from Davis et al. (1989) in the context of chatbots. **Quality** was evaluated by 4 items (very bad/very good quality) adapted from Fenko et al. (2016) for the context of chatbots. **Satisfaction** encompassed 5 items (e.g., the chatbot did a good job) from Chung et al. (2020). For ease of use and satisfaction, a 7-point Likert scale (1 = strongly disagree, 7 = strongly agree) was used, and for quality perception, a 7-point semantic differential scale was employed.

Construct **attitude** encompassed 3 items (e.g., favourable/unfavourable) adopted from MacKenzie and Lutz (1989) and validated in the chatbot context by Bialkova (2021, 2023a). **Intention to use** included 3 items (e.g., impossible/possible) and **recommendation** 4 items (e.g., say positive things about chatbots to other people) adapted from Bialkova and te Paske (2021) in the context of chatbot use (Bialkova, 2021, 2023a). For attitudes and intention to use, a 7-point semantic differential scale have been employed; and for recommendation, a 7-point Likert scale (1 = strongly disagree, 7 = strongly agree) was used.

Table 5.1 Summary of the constructs used, source, and reliability check

Construct	Measuring scale	Cronbach's α
Attitudes	3 items: e.g., Favourable/unfavourable, based on MacKenzie and Lutz (1989)	0.92
Functionality	3 items: e.g., chatbots are functional, validated in Bialkova (2021, 2023a)	0.84
Interactivity	3 items: e.g., I felt I could interact with the chatbot, validated by Bialkova (2021, 2023a)	0.78
Enjoyment	5 items: e.g., The interaction with chatbot(s) is sad/joyful based on Russell (2003), validated by Bialkova (2022b, 2023b)	0.87
Ease of use	5 items: e.g., Chatbots are easy to use, adapted from Davis et al. (1989)	0.92
Quality	4 items: e.g., Very bad/very good quality, adapted from Fenko et al. (2016)	0.88
Satisfaction	5 items: e.g., The chatbot did a good job adapted from Chung et al. (2020)	0.95
Intention to use	3 items: e.g., Impossible/possible, adapted from Bialkova and te Paske (2021)	0.97
Recommendation	4 items: e.g., Say positive things about chatbot to other people, adapted from Bialkova and te Paske (2021)	0.89

All the scales demonstrated high reliability, with all the Cronbach's $\alpha > 0.75$ (see Table 5.1).

5.1.3 Analytical Procedure

First, a reliability check was run. All the scales used were highly reliable (Cronbach's $\alpha > 0.75$). T-tests were subsequently run to probe whether there was a difference in the responses of the male and female participants. Such a difference was not reported (all p's > 0.1). ANOVAs were performed to test whether there was a difference in response depending on the frequency of chatbot use (1–2 vs. 3–5 vs. > 5 times). Such a deference was not reported (all p's > 0.1).

Regression modelling tested the relationship between the variables under investigation. Following the hypothesised direction of influence, we looked at (a) how functionality, interactivity and enjoyment influence, respectively, ease of use and quality perception; (b) how ease of use and quality perception influence satisfaction and attitudes; and (c) how attitudes and satisfaction predetermine intention to use and the willingness to recommend a chatbot.

5.2   Results

The results from the regression modelling are clear in showing the relationships between the factors investigated hereby. Ease of use and quality perception influenced the satisfaction and attitudes toward chatbots (see Table 5.2). Ease of use explained 29% of the variance in attitudes, $R^2 = 0.29$, $F(1, 58) = 24.28$, $p < 0.001$. Adding quality evaluation to the model significantly improved its explanatory power, $R^2 = 0.45$, $F(2, 57) = 23.03$, $p < 0.001$. The greater the ease of use ($\beta = 0.16$) and the quality ($\beta = 0.55$) were perceived to be, the more positive the attitudes toward chatbot(s) were. Satisfaction was also modulated by ease of use and quality perception, $R^2 = 0.78$, $F(2, 57) = 101$, $p < 0.001$. The higher the ease of use ($\beta = 0.61$) and the quality ($\beta = 0.35$) were perceived to be, the higher the satisfaction was. Ease of use also influenced the quality evaluation. The higher the ease of use ($\beta = 0.70$) was perceived to be, the better the quality was evaluated, $R^2 = 0.49$, $F(1, 58) = 55.77$, $p < 0.001$. Satisfaction modulated attitudes, $R^2 = 0.37$, $F(1, 58) = 33.49$, $p < 0.001$. The higher the satisfaction was ($\beta = 0.61$), the more positive the attitudes toward chatbot(s) were.

Attitudes explained 24% of the variance in future use intention, $R^2 = 0.24$, $F(1, 58) = 18.64$, $p < 0.001$. Adding satisfaction to the model doubled its explanatory power. The more positive the attitudes ($\beta = 0.15$) and the greater the satisfaction ($\beta = 0.57$) were perceived to be, the higher the intention to use a chatbot in future was, $R^2 = 0.45$, $F(2, 57) = 23.44$, $p < 0.001$. The more positive attitudes ($\beta = 0.36$) and the higher satisfaction ($\beta = 0.45$) led to greater willingness to recommend a chatbot, $R^2 = 0.52$, $F(2, 57) = 30.93$, $p < 0.001$ (see Table 5.3).

Table 5.2 Summary of the outcomes from the regression modelling encompassing ease of use and quality evaluation, and their effect on satisfaction (left panel) and attitudes (right panel)

	Satisfaction					Attitudes				
	$R^2 = 0.780$, $F = 101$					$R^2 = 0.447$, $F = 23.03$				
	b	SE	β	t	p	b	SE	β	t	p
Ease of use	0.66	0.09	0.61	7.26	< 0.001	0.21	0.18	0.16	1.18	0.248
Quality	0.40	0.10	0.35	4.17	< 0.001	0.73	0.18	0.55	3.96	< 0.001

Table 5.3 Summary of the outcomes from the regression modelling encompassing satisfaction and attitudes, and their effect on future use (left panel) and recommendation (right panel)

	Use (future)					Recommend				
	$R^2 = 0.451$, $F = 23.44$					$R^2 = 0.520$, $F = 30.93$				
	b	SE	β	t	p	b	SE	β	t	p
Attitudes	0.14	0.12	0.15	1.19	0.239	0.30	0.10	0.36	3.08	< 0.005
Satisfaction	0.64	0.14	0.57	4.65	< 0.001	0.44	0.11	0.45	3.90	< 0.001

Table 5.4 Summary of the outcomes from the regression modelling encompassing factors functionality, interactivity, enjoyment and their effect on ease of use (left panel) and quality (right panel) evaluation

	Ease of use					Quality				
	$R^2 = 0.616, F = 29.90$					$R^2 = 0.762, F = 59.87$				
	b	SE	β	t	p	b	SE	β	t	p
Functionality	0.35	0.15	0.28	2.95	< 0.05	0.35	0.12	0.30	3.10	< 0.005
Interactivity	0.34	0.13	0.32	2.72	< 0.01	0.05	0.09	0.05	0.48	0.635
Enjoyment	0.41	0.15	0.30	2.69	< 0.01	0.81	0.12	0.62	7.08	< 0.001

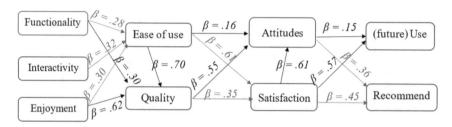

Fig. 5.1 Summary of the regression modelling (including regression coefficients)

Functionality explained 47% of the variance in the ease of use. Adding interactivity to the model increased its explanatory power to 57%, and including the emotional component improved the model further, $R^2 = 0.62$, $F(3, 56) = 29.90$, $p < 0.001$. Concerning the quality evaluation, functionality explained 52% of the variance in the model. Although interactivity itself modulated quality perception ($R^2 = 0.38$, $F(1, 58) = 35.69$, $p < 0.001$), adding interactivity to functionality in the model did not significantly change its power. However, including the emotional component increased the model significance, $R^2 = 0.76$, $F(3, 56) = 59.87$, $p < 0.001$. Table 5.4 provides a summary of the regression modelling encompassing factors functionality, interactivity, enjoyment and their effect, respectively, on ease of use and quality evaluation.

An illustrative summary of the model tested is provided in Fig. 5.1, including regression coefficients.

5.3 Discussion

The rapidly growing implementation of chatbots in everyday contexts and business practices such as branding, advertising and commerce aims at revolutionising and empowering these sectors with enhanced speed, insight-driven support, and personalised experiences. Surprisingly, however, chatbot technology seems to not always be accepted, and thus, further investigation on how to appropriately meet consumer

Table 5.5 Summary of the hypotheses tested

	Hypotheses	Status
H1	The higher the ease of use and the quality are perceived to be: H1a. the higher the satisfaction will be H1b. the more positive the attitudes toward chatbot(s) will be	Accepted
H2	The higher the satisfaction and the more positive the attitudes are, the higher the intention to use a chatbot in future will be	Accepted
H3	The higher the satisfaction and the more positive the attitudes are, the higher the willingness to recommend chatbots will be	Accepted
H4	The higher the functionality of a chatbot is perceived to be: H4a. the greater the ease of use H4b. the higher the quality will be	Accepted
H5	The better the interactivity is perceived to be: H5a. the greater the ease of use H5b. the higher the quality will be evaluated	Accepted
H6	The greater the enjoyment with chatbot interaction is: H6a. the greater the ease of use H6b. the higher the quality will be perceived	Accepted

needs and demands is invited. The present study embraced this challenge, aiming to provide the much-needed understanding of the factors shaping consumer satisfaction, attitudes, use and recommendation of a chatbot. Based on profound literature review, a survey addressed the factors hypothesised (see Table 5.5) as determinants of chatbot efficiency, and thus, crucial drivers of consumer attitudes and consequent behaviour toward chatbots. While previous lab studies have addressed chatbot mock-ups, hereby, the survey included responses from people who had used a chatbot at least once in their daily life. In this respect, the current study sheds light on the actual use of chatbots and therefore provides an authentic consumer evaluation of chatbots currently available on the market. The outcomes are summarised in a model and discussed in the framework of chatbot efficiency.

5.3.1   Key Drivers of Attitudes and Satisfaction

Attitudes were predetermined by the ease of use and quality. A similar pattern was also observed for **satisfaction**. The higher the **ease of use** and the **quality** were perceived to be, the higher the satisfaction was (**H1a—supported**), and the more positive the attitudes toward chatbots were (**H1b—supported**), see Table 5.2. These are very important findings providing useful arguments into the debate on how ease of use and quality perception influence chatbot acceptance. Note that prior studies have not been able to show an effect of ease of use on chatbot reuse (Meyer-Waarden et al., 2020). Other researchers even argued that if the ease of use is not provided at a level required by customers, it would be a barrier to chatbot use (Wirtz et al.,

2018). Concerning quality, although it is acknowledged that e-service quality must be smooth and satisfying (Zeithaml et al., 2002), in reality, e-agency might not necessarily provide such high-quality support (Bialkova, 2021). Despite the fact that chatbot quality has been questioned, researchers are not univocal (Lou et al., 2022). While recent studies have reported a positive relationship between quality and satisfaction (Chung et al., 2020), prior studies have not been able to show a direct effect on recommendation quality, and the perceived usefulness of the agent as a productivity output (Ben Mimoun et al., 2017). In this respect, our study is crucial, bringing new insights into the debate on how ease of use and quality perception enhance chatbot efficiency, and thus satisfaction and attitudes.

Furthermore, the higher the satisfaction and the more positive the attitudes were, the higher the **intention to use** a chatbot was (**H2—confirmed**). Similarly, the higher the willingness to **recommend** chatbots was (**H3—confirmed**), see Table 5.3. These findings cohere with the retail and service marketing literature showing that positive attitudes (Ramsey & Sohi, 1997; Zeithaml et al., 1996) lead to returning customers advocating for the company (Bettencourt, 1997; Reynolds & Arnold, 2000; Reynolds & Beatty, 1999). In the context of technology, it was also hypothesised that attitudes enhance the future system use (Davis et al., 1989). Implementing TAM (Davis et al., 1989) in various study contexts, e.g., online, mobile, AR, VR, etc., researchers have been able to show a positive relationship between recommendation adherence and attitudes. In the context of chatbot efficiency, such a tendency is also confirmed hereby, which is another contribution of the present paper.

We have to note, however, that the additional analyses we ran showed that consumers who are not satisfied with a chatbot will not use it in future. This is a crucial finding, especially given that the present outcomes are based on the actual use of chatbots. Although, it is well known that e-services should be satisfying (Zeithaml et al., 2002), in reality this might not necessarily be the case. From lab studies, there are further evidences that satisfying consumer expectations is a complex phenomenon. For example, when exploring chatbot anthropomorphic representations, research has not been able to show their mediation on attitudes toward a company, neither on satisfaction (Araujo, 2018). Furthermore, it is known that the interaction with bots might be judged in a different way than the interaction with human agents (Lou et al., 2022), especially considering the humanness characteristics, i.e., anthropomorphism (Miao et al., 2022). Based on the abovementioned puzzling findings, we can say that satisfaction needs to be examined closely. Brands should reconsider how to optimise the chatbots potential in order to satisfy consumer demands when it comes to the chatbot implementation.

Current study provides insights into this challenging issue, namely, a reflection on what could be improved to enhance quality and ease of use, emerging as crucial factors that load on satisfaction and attitudes toward chatbots.

5.3.2 Key Drivers of Quality and Ease of Use

The current work hypothesised that functionality, interactivity, and enjoyment are key determinants loading on ease of use and quality perception. The greater the level of **functionality** of a chatbot was perceived to be, the greater the ease of use (**H4a—confirmed**) and the higher the quality (**H4b—confirmed**) were perceived. This outcome is in line with earlier theories that functional characteristics might influence the end-user system evaluation (Davis et al., 1989). Advanced technology incorporating AI is expected to provide better functionality (Bialkova, 2021, 2023a). Hereby, we indeed see enhanced e-agency in terms of ease of use and quality perception with better functionality. Furthermore, functionality could be beneficial for saving time and easing the purchase process (Ben Mimoun et al., 2017). Feelings and loyalty toward the company have also been enhanced by functionality perception, as acknowledged for off and online shopping (Homburg et al., 2011; Xiao & Benbasat, 2007). Web functionality increased the visit duration and purchase likelihood (Mallapragada et al., 2016), and the implementation of virtual agents on a website enhanced e-consumer productivity and efficiency during online purchases (Ben Mimoun et al., 2017).

Concerning interactivity, the better it was, the greater the ease of use (**H5a—supported**) and the quality (**H5b—supported**) were evaluated. We must note that interactivity has been extensively studied before in the marketing and e-service context. Interactive communication with service agents and/or salespersons is an important determinant of consumer satisfaction (Qui & Benbasat, 2009), in forming attitudes toward a product and a company (Ramsey & Sohi, 1997; Reynolds & Arnold, 2000).

Interactivity and involvement with technology have been recognised as crucial components loading on the way experience with technology is evaluated and thus liked (Bialkova, 2019; Bialkova & Barr, 2022). In the context of chatbots, it was reported that avatars lead to positive attitudes toward the products (Holzwarth et al., 2006). Interaction facilitates the accuracy and credibility perception of a chatbot (Chung et al., 2020), provides feelings of connection between customer and company (Lee & Choi, 2017), and therefore navigates attitudes and consequent behaviour (Ben Mimoun et al., 2017). Hereby, we advance the knowledge by demonstrating how interactivity might enhance the ease of use and quality perception, recognised as prerequisites for satisfaction, attitude formation and consequent behaviour.

We further looked at the emotional aspect, and in particular, whether and how enjoyment plays a role. The results showed that the more **enjoyable** the interaction with a chatbot was, the higher the quality (**H6b—accepted**) and the greater the ease of use (**H6a—accepted**) were evaluated. These findings cohere with previous work showing that enjoyment could induce perceptions of ease of use (Venkatesh, 2000). It determines attitudes toward technology-based services (Dabholkar & Bagozzi, 2002), positively influences user attitudes toward e-commerce and commerce (Bialkova, 2021) and enhances the return of web shoppers (Bialkova & Barr, 2022). Current results are also in line with earlier lab experimentation, showing that humanoid embodiment influences users' perceptions of trust and enjoyment, as well as their intentions to use the agent as a decision aid (Qiu & Benbasat, 2009). Enjoyment loads on consumer experience evaluation, brand advocacy (Bialkova, 2019) and purchase intention (Bialkova & Barr, 2022). Pleasurable experience with the chatbot was acknowledged to modulate attitudes toward the brand and the intentions in terms of future use and recommendation (Bialkova, 2022a). Hereby, we have been able to further advance the knowledge base, by showing a causal relation between enjoyment, ease of use, and quality evaluation. This is a very important finding and contribution of the current work.

Moreover, as has been reported from the regression modelling performed hereby, functionality, interactivity, and enjoyment load jointly and positively on the way ease of use is perceived (see Table 5.4). Similarly, functionality and enjoyment had a joint and positive impact on quality perception. Note that, while previous studies have focused mainly on either cognitive or emotional aspects separately, hereby we have been able to address these in a single study looking at the actual use of chatbots, currently available on the market. The results clearly show that both cognitive and affective components are playing a role when it comes to chatbot performance evaluation, and thus the future use intention.

Based on the outcomes from the present work investigating consumer evaluation after actual use of chatbots currently employed as marketing and everyday applications, we have been able to distinguish key parameters shaping chatbot efficiency. These parameters we summarise in a conceptual framework (see Fig. 5.1) and suggest a toolkit aiming to facilitate the assessment of chatbot efficiency (see Table 5.6). Implementing the toolkit at prototyping stage and before the launch of (new) chatbots to the market is expected to help AI system developers and UX experts to anticipate pitfalls in design, and to elaborate better systems that appropriately meet the consumer demand for functional and enjoyable chatbot AI agency.

5.3.3 Interim Summary

The aim of the present study was to offer understanding on key drivers of chatbot efficiency, reflecting respectively, consumer satisfaction, attitudes, future use and recommendation of a chatbot. Chatbot performance was explored in a survey among consumers who had used a chatbot at least once in their daily life. Therefore, our study provides an objective picture of the actual use of chatbots currently available on the market.

The results are clear in chowing that: (1) The higher the quality and the ease of use were perceived to be, the greater the satisfaction was. (2) The higher the satisfaction was, the higher was the intention to use a chatbot and the willingness to recommend it. (3) The higher the quality and the ease of use were perceived to be, the more positive the attitudes toward chatbots were. (4) The more positive the attitudes toward the chatbots were, the greater was the intention to use a chatbot and the greater the willingness to recommend it. (5) Enhanced functionality leads

Table 5.6 Toolkit for assessing chatbot efficiency

Toolkit for assessing chatbot efficiency

Factor	Definition	Components	Validated in the chatbot context by studies from our lab
Functionality	Reflects a correct technical functioning (Parasuraman et al., 2005)	3 items The chatbot is: • Functional • Helpful • Knowledgeable 1= Strongly disagree–7= Strongly agree	Bialkova (2021, 2023a)
Interactivity	Extent to which users can manipulate technology (Bialkova & Barr, 2022) and/or control device	3 items Based on your experience with the chatbot, how do you feel? • I felt I could interact with the agent • I had the feeling that the agent was aware of me • I felt involved in 1= Strongly disagree–7= Strongly agree	Bialkova (2021, 2023a)

(continued)

Table 5.6 (continued)

Toolkit for assessing chatbot efficiency

Factor	Definition	Components	Validated in the chatbot context by studies from our lab
Enjoyment	Core affect (Russell, 1980), typically arising from connection or sensory pleasure, interchanged with happiness	5 items The interaction with the chatbot was: 1 = Unpleasant–7 = Pleasant 1 = Gloomy–7 = Exciting 1 = Unhappy–7 = Happy 1 = Sad–7 = Joyful 1 = Boring–7 = Entertaining	Bialkova (2022b, 2023b)
Ease of use	The degree to which the user expects the tech system to be free of effort (Davis et al., 1989)	5 items • Easy to use • User friendly • Efficient to use • Competent • Accurate 1 = Strongly disagree–7 = Strongly agree	Adapted from Davis et al. (1989) TAM, validated hereby for chatbot context Bialkova (2021, 2023a, 2023c)

(continued)

Table 5.6 (continued)

Toolkit for assessing chatbot efficiency

Factor	Definition	Components	Validated in the chatbot context by studies from our lab
Quality	Information, technical and overall service success (Trivedi, 2019, based on DeLone & McLean, 2003)	4 items I find the chatbot being: 1 = Very bad–7 = Very good 1 = Very unattractive–7 = Very attractive 1 = Very rejecting–7 = Very inviting 1 = Very bad quality–7 = Very good quality	Adapted from Fenko et al. (2016), validated hereby for chatbot context Bialkova (2021, 2023a, 2023c)

(continued)

Table 5.6 (continued)

Toolkit for assessing chatbot efficiency

Factor	Definition	Components	Validated in the chatbot context by studies from our lab
Satisfaction	Occurs when customers find that products or services meet or exceed their positive expectations (Chung et al., 2020; Zeithaml et al., 1996)	5 items How satisfied are you with the chatbot? • I am satisfied with the service agent • The chatbot did what I expected • The chatbot did a good job • I am happy with the service agent • I am satisfied with the experience I had with the chatbot 1= Strongly disagree–7 = Strongly agree	Bialkova (2022b, 2023b)

(continued)

Table 5.6 (continued)

Toolkit for assessing chatbot efficiency

Factor	Definition	Components	Validated in the chatbot context by studies from our lab
Attitudes	Beliefs about an object/person are evaluated, affecting intention to behave and actual behaviour (Theory of Planned Behaviour, TPB; Ajzen, 1991)	3 items My attitude toward the chatbot is 1 = Unfavourable–7 = Favourable 1 = Negative–7 = Positive 1 = I dislike chatbots–7 = I like chatbots	Bialkova (2021, 2023a)
Intention to use	Willingness to use the system, in this case chatbot	3 items What is the likelihood to use this chatbot in future? 1 = Very unlikely–7 = Very likely 1 = Improbable–7 = Probable 1 = Possible–7 = Impossible	Bialkova (2021, 2022b, 2023b)

to more positive evaluation of chatbot quality and ease of use. (6) Interactivity is a crucial factor in ease of use and quality perception. (7) Enjoyment also emerged to play a role in perceived quality and ease of use. (8) Although their satisfaction was relatively good, consumers who were not satisfied with the chatbots will not use them in future. This is a warning call to industry: to look for better techniques for assembling machine learning, natural language processing, and reasoning to appropriately meet customers' needs and demands in regard to chatbot implementation. Current outcomes provide a key to unlocking the potential of such techniques in order to incorporate best chatbot applications in everyday contexts and marketing business practices such as branding, advertising, and commerce.

5.4 Avenues for Future Research

We have to note hereby that, as part of the survey design, we have also asked participants whether they preferred a chatbot or a human agent to communicate with. Although our respondents reported relatively positive attitudes toward chatbots and in general were satisfied with the performance, they still preferred to communicate with a human agent (rather than with an AI system). This is a crucial finding inviting further investigations in direction of humanised agents. We also know from the latest research that systems characterised with high anthropomorphism seem to be more efficient, as studied in service providing (for a review see Blut et al., 2021) and avatar marketing (for an overview see Miao et al., 2022). Anthropomorphic AI agents have been identified as being "cool", i.e., a state that conveys an energetic, extraordinary, aesthetically appealing, high status, reflecting original, authentic, rebellious, subcultural, iconic, popular relation with a brand (Guerreiro & Loureiro, 2023).

Recent studies, however, have not been able to demonstrate strong anthropomorphic characteristics (Fernandes & Oliveira, 2021), neither mediation of chatbot anthropomorphic characteristics on attitudes toward and satisfaction with the company (Araujo, 2018). Furthermore, investigating the conditions under which a service entity of a brand can optimise its potential, it was shown that interaction with chatbot might be judged in a different way than the interaction with a human agent, presumably due to differences in schemata activation (Lou et al., 2022). The above controversial findings lead to the conclusion that understanding how anthropomorphic characteristics enhance the interaction with chatbot and thus its agent effectiveness is crucial. Addressing this challenge opens avenues for future research. In Chaps. 6 and 7 (Bialkova, 2024b, 2024c), we zoom-in onto detail how anthropomorphism shapes chatbot agency.

References

Ajzen, I. (1991). The theory of planned behavior. *Organizational Behavior and Planned Decision Processes, 50*, 179–211.

Araujo, T. (2018). Living up to the chatbot hype: The influence of anthropomorphic design cues and communicative agency framing on conversational agent and company perceptions. *Computers in Human Behavior, 85*, 183–189.

Ben Mimoun, M. S., Poncin, I., & Garnier, M. (2017). Animated conversational agents and e-consumer productivity: The roles of agents and individual characteristics. *Information & Management, 54*(5), 545–559, 43.

Bettencourt, L. A. (1997). Customer voluntary performance: Customers as partners in service delivery. *Journal of Retailing, 73*(3), 383–406.

Bialkova, S. (2019). Consumers journey enhancement: The VR impact. In *European Marketing Academy Conference, EMAC 2019*, May 28–31, Hamburg, Germany.

Bialkova, S. (2021). Would you talk to me? The role of chatbots in marketing. In *ICORIA 2021*, June 26–28, Bordeaux, France.

Bialkova, S. (2022a). How may I help you? Chatbots implementation in marketing. In *European Marketing Academy Conference, EMAC 2022*, May 24–27, Budapest, Hungary.

Bialkova, S. (2022b). Interacting with chatbot: How to enhance functionality and enjoyment? In *AEMARK 2022*, September 7–10, 2022, Valencia, Spain.

Bialkova, S. (2023a). I want to talk to you: Chatbot marketing integration. In *Advances in advertising research* (Vol. XII, pp. 23–36). https://doi.org/10.1007/978-3-658-40429-1_2

Bialkova, S. (2023b). AI-driven customer experience: Factors to consider. In *Philosophy of artificial intelligence and its place in society* (pp. 341–357). IGI Global.

Bialkova, S. (2023c). I need your help: Key parameters guiding satisfaction with chatbots. In *European Marketing Academy Conference, EMAC2023*, May 23–26, 2023, Odense, Denmark.

Bialkova, S. (2024a). Shaping chatbot efficiency—How to build better systems? In *The rise of AI user applications: Chatbots integration foundations and trends*. (Chap. 4). Springer. https://doi.org/10.1007/978-3-031-56471-0_4

Bialkova, S. (2024b). Anthropomorphism—What is crucial? In *The rise of AI user applications: Chatbots integration foundations and trends*. (Chap. 6). Springer. https://doi.org/10.1007/978-3-031-56471-0_6

Bialkova, S. (2024c). Chatbot agency—Model testing. In *The rise of AI user applications: Chatbots integration foundations and trends*. (Chap. 7). Springer. https://doi.org/10.1007/978-3-031-56471-0_7

Bialkova, S., & Barr, C. (2022). Virtual try-on: How to enhance consumer experience? In *Proceedings of IEEEVR2022, 8th Workshop on Everyday Virtual Reality*, March 12–16, 2022, Christchurch, New Zealand.

Bialkova, S., & te Paske, S. (2021). Campaign participation, spreading e-WOM, purchase: How to optimise CSR effectiveness via social media? *European Journal of Management and Business Economics, 31*(1), 108–126.

Blut, M., Wang, C., Wünderlich, N., & Brock, C. (2021). Understanding anthropomorphism in service provision: A meta-analysis of physical robots, chatbots, and other AI. *Journal of the Academy of Marketing Science, 49*, 632–658.

Chung, M., Ko, E., Joung, H., & Kim, S. J. (2020). Chatbot e-service and customer satisfaction regarding luxury brands. *Journal of Business Research, 117*, 587–595.

Dabholkar, P. A., & Bagozzi, R. P. (2002). An attitudinal model of technology-based self-service: Moderating effects of consumer traits and situational factors. *Journal of the Academy of Marketing Science, 30*(3), 184–201.

Davis, F. D., Bagozzi, R. P., & Warshaw, P. R. (1989). User acceptance of computer technology: A comparison of two theoretical models. *Management Science, 5*(8), 982–1003.

DeLone, W. H., & McLean, E. R. (2003). The DeLone and McLean model of information systems success: A ten-year update. *Journal of Management Information System, 19*(4), 9–30.

Fenko, A., Kersten, L., & Bialkova, S. (2016). Overcoming consumer scepticism toward food labels: The role of multisensory experience. *Food Quality and Preference, 48*, 81–92.

Fernandes, T., & Oliveira, E. (2021). Understanding consumers' acceptance of automated technologies in service encounters: Drivers of digital voice assistants adoption. *Journal of Business Research, 122*, 180–191.

Guerreiro, J., & Loureiro, S. M. C. (2023). I am attracted to my cool smart assistant! Analyzing attachment-aversion in AI-human relationships. *Journal of Business Research, 161*, 113863.

Holzwarth, M., Janiszewski, C., & Neumann, M. M. (2006). The influence of avatars on online consumer shopping behavior. *Journal of Marketing, 70*(4), 19–36.

Homburg, C., Müller, M., & Klarmann, M. (2011). When does salespeople's customer orientation lead to customer loyalty? The differential effects of relational and functional customer orientation. *Journal of the Academy of Marketing Science, 39*, 795–812.

Lee, S., & Choi, J. (2017). Enhancing user experience with conversational agent for movie recommendation: Effects of self-disclosure and reciprocity. *International Journal of Human-Computer Studies, 103*, 95–105.

Lou, C., Kang, H., & Tse, C. H. (2022). Bots vs. humans: How schema congruity, contingency-based interactivity, and sympathy influence consumer perceptions and patronage intentions. *International Journal of Advertising, 41*(4), 655–684.

MacKenzie, S. B., & Lutz, R. I. (1989). An empirical examination of the structural antecedents of attitude toward the ad in an advertising pretesting context. *The Journal of Marketing, 53*, 48–65.

Mallapragada, G., Chandukala, S., & Liu, Q. (2016). Exploring the effects of "what" (product) and "where" (website) characteristics on online shopping behavior. *Journal of Marketing, 80*, 21–38.

Meyer-Waarden, L., Pavone, G., Poocharoentou, T., Prayatsup, P., Ratinaud, M., Tison, A., & Torn, S. (2020). How service quality influences customer acceptance and usage of chatbots? *Journal of Service Management Research, 4*(1), 35–51.

Miao, F., Kozlenkova, I. V., Wang, H., Xie, T., & Palmatier, R. W. (2022). An emerging theory of avatar marketing. *Journal of Marketing, 86*(1), 67–90.

Parasuraman, A., Zeithaml, V. A., & Malhotra, A. (2005). E-S-QUAL: A multiple-item scale for assessing electronic service quality. *Journal of Service Research, 7*(3), 213–233.

Qiu, L., & Benbasat, I. (2009). Evaluating anthropomorphic product recommendation agents: A social relationship perspective to designing information systems. *Journal of Management Information Systems, 25*(4), 145–181.

Ramsey, R., & Sohi, R. S. (1997). Listening to your customers: The impact of perceived salesperson listening behavior on relationship outcomes. *Journal of the Academy of Marketing Science, 25*, 127–137.

Reynolds, K. E., & Arnold, M. J. (2000). Customer loyalty to the salesperson and the store: Examining relationship customers in an upscale retail context. *Journal of Personal Selling & Sales Management, 20*, 89–98.

Reynolds, K. E., & Beatty, S. E. (1999). Customer benefits and company consequences of customer-salesperson relationships in retailing. *Journal of Retailing, 75*, 11–32.

Russell, J. A. (1980). A circumplex model of affect. *Journal of Personality and Social Psychology, 39*, 1161–1178.

Russell, J. A. (2003). Core affect and the psychological construction of emotion. *Psychological Review, 110*(1), 145–172.

Trivedi, J. (2019). Examining the customer experience of using banking chatbots and its impact on brand love: The moderating role of perceived risk. *Journal of Internet Commerce, 18*(1), 91–111.

Venkatesh, V. (2000). Determinants of perceived ease of use: Integrating control, intrinsic motivation, and emotion into the technology acceptance model. *Information Systems Research, 11*(4), 342–365.

Wirtz, J., Patterson, P. G., Kunz, W. H., Gruber, T., Lu, V. N., Paluch, S., & Martins, A. (2018). Brave new world: Service robots in the frontline. *Journal of Service Management, 29*(5), 907–931.

Xiao, B., & Benbasat, I. (2007). E-commerce product recommendation agents: Use, characteristics, and impact. *MIS Quarterly, 31*(1), 137–209.

Zeithaml, V. A., Berry, L. L., & Parasuraman, A. (1996). The behavioral consequences of service quality. *Journal of Marketing, 60,* 31–46.

Zeithaml, V. A., Parasuraman, A., & Malhotra, A. (2002). Service quality delivery through web sites: A critical review of extant knowledge. *Journal of the Academy of Marketing Science, 30*(4), 362–375.

Chapter 6
Anthropomorphism—What Is Crucial?

Abstract Despite the recognised need for human-centred design and human-like features to be assigned to chatbot AI systems, the practice is scarce on working technological solutions that incorporate anthropomorphic interface. Such lack of anthropomorphism will inevitably lead to failures in usability perception and thus adoption of chatbots, and AI systems in general. To anticipate this technological disruption, there is an emergent call to provide a better understanding of the factors determining anthropomorphic structures, i.e., what is crucial for the design of human-like chatbots that are well accepted by consumers. The current chapter addresses this challenge by testing a framework on chatbot agency. Parallel to the cognitive and emotional components, that have emerged in the current book as key drivers of chatbot efficiency, we focus our exploration on social aspects. Such exploration is expected to shed light on AI applications as intelligent systems that provide not only algorithmic thinking, but also incorporate empathic and social interaction. Special attention is dedicated to social presence and personal care, distinguished as pivotal social components, from the literature audit reported hereby. Social presence associated with the sense of human contact, warmth, and sociability has a facilitating role when interacting with others. Personal care seeking personal attention, understanding, and empathy might enhance consumer satisfaction. Translating the above parameters in the framework of chatbot agency, we aim to map the essential requirements for interactivity, advising design space for AI systems that appropriately meet user demand. The framework of the chatbot agency is presented in detail below.

Implementing anthropomorphic representations (e.g., photographs of people; or software-generated talking faces) was recognised to improve the social presence in online interactions (Go & Sundar, 2019; Qiu & Benbasat, 2009), to impact information gathering activities (Kannan et al., 2023; Lee & Cho, 2020), performance expectations (Kang et al., 2023), and task completion (Moriuchi, 2021). Chatbots with more human-like behaviour are supposed to enhance the user experience, and thus to lift the acceptance of the system used, as reported in human–computer interaction literature (e.g., Chaves & Gerosa, 2021). In laboratory experiments, it was

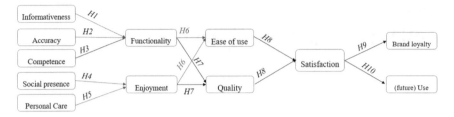

Fig. 6.1 Summary of the hypotheses tested on chatbot agency

demonstrated that humanoid embodiment and human-based communication influence user perception of social presence (e.g., Qui and Benbasat, 2009), which in turn increases trust, beliefs, and the intention to use recommendation agents. Human-like interfaces can improve the user's trust in technology (Bickmore & Picard, 2005) and attitudes toward the virtual assistants (Munnukka et al., 2022). As a result, it is observed enhancement of perceived enjoyment and the intentions to engage with the agent (Tsai et al., 2021). Increased purchase intention with increased social presence has also been acknowledged (Jin and Youn, 2020).

However, studies have not been able to substantiate the anthropomorphic effect on attitudes (Araujo, 2018) and future use of chatbot (Fernandes & Oliveira, 2021). A human-like communication style did not improve the ease of use, usefulness, or social presence as other researchers reported (de Sa Siqueira et al., 2023). Previous controversial findings invite further exploration. This exploration is especially relevant given the wide range of metrics employed to determine various anthropomorphic features. The current chapter addresses this issue by building upon research from diverse disciplines to create a holistic framework. The aim is to provide the much-needed understanding of how anthropomorphic characteristics enhance the interaction with chatbots, and thus their agency. In particular, we focus on cognitive, emotional, and social aspects, recognised in classical papers in service marketing to enhance the human agency evaluation. From psychology, i.e., human agency in Social Cognitive Theory (Bandura, 1989), we also know that personal agency operates within interactional causal structures involving cognitive, emotional, and social aspects.

In the following, we present details, and a summary of key hypotheses is provided in Table 6.2 (see also Fig. 6.1).

6.1 Cognitive Aspects

Quality and *ease of use* have already emerged as crucial parameters loading on the way chatbots efficiency have been perceived (see Chaps. 4 and 5, Bialkova, 2024c, 2024d). Functionality was also extensively studied in previous research and received significant attention hereby (see Chaps. 4 and 5). Enhanced functionality (see also

Bialkova, 2021, 2023a) was acknowledged to improve chatbot quality perception, and thus the e-agency. Quality itself was reported to reflect the system, e.g., what is the informativeness provided (e.g., Trivedi, 2019). How accurate (Bialkova, 2023c), skilful (Chung et al., 2020; Pitardi and Marriott, 2021), and competent (Bialkova, 2022b, 2023b) the chatbot is, also emerged as core parameters driving cognitive functioning and thus the evaluation of the chatbot performance (see Chap. 2, Bialkova, 2024a – for a detailed overview). Considering the importance of the abovementioned factors, we closely examine these, as described in detail below.

Informativeness was associated with the semantic success of the technology (Delone and McLean, 2003). It measures the quality of information. In order to manage a particular problem the user addresses, machine learning (ML) models, for example, are able to extract huge amount of information (Arrieta et al., 2020). Explainable ML models are expected to offer adequate information and knowledge, to provide the solution the user is looking for.

In particular, it was argued that high informativeness reflects the chatbot capability to provide timely, sufficient, and relevant information (Trivedi, 2019). Appropriately meeting the consumer demand for adequate information delivered on time was reported to further modulate how the experience with the chatbot was evaluated. As a consequence, positive experience led to enhanced brand-consumer relationship (Trivedi, 2019).

Positive experience with high tech applications was well recognised to foster purchase intention (Bialkova, 2019, 2022c) and brand advocacy (Bialkova & Barr, 2022). In the chatbot context, we have also seen that positive attitudes toward the bot lifted the intention to use it and to recommend it (see Chap. 5, Bialkova, 2024d).

What is much more interesting in line with the current discussion is whether and how *informativeness* modulates the functionality perception, and thus, further reflects quality and ease of use perception. Translating the abovementioned into the chatbot context, we propose the following hypothesis:

H1. The higher the informativeness is, the greater the degree to which the chatbot functionality will be evaluated.

We further look in determining how accuracy (Chung et al., 2020; Cheng & Jiang, 2021; Davis et al., 1989) and competence (Edwards et al., 2014; Yagoda & Gillan, 2012) of the AI system used reflects the chatbot functionality perception. Note that, earlier work examined these parameters in different (tech) contexts, in separate studies, often in isolation. In this respect, the current work has a major contribution to the advance of science, offering a holistic understanding, by encompassing these parameters under investigation in the context of chatbots. See Table 6.1 for a summary of the core parameters hypothesised in the chatbot agency evaluation.

Accuracy is the trueness and precision of the measurement method and results (ISO 5725). Hereby, we define accuracy as the precision of the system (Bialkova, 2023c). It is extensively examined in the usability literature. In AI context, accuracy was associated with extent to which the model accurately predicts unseen instances (Guidotti et al., 2018) and it is measured by accuracy score, reflecting the number of

Table 6.1 Core parameters in chatbot agency evaluation

Parameter	Definition	References
Informativeness	Reflects the quality of information (Delone and McLean, 2003)	Arrieta et al. (2020), Ashfaq et al. (2020), Bialkova (2023c), Trivedi (2019)
Accuracy	Precision of the system	Arrieta et al. (2020), Bialkova (2023c), Guidotti et al. (2018), Chung et al. (2020), Cheng and Jiang (2021)
Competence	Effective in accomplishing what was set out to do See Spitzberg (2006) for an overview on Computer-Mediated Communication Competence	Blut et al. (2021), Bialkova (2023b, c), Chopra (2019), Cheng and Jiang (2021), Chung et al. (2020) , Edwards et al. (2014), Meyer-Waarden et al. (2020), Pitardi and Marriott (2021), Roy and Naidoo (2021)
Social presence	A sense/feeling of being with another in a mediated environment Biocca et al. (2003)—see for an overview (Social Presence Theory) but see also Lombard and Ditton (1997)	Ben Mimoun et al. (2017), Bialkova (2022b, 2023b, c), Blut et al. (2021), Fernandes and Oliveira (2021), de Sa Siqueira et al. (2023), Edwards et al. (2019), Go and Sundar (2019), Gelbrich et al. (2021), Jain et al. (2022), Jin and Youn (2022), Landim et al. (2022), Liu-Thompkins et al. (2022), Lu et al. (2016), McLean and Osei-Frimpong (2019), Munnukka et al. (2022), Pitardi and Marriott (2021), Qiu and Benbasat (2009), Tsai et al. (2021), Xu et al. (2022)
Personal care	Requiring human touch, e.g., personal attention, seeking understanding, and empathy (Parasuraman et al., 2005; Zeithaml et al., 2002)	Bickmore and Picard (2005), Bialkova (2022b, 2023c), Cheng and Jiang (2021), Miao et al. (2022)

correct answers divided by the total number of questions (Huysmans et al., 2011). In the context of chatbot end-user applications, it was hypothesised to reflect the precision of the marketing information provided (Cheng & Jiang, 2021). Despite the enormous number of definitions and measuring scales in respect to the environments/scenarios the accuracy is assessed, ensuring timely and adequate e-agency is a prerequisite for accurate performance. Accuracy was therefore associated with agent functioning properly (Bialkova, 2023c).

It is expected from the AI system to be accurate and to provide adequate solutions (Arrieta et al., 2020), extracting interpretable decisions (Guidotti et al., 2018). A more

Table 6.2 Summary of the hypotheses tested

	Hypotheses tested
H1	The higher the informativeness is, the greater the degree to which the chatbot functionality will be evaluated
H2	The greater the accuracy is, the higher the chatbot functionality will be evaluated
H3	The greater the competence is, the higher the functionality will be evaluated
H4	The greater the social presence is, the greater the enjoyment from the interaction with the chatbot will be
H5	The better the personal care is, the greater the enjoyment from the interaction with the chatbot will be
H6	The higher the functionality and enjoyment are, the higher the ease of use will be perceived
H7	The higher the functionality and enjoyment are, the higher the quality will be perceived
H8	The higher the ease of use and the quality are perceived to be, the higher the satisfaction will be
H9	The greater the satisfaction is, the greater the brand loyalty will be
H10	The greater the satisfaction is, the higher the intention to use chatbot(s) in future will be

accurate system forecast is very likely to be recognised as being more useful, as noted a while ago (Davis et al., 1989). In contrast, lack of accuracy may preclude further communication with e-service robots (Yagoda & Gillan, 2012). In the chatbot context, recent study reported even negative feelings such as frustrations (de Sa Siqueira et al., 2023), when the chatbots are not able to understand the user questions, or do not provide suitable answers as expected. Based on the above theoretical notions, we therefore assume:

H2. The greater the accuracy is, the higher the chatbot functionality will be evaluated.

Competence also received significant attention in earliest studies in Computer-Mediated Communication (for an overview see Spitzberg, 2006). It was extensively explored in the context of robots (Edwards et al., 2014; Yagoda & Gillan, 2012) and chatbots applications (Blut et al., 2021; Chopra, 2019; Chung et al., 2020; Pitardi & Marriott, 2021; Roy & Naidoo, 2021). Previous research acknowledged the contextual and complex nature of competence (for an overview see Spitzberg, 2006). It drives peoples' responses to specific interaction (Fiske et al., 2007). The type of interaction is predetermined by the knowledge and skills translated into the mediated context, as noted in earlier studies (Edwards et al., 2014; Yagoda & Gillan, 2012).

The need for competent agency was also well documented in the service marketing literature. Having skills, knowledge, and being competent is a must to appropriately perform a service, as documented a long time ago (Parasuraman et al., 1988). With the rise of technology, it is obvious that competent (e.g., skilful and knowledgeable) agency is crucial in the evaluation of system performance. The need for competent e-services agents has been recognised, and thus, inspired the exploration of different scales, metrics and tools to adequately address competence (e.g., Edwards et al., 2014; Yagoda & Gillan, 2012).

In the context of chatbots, competent AI agency was reported to stimulate positive attitudes and to encourage trust toward technology (Pitardi & Marriott, 2021). Trust in AI (Chopra, 2019) and customer satisfaction (Chung et al., 2020) were positively influenced when the online service agents exhibited accurate and competent communication. However, research was not able to substantiate statistically the relationship between chatbot competence and its usefulness (Meyer-Waarden et al., 2020). One may argue that different scales have been used in these previous studies, and thus reflecting the discrepancies between earlier findings. Another plausible argument could be the lack of consumers' satisfaction regarding the AI agent performance. If this is the case, this is an important reason to closely investigate what exactly determines chatbot functionality evaluation. Therefore, we predict:

H3. The greater the competence is, the higher the functionality will be evaluated.

We are further interested in determining whether the parameters hypothesised to modulate functionality, quality, and ease of use also impact emotional components. One may expect that different factors predetermine cognitive and affective components, given that functionality, quality, and ease of use are cognitive components, while enjoyment is explained with emotional, affective response.

6.2   Emotional Components

Enjoyment, often associated with happiness, being a core affect (Russell, 2003) constructing emotions, is one of the most extensively studied in marketing and psychology literature when it comes to shopping. Linked with pleasurable experience, enjoyment was also addressed in exploring attitudes toward technology, in an earlier work (Dabholkar & Bagozzi, 2002). Acknowledged to influence how the system ease of use is perceived (Venkatesh, 2000), it was investigated in different studies exploring the tech system performance from online and digital, to augmented and virtual reality platforms. Enjoyment is a key factor in consumer experience evaluation when interacting with high tech platforms (Bialkova, 2019), reflecting further liking (Bialkova, 2022c, 2023d) and brand advocacy (Bialkova & Barr, 2022).

In the chatbot literature, it was addressed in line with attitudes (Bialkova, 2022a; Pitardi & Marriott, 2021), future use intention (Bialkova, 2022b; Lee & Choi, 2017; Rese et al., 2020), and shopping intention at AI-powered retail (Pillai et al., 2020). Enjoyment was found to interplay with chatbot quality perception and ease of use (see Chap. 5, Bialkova, 2024d). This outcome nicely coheres with earlier work from our lab (Bialkova, 2022b, 2023b), acknowledging essential role of enjoyment in chatbot performance evaluation.

What is much more interesting in the present context is what factors drive enjoyable experience regarding interaction with chatbots. We have to note that some of the previous work has addressed the role of emotions in chatbot efficiency (see Chap. 2, Bialkova, 2024a – for an overview). In particular, affective response was investigated in line with the incorporation of anthropomorphic features. Considering that chatbots are used to replace the human–human interaction in an increasing number of everyday situations, they are expected to deliver a pleasant and valuable experience to meet the consumer demand. In reality, however, AI applications may not necessarily deliver human-like and enjoyable interactions. One may, therefore, argue whether it is needed to enhance the anthropomorphic features in an AI system. This is a serious question worth further attention, especially given the way in which chatbot performance is judged. It was acknowledged already that the interaction with a chatbot might be evaluated in a different way than the interaction with a human agent (Baek et al., 2021; Lou et al., 2022).

Alternatively, low anthropomorphism of the chatbot agent itself could possibly be explanation for the lack of enjoyment (de Sa Siqueira et al., 2023) and even anxiety (Ali et al., 2023) when interacting with technology. As a recent study reported, AI marketing agents are often perceived as cold and uncaring (Liu-Thompkins et al., 2022). Although the authors claimed the need for artificial empathy to become a core design consideration in the next generation of AI marketing applications, the AI-human gap in affective and social customer experience has been noted. To close this gap, further investigation is invited, to disentangle the factors determining these social aspects.

6.3 Social Aspects—Presence and Personal Care

Social agency has been extensively explored since the earliest research in human–computer interaction (see Chap. 2, Bialkova, 2024a – for a detailed overview). For the AI systems to have human-like behaviour means to poses anthropomorphism, i.e., from the Greek words anthropos (for man) and morphe (form/structure). Chatbots, being one of these systems, are designed and expected to behave in a human-like manner (e.g., Blut et al., 2021; Chaves & Gerosa, 2021; Chong et al., 2021; Fernandes & Oliveira, 2021; Guerreiro & Loureiro, 2023; Lim et al., 2022; Liu-Thompkins et al., 2022; Miao et al., 2022; Pillai and Sivathanu, 2020; Qui and Benbasat, 2009; Tsai et al., 2021). In Bialkova, 2024b, Chap. 3, we already outlined core social theories, paradigms, and terms as emerging from the literature audit reflecting the chatbot context. Hereby, we focus our attention to two aspects (being the most frequently explored in earlier work), namely social presence and personal care.

Social presence defined as the "sense of being with another in a mediated environment" (Biocca et al., 2003) is achieved through interactions with others (Hess et al., 2009). Earlier work acknowledging the importance of mediated environment on how social presence is perceived (Witmer & Singer, 1998), noted the urgency for sociable, warm, sensitive, personal, or intimate interaction (Lombard & Ditton, 1997).

Note surprisingly then, to establish and maintain long-term relationships with the users, the human–computer interaction studies recognised the need for social-emotional agents, a long time ago (e.g., Bickmore & Picard, 2005). Enhanced user satisfaction with lifted social presence was reported from consumers applications (He et al., 2012). Perceived social presence had a positive impact on attitudes and consumer purchase behaviour (Dahl et al., 2001). Augmented social presence of website has further influenced consumer trust, as well as enjoyment and loyalty (Cyr et al., 2007), recognised to play a crucial role in agent and e-service evaluation (Gefen & Straub, 2003).

In the chatbot context, human contact, warmth, and sociability were also hypothesised to reflect social presence (Ben Mimoun et al., 2017). Social presence influenced the user perception of trust (Tsai et al., 2021), the interactivity (Bialkova, 2023b), and to further shape attitudes (de Sa Siqueira et al., 2023). Increased social presence and empathy were hypothesised to lift the social experience with AI-based marketing applications (Liu-Thompkins et al., 2022). Moreover, the warmth of the digital assistant was perceived as a mediator of its emotional support, and thus, modulated satisfaction (Gelbrich et al., 2021).

Note, however, social presence was higher in face-to-face than in mediated communication (Gefen & Straub, 2003). Recent work provides a plausible explanation of this outcome in terms of emotional information shown via facial expression, posture, and non-verbal cues contributing to the social presence (de Sa Siqueira et al., 2023). Put differently, the chatbot AI systems need to provide social presence as expected by the end users. Only well-demonstrated social presence may satisfy consumers experience with the AI system and to have a positive impact on the way the chatbot is perceived. We therefore hypothesise:

H4. The greater the social presence is, the greater the enjoyment from the interaction with the chatbot will be.

Personal care reflects the need for personal attention, understanding, and empathy. Adding personal touch to e-service was acknowledged to reflect social presence (Gefen & Straub, 2003). It further shapes consumer satisfaction, as it was well documented in service marketing literature (Parasuraman et al., 2005; Zeithaml et al., 2002). The researchers pointed out the need for personalisation, as it may have a beneficial role for the advancement of the service provided.

Recent work in the AI context already mentioned that personalisation (Greene & Shmueli, 2023; Lopes & Cavique, 2023) is important for lifting customers social engagement (Yang et al., 2022). In the chatbot context, better interaction, customisation, and thus direct effect on consumer-brand relationship was also reported when the service agent offered to customers individual attention and care (Cheng & Jiang, 2021). Enhanced purchase intent was associated with agent social response (e.g., social presence, personalisation), and enjoyable interaction with avatar exhibiting anthropomorphic features (Miao et al., 2022). Based on the above mentioned, we assume:

H5. The better the personal care is, the greater the enjoyment from the interaction with the chatbot will be.

We have to note, however, that personification of an interface by itself was not a sufficient condition to build trust with a user (Bickmore & Picard, 2005). The researchers claimed that other interface features and specific behaviour by the agent may change the user's perception. Therefore, it is crucial to determine which are these features and how social aspects interplaying with other factors as enumerated hereby impact chatbot performance, and thus, the way it is perceived by the user.

6.4   Factors Interplay: The Effect of Agency on Chatbot Evaluation

It is worth pointing out hereby that attractive avatars were found to be effective sales agents at moderate levels of product involvement (Holzwarth et al., 2006). By contrast, at high levels of product involvement, expert avatars were more effective sales agents. Put differently, both cognitive and affective components seem to modulate the way chatbot performance is perceived. Recent work from our laboratory supported the notion that affective (e.g., enjoyment) and cognitive (e.g., functionality, interactivity) components interplay, and thus enhance the chatbot evaluation (Bialkova, 2022a, 2023a). Therefore, in the current work, we look at how these influence chatbot perception.

As we have already discussed in Chap. 5 (Bialkova, 2024d), the ease of use is determined by functionality and enjoyment. Quality perception was also modulated by functionality and enjoyment. Enhanced e-agency in terms of ease of use and quality perception with greater functionality was reported as outcome of the empirical work (see the previous chapter). Based on the earlier studies (Bialkova, 2021, 2023a) and to be consistent with Chap. 5, we test hereby the following hypotheses:

H6. The higher the functionality and enjoyment are, the higher the ease of use will be perceived.

H7. The higher the functionality and enjoyment are, the higher the quality will be perceived.

Quality and ease of use emerged as crucial predictors of satisfaction (see Chap. 5, Bialkova, 2024d), associated with appropriately meeting customer expectations for products or services provided (e.g., Chung et al., 2020; Zeithaml et al., 2002). For fluency of the current model, and to be consistent with Chap. 5 outcomes, we therefore incorporate a relevant hypothesis:

H8. The higher the ease of use and the quality are perceived to be, the higher the satisfaction will be.

User satisfaction was recognised as a predictor for acceptance of technology (Wixom & Todd, 2005), a long time ago (Davis et al., 1989). In human–computer interaction literature, it has been acknowledged the need to make chatbots showing more human-like behaviour, as a prerequisite to improve user experience, satisfaction, and thus possibility to achieve acceptance of the system used (e.g., Chaves & Gerosa, 2021). Utilitarian and hedonic features were hypothesised to modulate satisfaction with the AI system used (Xie et al., 2022). In marketing literature, it was shown that enjoyment is a mediator in the relationship between user satisfaction and intention to use a chatbot (Lee & Choi, 2017). Recent studies from our lab reported that the level of satisfaction indeed modulated the way chatbot is experienced (Bialkova, 2022b, 2023e), and thus the user willingness to use the system in future (Bialkova, 2023b). While highly satisfied consumers found the interaction as pleasant and enjoyable, consumers reporting low satisfaction found the system to be useless. Hereby (see Chap. 5, Bialkova, 2024d), we confirm that satisfaction is a key predictor of the future use intention.

Given the increasing number of chatbots AI applications, it is interesting to further determine whether and how satisfaction with chatbots influences the brand perception itself. From classical marketing theories, we know that satisfaction is a crucial factor shaping the customers return. From service marketing literature, we also know that consumers satisfied with service quality have favourable intentions (e.g., Zeithaml et al., 2002). In the context of high-tech environments, recent papers reported that highly satisfied consumers recognise more positive hedonic and utilitarian values concerning the brand (Bialkova and Barr, 2022), as a prerequisite for increase in the purchase intention (Bialkova, 2022c). Translating these findings in the current context, we therefore predict:

H9. The greater the satisfaction is, the greater the brand loyalty will be.

H10. The greater the satisfaction is, the higher the intention to use chatbot(s) in future will be.

6.5 Conceptual Model of Chatbot Agency

Parallel to the cognitive and emotional components, that have emerged in the current book as key drivers of chatbot efficiency, we focus our exploration on social aspects. Such exploration is expected to shed light on AI applications as intelligent systems that provide not only algorithmic thinking, but also incorporate empathic and social interaction.

The above enumerated hypotheses are summarised in a conceptual model as presented in Fig. 6.1 (see also Table 6.2) and are tested in an empirical study as described in detail in Chap. 7 (Bialkova, 2024e). The conceptual model focuses at providing the much-needed understanding on chatbot agency. We aim to map the essential requirements for interactivity, advising design space for AI systems that appropriately meet user demand for efficient chatbot agency.

References

Ali, F., Zhang, Q., Tauni, M. Z., & Shahzad, K. (2023). Social chatbot: My friend in my distress. *International Journal of Human-Computer Interaction*. https://doi.org/10.1080/10447318.2022. 2150745

Araujo, T. (2018). Living up to the chatbot hype: The influence of anthropomorphic design cues and communicative agency framing on conversational agent and company perceptions. *Computers in Human Behavior, 85*, 183–189.

Arrieta, A. B., Díaz-Rodríguez, N., del Ser, J., Bennetot, A., et al. (2020). Explainable Artificial Intelligence (XAI): Concepts, taxonomies, opportunities and challenges toward responsible AI. *Information Fusion, 58*, 82–115.

Ashfaq, M., Yun, J., Yu, S., & Loureiro, S. M. (2020). I, Chatbot: Modeling the determinants of users' satisfaction and continuance intention of AI-powered service agents. *Telematics Informatics, 54*, 101473.

Baek, T. H., Bakpayev, M., Yoon, S., & Kim, S. (2021). Smiling AI agents: How anthropomorphism and broad smiles increase charitable giving. *International Journal of Advertising, 41*, 850–867.

Bandura, A. (1989). Human agency in social cognitive theory. *American Psychologist, 44*(9), 1175–1184.

BenMimoun, M. S., Poncin, I., & Garnier, M. (2017). Animated conversational agents and e-consumer productivity: The roles of agents and individual characteristics. *Information and Management, 54*(5), 545–559.

Bialkova, S. (2019). Consumers journey enhancement: The VR impact. In *European Marketing Academy Conference*, EMAC2019, May 28–31, Hamburg, Germany.

Bialkova, S. (2021). Would you talk to me? The role of chatbots in marketing. In *ICORIA2021*, June 26–28, in Bordeaux, France.

Bialkova, S. (2022a). How may I help you? Chatbots implementation in marketing. In *European Marketing Academy Conference*, EMAC2022, May 24–27, in Budapest, Hungary.

Bialkova S. (2022b). Interacting with Chatbot: How to enhance functionality and enjoyment? In *AEMARK2022*, 7–10 September 2022, Valencia, Spain.

Bialkova, S. (2022c). From attention to action: Key drivers to augment VR experience for everyday consumer applications. In *2022 IEEE Conference on Virtual Reality and 3D User Interfaces Abstracts and Workshops (VRW)*, Christchurch, New Zealand (pp. 247–252).

Bialkova, S. (2023a). I want to talk to you: Chatbot marketing integration. *Advances in Advertising Research*, (Vol. XII, pp. 23–36). https://doi.org/10.1007/978-3-658-40429-1_2

Bialkova, S. (2023b). AI-driven customer experience: Factors to consider. In L. Moutinho, L. Cavique, & E. Bigné (Eds.), *Philosophy of artificial intelligence and its place in society* (pp. 341–357). IGI Global.

Bialkova, S. (2023c). How to optimise interaction with chatbots? Key parameters emerging from actual application. *International Journal of Human–Computer Interaction*. https://doi.org/10.1080/10447318.2023.2219963

Bialkova, S. (2023d). Enhancing multisensory experience and brand value: Key determinants for extended, augmented, and virtual reality marketing applications. In A. Simeone, B. Weyers, S. Bialkova, & R. W. Lindeman (Eds.), *Everyday virtual and augmented reality. Human–Computer Interaction Series* (pp. 181–195). Springer.

Bialkova, S. (2023e). I need your help: Key parameters guiding satisfaction with chatbots. In *European Marketing Academy Conference, EMAC2023*, 23–26 May 2023, in Odense, Denmark.

Bialkova, S. (2024a). Audit of literature on chatbot applications. In *The rise of AI user applications: Chatbots integration foundations and trends*. Springer (Chapter 2), https://doi.org/10.1007/978-3-031-56471-0_2

Bialkova, S. (2024b). Core theories applied in chatbot context. In *The rise of AI user applications: Chatbots integration foundations and trends*. Springer (Chapter 3), https://doi.org/10.1007/978-3-031-56471-0_3

Bialkova, S. (2024c). Shaping chatbot efficiency—How to build better systems? In *The rise of AI user applications: Chatbots integration foundations and trends*. Springer (Chapter 4), https://doi.org/10.1007/978-3-031-56471-0_4

Bialkova, S. (2024d). Chatbot efficiency—Model testing. In *The rise of AI user applications: Chatbots integration foundations and trends*. Springer (Chapter 5), https://doi.org/10.1007/978-3-031-56471-0_5

Bialkova, S. (2024e). Chatbot agency—Model testing. In *The rise of AI user applications: Chatbots integration foundations and trends*. Springer (Chapter 7), https://doi.org/10.1007/978-3-031-56471-0_7

Bialkova, S., & Barr, C. (2022). Virtual try-on: How to enhance consumer experience? In *Proceedings of IEEEVR2022, 8th Workshop on Everyday Virtual Reality*, March 12–16, Chritschurch, New Zealand.

Bickmore, T. W., & Picard, R. W. (2005). Establishing and maintaining long-term human–computer relationships. *ACM Transactions on Computer–Human Interaction, 12*(2), 293–327.

Biocca, F., Harms, C., & Burgoon, J. K. (2003). Toward a more robust theory and measure of social presence: Review and suggested criteria. *Presence: Teleoperators and Virtual Environments, 12*, 456–480.

Blut, M., Wang, C., Wünderlich, N., & Brock, C. (2021). Under-standing anthropomorphism in service provision: A meta-analysis of physical robots, chatbots, and other AI. *Journal of the Academy of Marketing Science, 49*, 632–658.

Chaves, A. P., & Gerosa, M. A. (2021). How should my chatbot interact? A survey on social characteristics in human–chatbot interaction design. *International Journal of Human-Computer Interaction, 37*(8), 729–758.

Cheng, Y., & Jiang, H. (2021). Customer brand relationship in the era of artificial intelligence: Understanding the role of chatbot marketing efforts. *Journal of Product and Brand Management, 31*(2), 252–264.

Chong, T., Yu, T., Keeling, D. I., & de Ruyter, K. (2021). AI-chatbots on the services frontline addressing the challenges and opportunities of agency. *Journal of Retailing and Consumer Services, 63*, 102735.

Chopra, K. (2019). Indian shopper motivation to use artificial intelligence: Generating Vroom's expectancy theory of motivation using grounded theory approach. *International Journal of Retail & Distribution Management, 47*(3), 331–347.

Chung, M., Ko, E., Joung, H., & Kim, S. J. (2020). Chatbot e-service and customer satisfaction regarding luxury brands. *Journal of Business Research, 117*, 587–595.

Cyr, D., Hassanein, K., Head, M., & Ivanov, A. (2007). The role of social presence in establishing loyalty in e-service environments. *Interacting with Computers, 19*(1), 43–56.

Dabholkar, P. A., & Bagozzi, R. P. (2002). An attitudinal model of technology-based self-service: Moderating effects of consumer traits and situational factors. *Journal of the Academy of Marketing Science, 30*(3), 184–201.

Dahl, D. W., Manchanda, R. V., & Argo, J. J. (2001). Embarrassment in consumer purchase: The roles of social presence and purchase familiarity. *Journal of Consumer Research, 28*(3), 473–481.

Davis, F. D., Bagozzi, R. P., & Warshaw, P. R. (1989). User acceptance of computer technology: A comparison of two theoretical models. *Management Science, 5*(8), 982–1003.

DeLone, W. H., & McLean, E. R. (2003). The DeLone and McLean model of information systems success: A ten-year update. *Journal of Management Information System, 19*(4), 9–30.

de Sa Siqueira, M., Muller, B. C., & Bosse, T. (2023). When do we accept mistakes from chatbots? The impact of human-like communication on user experience in chatbots that make mistakes. *International Journal of Human–Computer Interaction*. https://doi.org/10.1080/10447318.2023.2175158

Edwards, C., Edwards, A., Spence, P. R., & Shelton, A. K. (2014). Is that a bot running the social media feed? Testing the differences in perceptions of communication quality for a human agent and a Bot Agent on Twitter. *Computers in Human Behavior, 33*, 372–376.

Fernandes, T., & Oliveira, E. (2021). Understanding consumers' acceptance of automated technologies in service encounters: Drivers of digital voice assistants adoption. *Journal of Busi-Ness Research, 122*, 180–191.

Fiske, S. T., Cuddy, A. J., & Glick, P. (2007). Universal dimensions of social cognition: Warmth and competence. *Trends in Cognitive Sciences, 11*(2), 77–83.

Gefen, D., & Straub, D. (2003). Managing user trust in B2C e-services. *e-Service Journal, 2*(2), 7–24.

Gelbrich, K., Hagel, J., & Orsingher, C. (2021). Emotional support from a digital assistant in technology-mediated services: Effects on customer satisfaction and behavioral persistence. *International Journal of Research in Marketing, 38*, 176–193.

Go, E., & Sundar, S. S. (2019). Humanizing chatbots: The effects of visual, identity and conversational cues on humanness perceptions. *Computers in Human Behavior, 97*, 304–316.

Greene, T., & Shmueli, G. (2023). Persons and personalization on digital platforms: A philosophical perspective. In L. Moutinho, L. Cavique, & E. Bigné (Eds.), *Philosophy of artificial intelligence and its place in society* (pp. 214–270). IGI global.

Guerreiro, J., & Loureiro, S. M. C. (2023). I am attracted to my Cool Smart Assistant! Analyzing attachment-aversion in AI-human relationships. *Journal of Business Research, 161*, 113863.

Guidotti, R., Monreale, A., Ruggieri, S., Turini, F., Giannotti, F., & Pedreschi, D. (2018). A survey of methods for explaining black box models. *ACM Computing Surveys, 51*(5), 93.

He, Y., Chen, Q., & Alden, D. L. (2012). Consumption in the public eye: The influence of social presence on service experience. *Journal of Business Research, 65*, 302–310.

Hess, T., Fuller, M., & Campbell, D. (2009). Designing interfaces with social presence: Using vividness and extraversion to create social recommendation agents. *Journal of the Association of Information Systems, 10*(12), 889–919.

Holzwarth, M., Janiszewski, C., & Neumann, M. M. (2006). The influence of avatars on online consumer shopping behavior. *Journal of Marketing, 70*(4), 19–36.

Huysmans, J., Dejaeger, K., Mues, C., Vanthienen, J., & Baesens, B. (2011). An empirical evaluation of the comprehensibility of decision table, tree and rule based predictive models. *Decision Support Systems, 51*, 141–154.

Jain, S., Basu, S., Dwivedi, Y. K., & Kaur, S. (2022). Interactive voice assistants—Does brand credibility assuage privacy risks? *Journal of Business Research, 139*, 701–717.

Jin, S. V., & Youn, S. (2022). Social presence and imagery processing as predictors of chatbot continuance intention in Human–AI-interaction. *International Journal of Human-Computer Interaction, 39*(9), 1874–1886.

Kannan, P. K., Yang, Y., & Zhang, K. (2023). Unlocking deeper insights into customer engagement through AI-powered analysis of social media. *Data Management and Business Review, 3*(1 & 2).

Kang, E., & Kang, Y. A. (2023). Counseling chatbot design: The effect of anthropomorphic chatbot characteristics on user self-disclosure and companionship. *International Journal of Human-Computer Interaction.* https://doi.org/10.1080/10447318.2022.2163775

Landim, A. R. D. B., Pereira, A. M., Vieira, T., Costa, E. B., Moura, J. A., Wanick, B. V., & Bazaki, E. (2022). Chatbot design approaches for fashion E-commerce: An interdisciplinary review. *International Journal of Fashion Design, Technology and Education, 15*(2), 200–210.

Lee, H., & Cho, C. H. (2020). Uses and gratifications of smart speakers: Modelling the effectiveness of smart speaker advertising. *International Journal of Advertising, 39*(7), 1150–1171.

Lee, S., & Choi, J. (2017). Enhancing user experience with conversational agent for movie recommendation: Effects of self-disclosure and reciprocity. *International Journal of Human-Computer Studies, 103*, 95–105.

Lim, W. M., Kumar, S., Verma, S., & Chaturvedi, R. (2022). Alexa, what do we know about conversational commerce? Insights from a systematic literature review. *Psychology and Marketing, 39*, 1129–1155.

Liu-Thompkins, Y., Okazaki, S., & Li, H. (2022). Artificial empathy in marketing interactions: Bridging the human AI gap in affective and social customer experience. *Journal of the Academy of Marketing Science, 50*(6), 1198–1218.

Lombard, M., & Ditton, T. (1997). At the heart of it all: The concept of presence. *Journal of Computer Mediated Communication, 3*(2), 321.

Lopes, N. C., & Cavique, L. (2023). Causal machine learning in social impact assessment. In L. Moutinho, L. Cavique, & E. Bigné (Eds.), *Philosophy of artificial intelligence and its place in society* (pp. 214–270). IGI Global.

Lou, C., Kang, H., & Tse, C. H. (2022). Bots vs. humans: How schema congruity, contingency-based interactivity, and sympathy influence consumer perceptions and patronage intentions. *International Journal of Advertising, 41*, 655–684.

Lu, B., Fan, W., & Zhou, M. (2016). Social presence, trust, and social commerce purchase intention: An empirical research. *Computers in Human Behavior, 56*, 225–237.

McLean, G., & Osei-Frimpong, K. (2019). Hey Alexa … examine the variables influencing the use of artificial intelligent in-home voice assistants. *Computers in Human Behavior, 99*, 28–37.

Meyer-Waarden, L., Pavone, G., Poocharoentou, T., Prayatsup, P., Ratinaud, M., Tison, A., & Torn, S. (2020). How service quality influences customer acceptance and usage of chatbots? *Journal of Service Management Research, 4*(1), 35–51.

Miao, F., Kozlenkova, I. V., Wang, H., Xie, T., & Palmatier, R. W. (2022). An emerging theory of avatar marketing. *Journal of Marketing, 86*(1), 67–90.

Moriuchi, E. (2021). An empirical study on anthropomorphism and engagement with disembodied AIs and consumers' re-use behavior. *Psychology and Marketing, 38*(7), 21–42.

Munnukka, J., Talvitie-Lamberg, K., & Maity, D. (2022). Anthropomorphism and social presence in Human-Virtual service assistant interactions: The role of dialog length and attitudes. *Computers in Human Behavior, 135*, 107343.

Parasuraman, A., Zeithaml, V. A., & Berry, L. (1988). SERVQUAL: A multiple-item scale for measuring consumer perceptions of service quality. *Journal of Retailing, 61*(1), 12–40.

Parasuraman, A., Zeithaml, V. A., & Malhotra, A. (2005). E-S-QUAL: A multiple-item scale for assessing electronic service quality. *Journal of Service Research, 7*(3), 213–233.

Pillai, R., Sivathanu, B., & Dwivedi, Y. K. (2020). Shopping intention at AI-powered automated retail stores (AIPARS). *Journal of Retailing and Consumer Services, 57*, 102207.

Pitardi, V., & Marriott, H. R. (2021). Alexa, she's not human but… Unveiling the drivers of consumers' trust in voice-based artificial intelligence. *Psychology and Marketing, 38*, 626–642.

Qiu, L., & Benbasat, I. (2009). Evaluating anthropomorphic product recommendation agents: A social relationship perspective to designing information systems. *Journal of Management Information Systems, 25*(4), 145–181.

Rese, A., Ganster, L., & Baier, D. (2020). Chatbots in retailers' customer communication: How to measure their acceptance? *Journal of Retailing and Consumer Services, 56*, 102176.

Roy, R., & Naidoo, V. (2021). Enhancing chatbot effectiveness: The role of anthropomorphic conversational styles and time orientation. *Journal of Business Research, 126*, 23–34.

Russell, J. A. (2003). Core affect and the psychological construction of emotion. *Psychological Review, 110*(1), 145–172.

Spitzberg, B. H. (2006). Preliminary development of a model and measure of Computer-mediated communication (CMC) competence. *Journal of Computer-Mediated Communication, 11*(2), 629–666.

Trivedi, J. (2019). Examining the customer experience of using banking chatbots and its impact on brand love: The moderating role of perceived risk. *Journal of Internet Commerce, 18*(1), 91–111.

Tsai, W. H. S., Liu, Y., & Chuan, C. H. (2021). How chatbots' social presence communication enhances consumer engagement: The mediating role of parasocial interaction and dialogue. *Journal of Research in Interactive Marketing, 15*(3), 460–482.

Venkatesh, V. (2000). Determinants of perceived ease of use: Integrating control, intrinsic motivation, and emotion into the technology acceptance model. *Information Systems Research, 11*(4), 342–365.

Witmer, G., & Singer, M. J. (1998). Measuring presence in virtual environments: A presence questionnaire. *Presence: Teleoperators and Virtual Environments, 7*(3), 225–240.

Wixom, B., & Todd, P. (2005). A theoretical integration of user satisfaction and technology acceptance. *Information Systems Research, 16*(1), 85–102.

Xie, C., Wang, Y., & Cheng, Y. (2022). Does artificial intelligence satisfy you? A meta-analysis of user gratification and user satisfaction with AI-powered chatbots. *International Journal of Human–Computer Interaction.*

Xu, K., Chan-Olmsted, S., & Liu, F. (2022). Smart speakers require smart management: Two Routes from user gratifications to privacy settings. *International Journal of Communication, 16*, 192–214.

Yagoda, R., & Gillan, D. (2012). You want me to trust ROBOT? The development of a human–robot interaction trust scale. *International Journal of Social Robotics, 4*(3), 235–248.

Yang, Y., Zhang, K., & Kannan, P. K. (2022). Identifying market structure: A deep network representation learning of social engagement. *Journal of Marketing, 86*(4), 37–56.

Zeithaml, V. A., Parasuraman, A., & Malhotra, A. (2002). Service quality delivery through web sites: A critical review of extant knowledge. *Journal of the Academy of Marketing Science, 30*(4), 362–375.

Chapter 7
Chatbot Agency—Model Testing

Abstract The factors hypothesised in the conceptual model on chatbot agency are tested in an empirical study hereby. We have invited consumers who had used a chatbot at least once in their daily life to complete a survey, sharing their opinion about the experience they had concerning chatbot agency. The chatbots were used to contact the customer services in 91% of the cases, demonstrating the increasing role of chatbot agents as front service line providers. The results from the regression modelling are clear in showing that: (1) Informativeness and accuracy predetermine chatbot functionality perception. (2) The higher the social presence was perceived to be, the higher was the enjoyment of interacting with a chatbot. (3) Functionality and enjoyment had positive impact on ease of use and quality perception, and thus, on satisfaction. (4) The greater the satisfaction was, the higher the brand loyalty was and the intention to use chatbots in future. Interestingly, however, personal care did not play a role hereby, opposite to the proposition we had. Competence did not load on functionality, but modulated enjoyment. Given, we have asked about user experience after the actual use of a chatbot in a daily life situation, a reasonable question arising hereby is whether chatbots currently available on the market offer the desired personal care and competence. This is a serious question challenging the UX design to reconsider the contemporary AI systems, and to ensure that these provide the desired agency, distinguishable with intelligence, empathy, and social interaction.

7.1 Methodology

The conceptual model as presented in Chap. 6 (Bialkova, 2024d) is tested hereby, aiming at providing the much-needed understanding on chatbot agency. In addition to the cognitive and affective components that have been discussed in the current book as core determinants of chatbot efficiency, we also investigate relevant social aspects. Current approach is expected to bring new insights into the development of AI applications as intelligent systems offering algorithmic thinking, as well as operating empathic and social interaction. The model is explored in an empirical study as described in detail below.

7.1.1 Participants

A random sample (different from the one reported in Chap. 5) completed a survey online. Again, participants were recruited via social media, and invitations sent via emails. They have been explicitly informed that could take part in the study only if they have used a chatbot at least once in their daily life. The study was approved by the ethics board of the home university, accordingly. Participation was anonymous and voluntary. Participants completed an informed consent prior to the study.

42 people (22 women) completed the survey. The youngest was 20 years old and the oldest 48 years old. 42% of the respondents had a MSc degree. All have experienced a chatbot before: 31% at least once, 50% more than 5 times, and the rest between 3 and 5 times. The chatbot was used to contact the customer services in 91% of the cases. Respondents also experienced chatbots in product purchase (31% of the sample). 65% of the respondents reported to have experienced chatbots in telecommunication sector. Fashion also scored 65%, followed by entertainment (62%), and banking (60%) sector.

7.1.2 Procedure and Instrument

The survey was presented after a short introduction and a consent form provided. The core concepts addressed concerned the informativeness, accuracy, competence, personal care, and social presence. We further looked how these factors enhance functionality and enjoyment when interacting with chatbots. As part of the design (and in line with the study presented in Chap. 4, Bialkova, 2024b), we have looked how functionality and enjoyment shape the ease of use and quality perception, and thus satisfaction. Brand loyalty (including attitudes) and intention to use the chatbot in future have been also addressed. At the end, sociodemographics were collected, e.g., age, gender, highest education completed. Questions about chatbot actual use were also asked (as reported in the previous section).

Informativeness scale encompassed 4 items (e.g., The chatbot agent provided the necessary information), adapted from Trivedi (2019). Accuracy and competence were self-developed constructs. These have been tested and validated from pilots in our lab, accordingly (Bialkova, 2022b, 2023b, 2023c). Accuracy (e.g., The chatbot was accurate), and competence scales (e.g., The chatbot was competent) had 3 items each. Personal care also encompassed 3 items (e.g., The chatbot provided individual attention), adapted from Cheng and Jiang (2021), validated by Bialkova (2023b). Social presence had 5 items (e.g., I felt a sense of human contact in the agent), adapted from Ben Mimoun et al. (2017), and validated by Bialkova (2023c). Loyalty encompassed 5 items (e.g., The chatbot service enhanced my attitudes toward the brand), based on Cheng and Jiang (2021). All constructs were evaluated by Likert scales (1 = strongly disagree, 7 = strongly agree).

Functionality scale encompassed 3 items (e.g., Chatbots are functional) based on Bialkova (2023a). Enjoyment encompassed 5 items (e.g., sad/joyful) based on Russell (2003), validated for UX in new tech context (Bialkova, 2019, 2023d) and in the chatbot context (Bialkova, 2022b, 2023b). For functionality, 7-point Likert scale (1 = strongly disagree, 7 = strongly agree) was used; and for enjoyment, 7-point semantic differential scale was used.

Constructs ease of use, quality, satisfaction, future use have been the same as reported for the study in Chap. 5, Bialkova, 2024c (for completeness and coherence, we incorporate these in Table 7.1). All scales demonstrated a high reliability, all Cronbach's $\alpha > 0.75$. See Table 7.1 for a summary of the constructs used and the reliability check.

7.1.3 Analytical Procedure

Data were first submitted for reliability check. All scales used were highly reliable (Cronbach's $\alpha > 0.75$). T-tests were then run to probe whether there is a difference in the response from male and female participants. Such difference was not reported (all p's > 0.1). ANOVAs were run to test whether there is a difference in response depending on the frequency of chatbot use (1–2 versus 3–5 versus > 5 times). Such deference was not reported either (all p's > 0.1).

Regression modelling tested the relationship between variables under investigation. Following the hypothesised direction of influence, we looked at (a) how informativeness, accuracy, and competence impact the chatbot functionality; (b) how personal care and social presence enhance enjoyment when interacting with chatbot; (c) how satisfaction predetermines brand loyalty and intention to use chatbots in future. As part of the design (and in line with Chaps. 5 and 6, Bialkova, 2024c, 2024d), we also looked at (d) how functionality and enjoyment influence, respectively, ease of use and quality perception; and (e) how ease of use and quality perception influence satisfaction.

7.2 Results

Informativeness explained 55% of the variance in functionality. Adding accuracy to the model improved its explanatory power to 61%. The higher the informativeness ($\beta = 0.59$) and the accuracy ($\beta = 0.44$) were, the better the functionality was perceived to be, $R^2 = 0.61$, $F(2, 39) = 30.26$, $p < 0.001$. Competence, however, did not have effect on model empowering (see Table 7.2, bottom line). Table 7.2 presents

Table 7.1 Summary of the constructs used, sources, and reliability check

Construct	Measuring scale	Cronbach's α
Informativeness	4 items: e.g., "The chatbot agent provided the necessary information", adapted from Trivedi (2019), validated by Bialkova (2023b)	0.75
Accuracy	3 items: e.g., "The chatbot was accurate", self-developed, validated in Bialkova (2023b, c)	0.85
Competence	3 items: e.g., "The chatbot was competent", self-developed, validated by Bialkova (2023b, c)	0.82
Social presence	5 items: e.g., "I felt a sense of human contact in the agent", adapted from Ben Mimoun et al. (2017), validated by Bialkova (2023b, c)	0.88
Personal care	3 items: e.g., "The chatbot provided individual attention", adapted from Cheng and Jiang (2021), validated by Bialkova (2023c)	0.78
Functionality	3 items: e.g., "Chatbots are functional", based on Bialkova (2021, 2023a)	0.88
Enjoyment	5 items: e.g., "The interaction with chatbot(s) is sad/joyful", based on Russell (2003), validated for the chatbot context by Bialkova (2022b, 2023b)	0.92
Ease of use	5 items: e.g., "Chatbots are easy to use", adapted from Davis et al. (1989)	0.88
Quality	4 items: e.g., "very bad/ very good quality", adapted from Fenko et al. (2016), validated for the chatbot context by Bialkova (2021, 2023a)	0.93
Satisfaction	5 items: e.g., "The chatbot did a good job", adapted from Chung et al. (2020)	0.92
Future use	3 items, e.g., "impossible/possible", based on Bialkova (2021, 2023a)	0.93
Loyalty	5 items: e.g., "The chatbot service enhanced my attitudes toward the brand", based on Cheng and Jiang (2021)	0.89

a summary of regression modelling concerning the effect of informativeness, accuracy, and competence on functionality perception. For completeness, in Table 7.2, we also report the effect of the above-mentioned factors on enjoyment, as results from the additional regression modelling.

Concerning the factors hypothesised to impact the affective response, personal care explained 27% of the variance of enjoyment. Adding social presence improved the model power to 38%, $R^2 = 0.38$, $F(2, 39) = 12.09$, $p < 0.001$. What is much more interesting hereby, adding competence, significantly enhanced the model power, $R^2 = 0.46$, $F(3, 38) = 10.81$, $p < 0.001$. We have run additional modelling, which will be addressed in detail in Sect. 7.3. Table 7.3 presents a summary of regression modelling concerning the effect of personal care and social presence on enjoyment. For completeness, in Table 7.3, we also report the effect of the above factors on

Table 7.2 Summary of the outcomes from the regression modelling encompassing the factors informativeness, accuracy, and competence, and their effect on functionality (left panel) and enjoyment (right panel)

	Functionality			Enjoyment		
	$R^2 = 0.617, F = 13.99$			$R^2 = 0.382, F = 7.83$		
	b	β	p	b	β	p
Informativeness	0.68	0.59	0.001	0.20	0.19	0.259
Accuracy	0.44	0.44	0.040	0.03	0.04	0.896
Competence	−0.19	−0.19	0.359	0.43	0.46	0.092

functionality. Note that personal care seems to be a predictor for functionality. We turn to this point in the discussion.

Concerning the factors hypothesised for ease of use and quality perception, results confirmed the tendencies emerging in Chap. 5 (Bialkova, 2024c). Functionality explained 31% of the variance in ease of use. Adding enjoyment to the model lifted its explanatory power to 46%, $R^2 = 0.46$, $F(2, 39) = 16.85$, $p < 0.001$. The higher the functionality ($\beta = 0.35$) and the enjoyment ($\beta = 0.44$) were, the higher the ease of use was perceived to be. Quality perception also was determined by functionality and enjoyment, $R^2 = 0.54$, $F(2, 39) = 22.41$, $p < 0.001$. The higher the functionality ($\beta = 0.26$) and the enjoyment ($\beta = 0.58$) were, the higher the quality was perceived to be. See Table 7.4 for a summary of the regression modelling concerning the effect of functionality and enjoyment on ease of use and quality. For completeness, the effect on satisfaction is also included in Table 7.4.

Table 7.3 Summary of the outcomes from the regression modelling encompassing the factors personal care and social presence, and their effect on functionality (left panel) and enjoyment (right panel)

	Functionality			Enjoyment		
	$R^2 = 0.233, F = 5.93$			$R^2 = 0.383, F = 12.09$		
	b	β	p	b	β	p
Personal care	0.48	0.45	0.023	0.18	0.18	0.303
Social presence	0.03	0.03	0.895	0.47	0.48	0.010

Table 7.4 Summary of the outcomes from the regression modelling encompassing the factors functionality and enjoyment and their effect on ease of use (left panel), quality (middle panel), and satisfaction (right panel)

	Ease of use			Quality			Satisfaction		
	$R^2 = 0.464, F = 16.85$			$R^2 = 0.535, F = 22.41$			$R^2 = 0.494, F = 19.13$		
	b	β	p	b	β	p	b	β	p
Functionality	0.38	0.35	0.010	0.26	0.26	0.042	0.38	0.35	0.009
Enjoyment	0.49	0.44	0.002	0.61	0.58	0.001	0.52	0.47	0.001

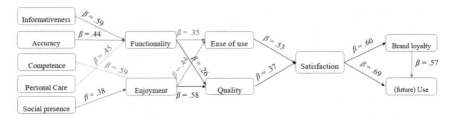

Fig. 7.1 Summary of the regression modelling of chatbot agency (including regression coefficients)

Ease of use explained 56% of the variance in satisfaction, $R^2 = 0.56$, $F(1, 40)$ $= 51.23$, $p < 0.001$. Adding quality to the model improved its explanatory power, $R^2 = 0.65$, $F(2, 39) = 25.06$, $p < 0.001$. In line with the hypotheses tested, the higher the ease of use ($\beta = 0.53$) and the quality ($\beta = 0.37$) were perceived to be, the higher was the satisfaction.

Satisfaction explained 36% of the variance in brand loyalty, $R^2 = 36$, $F(1, 40) =$ 22.65, $p < 0.001$. The more satisfied the consumers were ($\beta = 0.60$), the higher the brand loyalty was. Loyalty determined 33% of the variance in future use intention, $R^2 = 32$, $F(1, 40) = 19.27$, $p < 0.001$. Furthermore, the higher the satisfaction was ($\beta = 0.69$), the higher was the intention to use a chatbot in future, $R^2 = 0.48$, $F(1, 40) = 36.29$, $p < 0.001$.

An illustrative summary of the model tested is provided on Fig. 7.1, including significant regression coefficients.

7.3 Discussion

7.3.1 Informativeness and Accuracy as Drivers of Functionality

Results were clear in showing that informativeness (**H1—accepted**) and accuracy (**H2—accepted**) are crucial parameters determining chatbot functionality (For a summary of the hypotheses tested, see Table 7.5). Current findings cohere with earlier work from our lab investigating the role of informativeness and accuracy in chatbot evaluation (Bialkova, 2023b, 2023c). These outcomes are very important as there is a high demand for good quality, relevant and sufficient information to be provided by chatbots.

Informativeness reflecting the quality of information and system semantic success (DeLone and McLean, 2003) is addressed in machine learning, ML, models aiming at providing adequate information and solutions to problems/questions the user addresses (Arrieta et al., 2020). In the chatbot end-user applications, quality of information was also acknowledged as a prerequisite for positive chatbot evaluation, as well as reflecting sustainable brand-consumer relationship (Trivedi, 2019).

Table 7.5 Summary of the hypotheses tested

	Hypotheses tested	Status
H1	The higher the informativeness is, the greater the degree to which the chatbot functionality will be evaluated	Accepted
H2	The greater the accuracy is, the higher the chatbot functionality will be evaluated	Accepted
H3	The greater the competence is, the higher the functionality will be evaluated	Rejected
H4	The greater the social presence is, the greater the enjoyment from the interaction with the chatbot will be	Accepted
H5	The better the personal care is, the greater the enjoyment from the interaction with the chatbot will be	Rejected
H6	The higher the functionality and enjoyment are, the higher the ease of use will be perceived	Accepted
H7	The higher the functionality and enjoyment are, the higher the quality will be perceived	Accepted
H8	The higher the ease of use and the quality are perceived to be, the higher the satisfaction will be	Accepted
H9	The greater the satisfaction is, the greater the brand loyalty will be	Accepted
H10	The greater the satisfaction is, the higher the intention to use chatbot(s) in future will be	Accepted

Accuracy was questioned in earlier work regarding the performance of various technologies (e.g., Chung et al., 2020; Cheng & Jiang, 2021; Davis et al., 1989; Spitzberg, 2006). Note, however, different scales have been used and in different contexts. In this respect, the current study provides a unified model, identifying the key parameters driving accuracy as a prerequisite for functionality. Such outcome is especially relevant given that lack of accuracy was a possible pitfall, precluding the communication with a robot (Yagoda & Gillan, 2012). Another note of caution comes from researchers mentioning feelings of frustration, taken the users complains that chatbot cannot understand their questions and does not provide suitable answers (de Sa Siqueira et al., 2023). Put differently, the accuracy of communication and competence of online service agents seems to significantly influence customer satisfaction (Chung et al., 2020). As reported in earlier studies from our lab, only satisfied consumers found the chatbots to be accurate and competent (Bialkova, 2023b, 2023e).

We have to note, however, that *competence* did not improve the model power on functionality (**H3—not confirmed**), see Table 7.2, bottom line. This is an interesting outcome, taken that competence loaded on enjoyment, as the additional modelling showed hereby (see Fig. 7.1). Note also that competence has been acknowledged as crucial in system evaluation (e.g., Edwards et al., 2014; Yagoda & Gillan, 2012). There is no doubt that the service agent should be competent, as well documented in service marketing literature a while ago (e.g., Parasuraman et al., 1988). Nevertheless, previous work was not able to substantiate statistically a relationship between chatbot competence and its usefulness (Meyer-Waarden et al., 2020). Chatbot competence did not affect satisfaction, opposite to what the researchers expected (Chung et al.,

2020). In this respect, the present study provides new insights, especially given the role competence has for enjoyable interaction, as discussed in detail below.

7.3.2   Competence and Social Presence as Drivers of Enjoyable Interaction

Social presence played a significant role for enjoyable interaction (**H4—confirmed**). This finding nicely coheres with earlier work from our lab (Bialkova, 2022b, 2023b, 2023c) recognising social presence as a predictor for enhanced user experience. Associated with the sense of human contact, warmth, and sociability (Ben Mimoun et al., 2017), social presence and enjoyable conversations increased the feeling of others being present via mediated environment (de Sa Siqueira et al., 2023). It was a prerequisite for satisfaction (Gelbrich et al., 2021; He et al., 2012), and willingness to purchase (Dahl et al., 2001; Jin & Youn, 2022), as already noted in service marketing literature. Other researchers (Tsai et al., 2021) reported that social presence influences trust and the intention to engage with the agent (for details, see Chap. 2).

What is much more interesting hereby, is the outcome of the additional modelling concerning enjoyment, showing that the greater the competence ($\beta = 0.59$) and the social presence were perceived to be ($\beta = 0.38$), the more enjoyable was the interaction with a chatbot, $R^2 = 0.46$, $F(2, 39) = 16.59$, $p < 0.001$. This finding brings new assets to better understand the way chatbots are perceived. Namely, the competence is a crucial determinant for enjoying the interaction with chatbot. Furthermore, competence combined with enhanced social presence is lifting the enjoyment, and thus the chatbot evaluation. While enjoyable interaction was a prerequisite for a positive system evaluation (Bialkova, 2022c), and thus, lifted user experience within high tech environments (Bialkova & Barr, 2022; Bialkova, 2023d), in the context of chatbots, enjoyment was hardly reported. Some authors even reported negative emotional reactions to AI (Ciechanowski et al., 2019; Shank et al., 2021). Therefore, the present work is pivotal in the scientific debate, revealing new insights on the factors modulating emotional components, when it comes to the interaction with chatbots. See Table 7.5 for a summary of the hypotheses tested and the outcomes as substantiated per statistical analyses.

We have to also mention that ***personal care*** did not affect the enjoyment component hereby (**H5—not supported**). This is very important finding, especially taken the very early papers in HCI arguing that personalisation of an interface alone is not a sufficient condition to build trust with a user (Bickmore & Picard, 2005), but rather specific behaviour by the agent combined with other interface features may change the user's perception. On a further note, although in service marketing literature it has been recognised that providing personal care, in terms of personal attention, understanding, and empathy could enhance consumer satisfaction (Parasuraman et al., 2005; Zeithaml et al., 2002), this does not necessarily mean that chatbots currently available on the market provide such personalisation. This lacuna is a warning call to look for appropriate tools for personalisation, in order to accelerate the service provided.

We have to also note hereby that the additional analyses we ran showed that personal care impacts functionality (see Table 7.3, top line). This is another interesting outcome. It seems consumers are sensitive to the personal care provided by chatbots. Such outcome coheres with earlier work arguing that service agents offering customers individual attention and personal care are expected to improve interaction (Bialkova, 2022b) and to lift satisfaction (Bialkova, 2023b).

Naturally then, personalisation is addressed by marketing as well as AI studies. Enhanced personalisation was claimed to increased customisation, and thus, to have a direct impact on consumer-brand relationship (Cheng & Jiang, 2021). Note however, these previous studies were mainly lab experimentations, using mock-ups, and thus, showing the intention to behave, but lacking actual behaviour in real-life scenarios. A recent study even reported that AI marketing agents are often perceived as cold and uncaring (Liu-Thompkins et al., 2022).

Therefore, we have to point out that it may be possible that chatbots currently available on the market to do not provide the personal care demanded by consumers. If this is the case, there is an urgent need for designing and launching AI systems that appropriately meet the consumer demand regarding efficient chatbot agency.

7.3.3 Satisfaction and Its Impact on Chatbot Agency

Designing chatbots meeting consumer demand, however, is not an easy task. As discussed in the current study, several parameters load on satisfaction, directly or through mediation. We have been able to bring into one model these parameters, which is a significant contribution of the present work. In particular, functionality and enjoyment had a positive impact on the ease of use (**H6—supported**) and quality perception (**H7—supported**) when interacting with chatbots. These findings confirm the outcomes reported in Chap. 5 (Bialkova, 2024c). Furthermore, the higher the ease of use and the quality were perceived, the greater the satisfaction was (**H8—confirmed**). This outcome well aligns with earlier work from our lab, reporting that only satisfied consumers find the chatbot to be of good quality and easy to use (Bialkova, 2023b, 2023d).

Note, however, some of the previous studies from other laboratory experiments have not been able to demonstrate an effect of ease of use on chatbot reuse (Meyer-Waarden et al., 2020), neither a relation between quality and the perceived usefulness of the agent (Ben Mimoun et al., 2017).

Previous studies, nevertheless, acknowledged the mediating role of enjoyment for user satisfaction (Lee & Choi, 2017; Xie et al., 2022). The need for human-like communication (Chaves & Gerosa, 2021; Fernandes & Oliveira, 2021; Lim et al., 2022) and human-like style of expression (Go & Sundar, 2019; Munnukka et al., 2022), which may lift the enjoyment when interacting with chatbots (de Sa Siqueira et al., 2023) was also discussed. Enjoyable interaction with avatar exhibiting anthropomorphic features was argued to further boost the purchase intent (Miao et al., 2022).

Hereby, we have zoomed-in into details and were able to demonstrate that enjoyment enhanced ease of use and quality perception, and thus, shaped satisfaction. Functionality also played a crucial role. Both, ease of use and quality perception have been modulated by functionality perception. These findings confirm the outcomes from Chap. 5 (Bialkova, 2024c), which is very important in the debate concerning factors determining satisfaction when interacting with chatbots AI agents.

Note, however, in some of the earlier studies, researchers failed to substantiate an effect of quality of communication on satisfaction, opposite to what they expected (Chung et al., 2020). A recent study, closely looking at consumers response when actually interacting with chatbots showed that only satisfied consumers are in fact the ones who find the chatbot to provide good quality and being easy to use (Bialkova, 2022b, 2023b). By contrast, consumers reporting low quality, and difficulty to use chatbots, have not been satisfied with the experience they had when interacting with chatbots. Put differently, the interplay between ease of use, quality, and satisfaction is an important indicator to how chatbots will be perceived by consumers.

Satisfaction was crucial component for also forming positive attitudes, and thus enhancing brand loyalty (**H9—confirmed**). Brand loyalty was a predictor for future use (see Fig. 7.1). Social interaction led to engagement and brand intimacy (Lin & Wu, 2023), as well as to chatbot related intention (Bialkova, 2022b). Satisfied consumers enjoyed the interaction with chatbots (Bialkova, 2023b, 2023e) and developed loyalty toward the brand (Bialkova, 2022b; Klaus & Zaichkowsky, 2020). Trust in e-agency (Pitardi & Marriott, 2021; Tsai et al., 2021; Yen & Chiang, 2021) and willingness to purchase (Bialkova, 2021, 2022b) were also reported by consumers satisfied with the chatbot interaction.

As part of the design, we further tested how satisfaction predicts the future use intention. It has been confirmed that the more satisfied the consumers were, the higher was the intention to use a chatbot in future (**H10—accepted**). This outcome is in line with Chap. 5, but also coheres nicely with pervious work from our lab for system evaluation and future use intention (e.g., Bialkova, 2022a, 2023a, 2023e).

Interim Summary

The aim of the present study was to offer understanding on key parameters of chatbot agency, reflecting respectively, cognitive, affective, and social aspects. Chatbot performance was explored in a survey among consumers who have used a chatbot at least once in their daily life. The study confirmed the general tendencies emerging in Chap. 5 (Bialkova, 2024c), concerning the positive effect of ease of use and quality perception on satisfaction.

What is further interesting in the present work is the role of chatbot agency, and therefore, how intelligent systems can provide not just algorithmic thinking, but also to incorporate empathic and social response. Current results are clear in chowing that (1) informativeness and accuracy predetermine chatbot functionality perception. (2) The higher the social presence was perceived to be, the higher was the enjoyment when interacting with chatbot. (3) Functionality and enjoyment had positive impact on ease of use and quality perception, and thus, satisfaction. (4) The higher the satisfaction, the higher the brand loyalty was and the intention to use chatbots in future.

Interestingly, however, competence did not load on functionality perception, but modulated enjoyment. Furthermore, the role of personal care was not substantiated statistically on enjoyment, opposite to the hypothesised effect. Personal care, nevertheless, was associated with functionality. As noted several times, competent and caring AI agency is a prerequisite for empathic and satisfactory experience.

Obviously, the chatbots currently available on the market do not provide the competence and personal care as desired and expected by consumers. This outcome is very important, calling reconsideration of the UX design on how to enhance the agent competence and personal care, when creating new AI systems, ready to be launched.

Based on the outcomes from the present work investigating consumer evaluation after actual use of chatbots currently employed in various marketing applications, we have been able to define core parameters shaping chatbot agency. These parameters we summarise in a conceptual framework (see Fig. 7.1) and suggest a toolkit aiming to facilitate the assessment of chatbot agency (see Table 7.6). Implementing the toolkit at prototyping stage and before the launch of (new) chatbots to the market is expected to facilitate the development of human-like AI systems to adequately face the user demand for functional and enjoyable interaction, a core objective for UX as well as AI and consumer scientists.

Table 7.6 Chatbot agency toolkit (ChAT)

Toolkit for accessing chatbot agency

Factor	Definition	Components	Validated in the chatbot context by studies from our lab
Informativeness	Reflects the quality of information and semantic success (Delone and McLean, 2003)	4 items The chatbot provided: • Timely response • Necessary information • Sufficient information • Helpful information regarding my queries 1 = Strongly disagree–7 = Strongly agree	Bialkova (2022b, 2023b, c)
Accuracy	Precision of the system	3 items The chatbot agent was: • Accurate • Adequate • Correct 1 = Strongly disagree–7 = Strongly agree	Bialkova (2022b, 2023b, c)
Competence	Effective in accomplishing what was set out to do (Spitzberg, 2006)	3 items The chatbot was: • Competent • Skilful • Explained things well 1 = Strongly disagree–7 = Strongly agree	Bialkova (2022b, 2023b)
Social presence	Being with another in a mediated environment (Biocca et al. 2003, but see also Lombard and Ditton, 1997)	5 items In the agent, I felt a sense of • Human contact • Personalness • Human warmth • Sociability • Human sensitivity, 1 = Strongly disagree–7 = Strongly agree	Bialkova (2023b, c)

(continued)

Table 7.6 (continued)

Toolkit for accessing chatbot agency

Factor	Definition	Components	Validated in the chatbot context by studies from our lab
Personal care	Requiring human touch, e.g., personal attention, seeking understanding, empathy (Parasuraman et al., 2005; Zeithaml et al., 2002)	3 items The chatbot agent was: • Sensitive to my customer needs • Provided individual attention • Showed sincere interest in solving my problems 1 = Strongly disagree–7 = Strongly agree	Bialkova (2023b, c)
Functionality	Reflects a correct technical functioning (Parasuraman et al., 2005)	3 items The chatbots are: • Functional • Helpful • Knowledgeable 1 = Strongly disagree–7 = Strongly agree	Bialkova (2021, 2023a)
Enjoyment	Core affect (Russell 1980) typically arising from connection or sensory pleasure, interchanged with happiness	5 items The interaction with the chatbot was: 1 = Unpleasant–7 = Pleasant 1 = Gloomy–7 = Exciting 1 = Unhappy–7 = Happy 1 = Sad–7 = Joyful 1 = Boring–7 = Entertaining	Bialkova (2022b, 2023b)

(continued)

Table 7.6 (continued)

Toolkit for accessing chatbot agency

Factor	Definition	Components	Validated in the chatbot context by studies from our lab
Ease of use	The degree to which the user expects the tech system to be free of effort (Davis et al., 1989)	5 items • Easy to use • User friendly • Efficient to use • Competent •Accurate 1 = Strongly disagree–7 = Strongly agree	Adapted from Davis et al. (1989) TAM, validated hereby for chatbot context Bialkova (2021, 2023a, e)
Quality	Information, technical, and overall service success (Trivedi, 2019, based on DeLone and McLean, 2003)	4 items I find the chatbot being: 1 = Very bad–7 = Very good 1 = Very unattractive–7 = Very attractive 1 = Very rejecting–7 = Very inviting 1 = Very bad quality–7 = Very good quality	Adapted from Fenko et al. (2016), validated hereby for chatbot context Bialkova (2021, 2023a, e)
Satisfaction	Occurs when customers find that products or services meet or exceed their positive expectations (Chung et al., 2020; Zeithaml et al., 1996, 2002)	5 items How satisfied are you with the chatbot? • I am satisfied with the service agent • The chatbot did what I expected • The chatbot did a good job • I am happy with the service agent • I am satisfied with the experience I had with the chatbot 1 = Strongly disagree–7 = Strongly agree	Bialkova (2022b, 2023b)

(continued)

Table 7.6 (continued)

Toolkit for accessing chatbot agency

Factor	Definition	Components	Validated in the chatbot context by studies from our lab
Additional items (in line with Chap. 5, Bialkova, 2024c)			
Interactivity	Extent to which users can manipulate technology (Bialkova & Barr, 2022) and/or control device	3 items Based on your experience with the chatbot, how do you feel? • I felt I could interact with the agent • I had the feeling that the agent was aware of me • I felt involved in 1 = Strongly disagree–7 = Strongly agree	Bialkova (2021, 2023a)
Attitudes	Beliefs about an object/person are evaluated, affecting intention to behave and actual behaviour (Theory of Planned Behaviour, TPB; Ajzen, 1991)	3 items My attitude toward the chatbot is 1 = Unfavourable–7 = favourable 1 = Negative–7 = positive 1 = I dislike chatbots–7 = I like chatbots	Bialkova (2021, 2023a)
Intention to use	Willingness to use the system, in this case chatbot	3 items What is the likelihood to use this chatbot in future? 1 = very unlikely–7 = very likely 1 = improbable–7 = probable 1 = possible–7 = impossible	Bialkova (2021, 2022b, 2023b, 2023e)

References

Ajzen, I. (1991). The theory of planned behavior. *Organizational Behavior and Planned Decision Processes, 50*, 179–211.

Arrieta, A. B., Díaz-Rodríguez, N., del Ser, J., Bennetot, A., et al. (2020). Explainable artificial intelligence (XAI): Concepts, taxonomies, opportunities and challenges toward responsible AI. *Information Fusion, 58*, 82–115.

Ben Mimoun, M. S., Poncin, I., & Garnier, M. (2017). Animated conversational agents and E-consumer productivity: The roles of agents and individual characteristics. *Information & Management, 54*(5), 545–559.

Bialkova, S. (2019). Consumers journey enhancement: The VR impact. In *European Marketing Academy Conference*, EMAC2019, May 28–31, in Hamburg, Germany.

Bialkova, S. (2021). Would you talk to me? The role of chatbots in marketing. In *ICORIA2021*, June 26–28, in Bordeaux, France.

Bialkova, S. (2022a). How may I help you? Chatbots implementation in marketing. In *European Marketing Academy Conference*, EMAC2022, May 24–27, in Budapest, Hungary.

Bialkova S. (2022b). Interacting with Chatbot: How to enhance functionality and enjoyment? In *AEMARK2022*, 7–10 September 2022, Valencia, Spain.

Bialkova, S. (2022c). From attention to action: Key drivers to augment VR experience for everyday consumer applications. In *2022 IEEE Conference on Virtual Reality and 3D User Interfaces Abstracts and Workshops (VRW)*, Christchurch, New Zealand, 2022, pp. 247–252.

Bialkova, S. (2023a). I want to talk to you: Chatbot marketing integration. *Advances in Advertising Research* (Vol. *XII*, pp. 23–36). https://doi.org/10.1007/978-3-658-40429-1_2

Bialkova, S. (2023b). AI-driven customer experience: factors to consider. In L. Moutinho, L. Cavique, & E. Bigné (Eds.), *Philosophy of Artificial Intelligence and Its Place in Society* (pp. 341–357). IGI Global.

Bialkova, S. (2023c). How to optimise interaction with chatbots? Key parameters emerging from actual application. *International Journal of Human–Computer Interaction*. https://doi.org/10.1080/10447318.2023.2219963

Bialkova, S. (2023d). Enhancing multisensory experience and brand value: Key determinants for extended, augmented, and virtual reality marketing applications. In A. Simeone, B. Weyers, S. Bialkova, & R. W. Lindeman (Eds.), *Everyday virtual and augmented reality. Human–Computer Interaction Series* (pp. 181–195). Springer.

Bialkova, S. (2023e). I need your help: Key parameters guiding satisfaction with chatbots. In *European Marketing Academy Conference*, EMAC2023, 23–26 May 2023, in Odense, Denmark.

Bialkova, S. (2024a). Audit of literature on chatbot applications. In *The rise of AI user applications: Chatbots integration foundations and trends*. Springer. (Chapter 2). https://doi.org/10.1007/978-3-031-56471-0_2

Bialkova, S. (2024b). Shaping chatbot efficiency—How to build better systems? In *The rise of AI user applications: Chatbots integration foundations and trends*. Springer. (Chapter 4). https://doi.org/10.1007/978-3-031-56471-0_4

Bialkova, S. (2024c). Chatbot efficiency—Model testing. In *The rise of AI user applications: Chatbots integration foundations and trends*. Springer. (Chapter 5). https://doi.org/10.1007/978-3-031-56471-0_5

Bialkova, S. (2024d). Anthropomorphism—What is crucial? In *The rise of AI user applications: Chatbots integration foundations and trends*. Springer. (Chapter 6). https://doi.org/10.1007/978-3-031-56471-0_6

Bialkova, S., & Barr, C. (2022). Virtual try-on: How to enhance consumer experience? In *Proceedings of IEEEVR2022, 8th Workshop on Everyday Virtual Reality*, March 12–16, 2022, in Chritschurch, New Zealand.

Bickmore, T. W., & Picard, R. W. (2005). Establishing and maintaining long-term human-computer relationships. *ACM Transactions on Computer–Human Interaction, 12*(2), 293–327.

Biocca, F., Harms, C., & Burgoon, J. K. (2003). Toward a more robust theory and measure of social presence: Review and suggested criteria. *Presence: Teleoperators and Virtual Environments, 12*, 456–480.

Chaves, A. P., & Gerosa, M. A. (2021). How Should my chatbot interact? A survey on social characteristics in human–chatbot interaction design. *International Journal of Human–Computer Interaction, 37*(8), 729–758.

Cheng, Y., & Jiang, H. (2021). Customer brand relationship in the era of artificial intelligence: Understanding the role of chatbot marketing efforts. *Journal of Product and Brand Management, 31*(2), 252–264.

Chung, M., Ko, E., Joung, H., & Kim, S. J. (2020). Chatbot e-service and customer satisfaction regarding luxury brands. *Journal of Business Research, 117*, 587–595.

Ciechanowski, L., Przegalinska, A., Magnuski, M., & Gloor, P. (2019). In the shades of the uncanny valley: An experimental study of human–chatbot interaction. *Future Generation Computer Systems, 92*, 539–548.

Dahl, D. W., Manchanda, R. V., & Argo, J. J. (2001). Embarrassment in consumer purchase: The roles of social presence and purchase familiarity. *Journal of Consumer Research, 28*(3), 473–481.

Davis, F. D., Bagozzi, R. P., & Warshaw, P. R. (1989). User acceptance of computer technology: A comparison of two theoretical models. *Management Science, 5*(8), 982–1003.

DeLone, W. H., & McLean, E. R. (2003). The DeLone and McLean model of information systems success: A ten-year update. *Journal of Management Information System, 19*(4), 9–30.

de Sa Siqueira, M., Muller, B. C., & Bosse, T. (2023). When do we accept mistakes from chatbots? The impact of human-like communication on user experience in chatbots that make mistakes. *International Journal of Human–Computer Interaction.* https://doi.org/10.1080/104 47318.2023.2175158

Edwards, C., Edwards, A., Spence, P. R., & Shelton, A. K. (2014). Is that a bot running the social media feed? Testing the differences in perceptions of communication quality for a human agent and a bot agent on Twitter. *Computers in Human Behavior, 33*, 372–376.

Fenko, A., Kersten, L., & Bialkova, S. (2016). Overcoming consumer scepticism toward food labels: The role of multisensory experience. *Food Quality and Preference, 48*, 81–92.

Fernandes, T., & Oliveira, E. (2021). Understanding consumers' acceptance of automated technologies in service encounters: Drivers of digital voice assistants adoption. *Journal of Busi-Ness Research, 122*, 180–191.

Gelbrich, K., Hagel, J., & Orsingher, C. (2021). Emotional support from a digital assistant in technology-mediated services: Effects on customer satisfaction and behavioral persistence. *International Journal of Research in Marketing, 38*, 176–193.

Go, E., & Sundar, S. S. (2019). Humanizing chatbots: The effects of visual, identity and conversational cues on humanness perceptions. *Computers in Human Behavior, 97*, 304–316.

He, Y., Chen, Q., & Alden, D. L. (2012). Consumption in the public eye: The influence of social presence on service experience. *Journal of Business Research, 65*, 302–310.

Jin, S.V., & Youn, S. (2022). Social presence and imagery processing as predictors of chatbot continuance intention in human–AI–Interaction. *International Journal of Human–Computer Interaction.*

Klaus, P., & Zaichkowsky, J. (2020). AI voice bots: A services marketing research agenda. *Journal of Services Marketing, 34*(3), 389–398.

Lee, S., & Choi, J. (2017). Enhancing user experience with conversational agent for movie recommendation: Effects of self-disclosure and reciprocity. *International Journal of Human-Computer Studies, 103*, 95–105.

Lim, W. M., Kumar, S., Verma, S., & Chaturvedi, R. (2022). Alexa, what do we know about conversational commerce? Insights from a systematic literature review. *Psychology and Marketing, 39*, 1129–1155.

Lin, J. S., & Wu, L. (2023). Examining the psychological process of developing consumer-brand relationships through strategic use of social media brand chatbots. *Computers in Human Behavior, 140*, 107488.

Liu-Thompkins, Y., Okazaki, S., & Li, H. (2022). Artificial empathy in marketing interactions: Bridging the human AI gap in affective and social customer experience. *Journal of the Academy of Marketing Science, 50*(6), 1198–1218.

Lombard, M., & Ditton, T. (1997). At the heart of it all: The concept of presence. *Journal of Computer Mediated Communication, 3*(2), JCM321.

Meyer-Waarden, L., Pavone, G., Poocharoentou, T., Prayatsup, P., Ratinaud, M., Tison, A., & Torn, S. (2020). How service quality influences customer acceptance and usage of chatbots? *Journal of Service Management Research, 4*(1), 35–51.

Miao, F., Kozlenkova, I. V., Wang, H., Xie, T., & Palmatier, R. W. (2022). An emerging theory of avatar marketing. *Journal of Marketing, 86*(1), 67–90.

Munnukka, J., Talvitie-Lamberg, K., & Maity, D. (2022). Anthropomorphism and social presence in Human–Virtual service assistant interactions: The role of dialog length and attitudes. *Computers in Human Behavior, 135*, 107343.

Parasuraman, A., Zeithaml, V. A., & Berry, L. (1988). SERVQUAL: A multiple-item scale for measuring consumer perceptions of service quality. *Journal of Retailing, 61*(1), 12–40.

Parasuraman, A., Zeithaml, V. A., & Malhotra, A. (2005). E-S-QUAL: A multiple-item scale for assessing electronic service quality. *Journal of Service Research, 7*(3), 213–233.

Pitardi, V., & Marriott, H. R. (2021). Alexa, she's not human but… Unveiling the drivers of consumers' trust in voice-based artificial intelligence. *Psychology and Marketing, 38*, 626–642.

Russell, J. A. (1980). A circumplex model of affect. *Journal of Personality and Social Psychology, 39*, 1161–1178.

Russell, J. A. (2003). Core affect and the psychological construction of emotion. *Psychological Review, 110*(1), 145–172.

Shank, D. B., Bowen, M., Burns, A., & Dew, M. (2021). Humans are perceived as better, but weaker, than artificial intelligence: A comparison of affective impressions of humans, AIs, and computer systems in roles on teams. *Computers in Human Behavior Reports, 3*, 100092.

Spitzberg, B. H. (2006). Preliminary development of a model and measure of Computer-mediated communication (CMC) competence. *Journal of Computer-Mediated Communication, 11*(2), 629–666.

Trivedi, J. (2019). Examining the customer experience of using banking chatbots and its impact on brand love: The moderating role of perceived risk. *Journal of Internet Commerce, 18*(1), 91–111.

Tsai, W. H. S., Liu, Y., & Chuan, C. H. (2021). How chatbots' social presence communication enhances consumer engagement: The mediating role of parasocial interaction and dialogue. *Journal of Research in Interactive Marketing, 15*(3), 460–482.

Xie, C., Wang, Y., & Cheng, Y. (2022). Does artificial intelligence satisfy you? A meta-analysis of user gratification and user satisfaction with AI-powered chatbots. *International Journal of Human–Computer Interaction.*

Yagoda, R., & Gillan, D. (2012). You want me to trust ROBOT? The development of a human–robot interaction trust scale. *International Journal of Social Robotics, 4*(3), 235–248.

Yen, C., & Chiang, M. C. (2021). Trust me, if you can: A study on the factors that influence consumers' purchase intention triggered by chatbots based on brain image evidence and self-reported assessments. *Behaviour and Information Technology, 40*(11), 1177–1194.

Zeithaml, V. A., Berry, L. L., & Parasuraman, A. (1996). *The behavioral consequences of service quality. Journal of Marketing, 60*, 31–46.

Zeithaml, V. A., Parasuraman, A., & Malhotra, A. (2002). Service quality delivery through web sites: A critical review of extant knowledge. *Journal of the Academy of Marketing Science, 30*(4), 362–375.

Part III
Implementing New Generation Systems

Chapter 8
AI Connecting Business and Consumers

Abstract AI technology has enabled new roles for machines and enhanced the processing of information by fuelling autonomous characteristics. Not surprisingly then, the potential of AI autonomous agents is embraced by brands to easily connect with consumers, to speed up management and operation processing. Entering the transformational era from conventional HCI systems focusing on human interaction with non-AI computing systems to human interaction with AI systems, companies could see a real upscale. Doing business is facilitated by substituting various manpower activities with human–machine systems mirroring human agency. AI agents are developed to exhibit unique behaviour, as well as to demonstrate autonomy with certain levels of human-like intelligence abilities. The development of usable and explainable AI systems as demonstrated in the two models suggested hereby (Chaps. 5 and 7) could spark the launch of AI applications that appropriately meet consumer needs and market demand. By assembling human and machine intelligence, AI technology may augment human capabilities by integrating human roles into human–machine systems. Introducing new channels, however, fosters some new challenges, and thus requires further exploration. For example, understanding under which conditions a mutual trust between humans and AI agents will be established is essential. Another puzzling question is whether an AI agent would be able to take over the control of a system for a human in specific domains and activities. In this respect, it is important to look at the open AI dialogue generative pre-trained transformer (GPT). Gaining enormous popularity, it is perhaps the most frequently used transformer for conversational AI and natural language generation. The current chapter will address several of these AI application challenges in an attempt to recommend channel deployment that integrates decision-making systems encompassing interpretable primitives. These should describe the decision-making steps in a human-understandable manner. Furthermore, human-driven decision making should be guaranteed. It is recognised as a success factor in implementing human-centred design processes and is discussed in detail below.

8.1 Applications

Various AI applications have been launched on the market. Chatbots being one of these are increasingly employed as recommendation agents by companies for providing services and to enhance experiences. AI agency could be incorporated at different stages during the consumer journey and combined with various channels. The purpose of new channels integration is to improve market performance, to enrich brand management, as well as to elevate customer relationship, encouraging positive customer sentiments and to enhance customer lifetime value. Table 8.1 provides a summary of core commerce opportunities as arising at different stages along the experiential journey, from pre-, actual, and post-use of AI agent.

Satisfied Consumers—Happy Brands

Consumers who were satisfied with chatbot performance reported their intention for future use, and to recommend chatbots, as seen hereby (Chap. 7). Furthermore, satisfaction is a core ingredient of brand attachment (Pererira et al., 2022; Bialkova, 2022b, 2023b). Not surprisingly then, many brands have invested in chatbot AI applications (Chap. 1, Bialkova, 2024a). A major body of academic papers has also dedicated significant attention to satisfaction with chatbots and use (Bialkova, 2021, 2022a, 2023a, 2023e). Future use intention was also explored extensively (Blut et al., 2021; Flavián et al., 2021; Landim et al., 2022; Pillai & Sivathanu, 2020). Although previous works have not achieved a consensus concerning parameters determining satisfaction, it is agreed that high quality is a prerequisite for elevating user satisfaction (DeLone & McLean, 2003; Trivedi, 2019), and consequent system adoption (Bialkova, 2023a, 2023c). Put differently, any brand aims at offering satisfactory experience. With AI user applications, it is expected to enhance satisfaction. From marketing classics, it is well known that satisfied consumers are not just returning

Table 8.1 Opportunities of chatbot use during the customer journey

Stage	Pre	Use	Post
Characteristics	• Attitudinal acceptance • Intentions • Behavioural intention • Continuance intention • Purchase intention • Word-of-mouth intention	• Actual use behaviour • Experience enhancement • Satisfaction • Price value	• Post-usage behaviour • Addiction • Continuance • Enhanced Loyalty • eWord-of-mouth
Benefits	Improved market performance Enriched brand management Elevated customer relationship Positive customer sentiments Enhanced customer lifetime value		

Table 8.2 Tasks with respect to AI agency and stakeholder needs

Stakeholder	Customer	Employer	Managers
Tasks and Objectives	• User's motivation to adopt AI-based technology • Meet needs and demand • Define expected outcome • Capability to interact properly • Ability in the context • Recognise emotions and feelings • Get insights	• Learn to work with AI • Understand AI • Feel human touch • People skills enhancement • Examine the critical role of AI in the success of application • Identify methods for segmentation and targeting • Clarify the user and AI roles • Get insights from customer data • Monitor user performance and continuously updates system taken into account user feedback • Design strategies to build trust in the AI system in use	• Prioritise organisational consideration when operationalising an AI project • Emphasise human-AI collaboration • People-oriented jobs focus • Monitor task performance and efficiency • Machine extracting information and rise of analytical ability • Explain applicability and potential challenges • Ensure employees understand, adopt, and use properly AI systems • Establish strategies for AI system adoption

Important: To elaborate on types of agency and control, and ways to delegate to drive user-centred human-AI collaboration

to the brand, but they could be its ambassadors. Thus, by enlarging the number of customers reached, increasing revenues, and lifting reputation, brands are also happy.

AI agents could perform various tasks, given the variabilities in needs of the stakeholders (i.e., end users, employers, managers). Also note that end users (Bialkova, 2021, 2023a), as well as employees have to adopt properly the AI systems (Choi, 2021), which often requires to predetermine specific roles and tasks. Table 8.2 provides an overview of tasks assigned in line with AI agency and stakeholder demands. In all of the cases, it is crucial to elaborate on types of agencies and control, and ways to delegate task activities to drive user-centred human-AI collaboration.

8.2 Channel Deployment and AI Integration

We focus on how the current work advances the understanding of consumer reactions to AI agencies, empowering insight-driven experiences through new channels deployment. In particular, AI should be used to extend chatbot capabilities. Such an extension would enhance the value of touch points for brand communication and advocacy, and thus, have a substantial effect on customer equity.

The following paragraph highlights the main recommendations for marketing practices based on our findings.

First, by increasing chatbot functionality, there should be a lift in ease of use and quality. Through functionality expansion, AI will not only accelerate technology implementation, but could also alter the communication between consumers and chatbots. Enhanced functionality will improve recommendation capacity, facilitate decision aid, and speedup purchases. One might, however, argue what actually loads on functionality. This is a crucial question we addressed in Chaps. 6 and 7 hereby (Bialkova, 2024d, 2024e). Considering the complexity of the functionality perception, upcoming studies may have a further look, especially exploring specific AI systems. The current outcomes could be translated to new contexts, and thus be a cornerstone to build around.

Second, brands should augment the interactivity of chatbots. Improved interaction will lead to more insightful knowledge about customers. Knowing customers better is beneficial for (re-)targeting and ads (re-)iteration. Such reiteration could lead to personalised and insightful customer experiences. Furthermore, turning chatbots to personal buddies could be highly advantageous. Chatbots could be friends, advisors, and thus trusted brand advocates. For example, knowing customer needs, interests, and past behaviour, AI could predict the desired product, and therefore recommend, e.g., a fashionable dress, delicious and healthy food. Knowing further details, e.g., time, location, hobbies, AI could advertise appropriate restaurants, favourite outdoor activities, places, and events.

Third, chatbots should provide more enjoyable agency. High interactivity and enjoyment proven to positively impact customer perceptions of quality and ease of use (Chaps. 5 and 7, Bialkova, 2024c, 2024e). This outcome brings extra value to the debate on how cognitive and affective components interplay with chatbot capacity, and thus shape consumer attitudes and (future) use. Positive emotional experiences could elevate the satisfaction of customers, thus turning them into delighted fans, who could advocate for the brand.

Fourth, proven to be key determinants of satisfaction as well as drivers of attitude formation and consequent behaviour, ease of use, and quality perception need special attention. According to the literature, when ease of use is not provided at the level required by customers, it is considered a barrier. The same holds true for the quality level which predetermines chatbot adoption, as shown by marketing practices. Brands should, therefore, offer high-quality and easy-to-use chatbots to assure successful adoption of technology.

8.3 AI Agency Enhancement

In the majority of high-end systems, chatbots are recognised as conversational agents. We organised these in a typology encompassing disembodied, embodied, and virtual agents. Figure 8.1 presents agency typology (for completeness, physical agency is

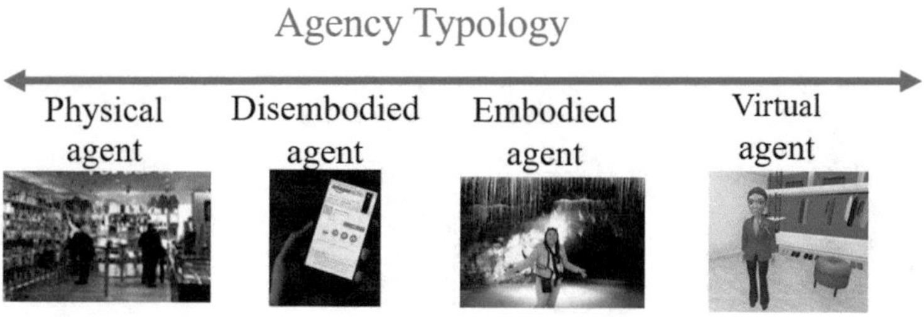

Agency Typology

Physical agent | Disembodied agent | Embodied agent | Virtual agent

Fig. 8.1 Agency typology

also included). Disembodied agents cannot rely on bodily behaviour when interacting with users. They primarily communicate via message-based interface, or voice assistance. Embodied agents demonstrate human-like behaviour as they can rely on interface mirroring human body and behaviour (Cassell, 2000), by incorporating the ability of verbal and non-verbal cues (Krämer et al., 2009). They demonstrate the ability to engage in face-to-face dialogues through speech, as well as modalities including face, gaze, gesture, posture, and body movement (Cassell & Bickmore, 2000). Embodied agents are three-dimensional human characters that employ rendered, embodied interfaces and audible responses (Derrick et al., 2011). While embodied agents may mirror real personas superimposed to virtual environment (for an overview of virtual reality, see Alcañiz et al., 2019), virtual agents could be entirely synthetic, computer-generated visual representations. Virtual agents representing animated embodiments can respond to users through verbal and non-verbal communication (Chattaraman et al., 2012). They exhibit human-like behaviour in various modalities, e.g., vision, audition, and body motion.

This typology is inspired by the environment where the agent is operating, i.e., in the real physical world (physical agent), in augmented virtuality features (disembodied agent), augmented virtuality (embodied agent), or virtual reality (virtual assistant). Figure 8.2 presents the agency typology in line with the environment in which the agent lives. The environment could be observable, dynamical and to contain various objects and other agents, as well as humans.

8.3.1 The AI Persuasive Power

Considering the recommendation power AI may exhibit, companies are massively investing in chatbots that provide purchase recommendations. It turns out, however, that customers are often resistant to recommendations by chatbots. Trustworthiness and persuasiveness (Luo et al., 2019) emerged as core reasons for consumer resistance. Insufficient content (Schwede et al., 2022), recommended advice, the level of message persuasiveness (Liao & Sundar, 2022), the source of persuasion (Luo et al., 2019), and the chatbot itself were also acknowledged.

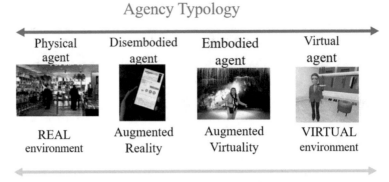

Fig. 8.2 Agency continuum

To overcome the above-enumerated gaps, further investigation is invited on the way the content of recommendation is composed, what communication strategy is implemented, how the message is designed, and which conversation style is offered by chatbot AI systems. From communication literature, it is well known that two-sided (rather than one-sided) messages are more efficient. In digital marketing, two-sided dialogue was acknowledged to be the preferred type of communication, leading to increased purchase intentions (Bialkova & te Paske, 2021). Hereby, we have also shown that consumers prefer interactive chatbot communication. Improved interactivity led to a more positive perception of ease of use (see Chap. 5, Bialkova, 2024c). Similarly, an online experiment reported that a two-sided recommendation message increases purchase intention (Schwede et al., 2022). The authors, however, noted that this outcome is valid only for chatbots having a warm or competent communication style (but not being neutral). The researchers further reported that a warm chatbot style results in higher purchase intentions as a result of the recommendation, especially when promoting the source of persuasiveness. A competent chatbot increased the recommendation impact by promoting message persuasiveness. These outcomes are in line with earlier work reporting that the expression of sympathy and empathy is preferred, over the unemotional provision of advice (Liu & Sundar, 2018). Based on the above mentioned, we could say that brands should carefully consider how to improve the persuasive power of chatbots, so that a purchase is guaranteed (business insight), but also meet the need to build trust in customers toward chatbots and AI recommender systems.

The notion of empathy/sympathy (Liu and Sundar 2018), was further positioned in line with the Computers as Social Actors, CASA, paradigm (Nass et al., 1994), as discussed in detail in Chap. 3, Bialkova, 2024b. This brings our attention to another important aspect of human-like agents, i.e., the exhibition of social characteristics and behaviours.

8.3.2 AI Social Empowerment

AI agents not only are anthropomorphised, but also try to interact in social manner. For example, *social media bots* (e.g., Lin & Wu, 2023; Youn & Jin, 2021) and various *branded chatbots* (e.g., eBay ShopBot; KLM BlueBot, Lufthansa Elisa chat assistant, etc.) provide personalised responses. Social bots are expected to offer content, and recommendations to consumers when a particular service is needed. Social (media) chatbots could be effectively implemented as recommender systems, even if the consumer did not explicitly ask for help. Moreover, enhancing the social characteristics of the implemented conversational agents could improve brand communication (as reported in Chap. 7, Bialkova, 2024e). and, thus, substantiate the marketing efforts, to scale up outcomes and boost revenues.

Moreover, maximising engagement via social media and incorporating techniques such as personalised searches, recommendation systems, and algorithmic curation are very likely to cause intellectual isolation with filter bubbles. In contrast, a lack of search engine optimisation, SEO techniques may preclude customer engagement, and thus, brand is easily outperformed by competitors.

We have to also note hereby the inherent capability to explain, interpretability, independent data, interactive learning, and inquisitiveness (the agent display of eagerness to learn) suggested as five principles of conversational agents (Wahde & Virgolin, 2023). These principles nicely cohere with what has been reported in empirical studies from our laboratory and reported in the current book. Our respondents noted the need for accurate and competent agents, who provide ample care and service (see Chap. 7 hereby, Bialkova, 2024e). Furthermore, our empirical work showed the demand for proper interaction that satisfies the consumer demand for quality and ease of use.

8.4 Autonomous Agents

Although the goal of AI agents is not to overtake people, but to empower their performance and facilitate decision making, the boost of new generation of applications raises questions about the level of agent autonomy. To give humans control over technology, therefore, brings another important aspect we must point out, i.e., the automation and control.

Hereby, we suggest an automation-control matrix (see Fig. 8.3) reflecting the different stages of agent performance, i.e., acquisition, analysis, decision, and action mirroring human performance from attention to action. The matrix is based on a literature audit, as described in detail below.

Various taxonomies concerning automation have been suggested over the years (for an overview see Vagia et al., 2016). With the rise of AI agency, the question about appropriateness of automation, autonomy, and the suitability for particular task attracted sufficient attention. Hereby we have to point what the distinction

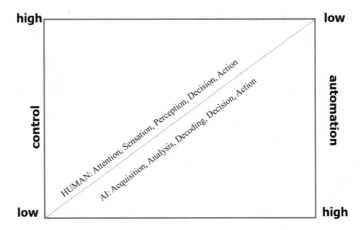

Fig. 8.3 Automation-control matrix

between automation and autonomy is, although some authors use the terms inter-changeably. Automation reflects the "automatic operation and the process of making things automatic" (Diebold, 1952), and is associated with the shift from manual to supervisory control (Sheridan & Verplank, 1978). The human–computer interaction is characterised by different levels of automation, LOA.

Autonomy originates from the Greek word "autonomia"—which means independent and self-governing, where "auto" means self and "nomos" means law. In the context of engineering systems, it reflects their capability to make their own decisions about their actions while performing different tasks and this happens irrespective of external systems or supervision involvement (Antsaklis, 1998). More recent definitions associate autonomy with the freedom of the AI system to take own deliberate decisions and thus to make free choices (Vagia et al., 2016).

With the rise of AI and its implementation to substitute not only physical but also intellectual manpower a crucial question is: *How to delegate agency?* In particular, given the fact that users need to perceive agent adequacy, a sufficient level of control in tasks performed is expected. System control was mentioned as a prerequisite for achieving autonomy a while ago (Antsaklis et al., 1990). Not surprisingly, then, the notion of control received significant attention.

It was suggested that machines should only help humans. In this respect, three core principles of beneficial machines were outlined, namely to be altruistic, humble, and learning to predict human preference (Russell, 2019; but see also Russell & Norvig, 2022). For altruistic machines, the only objective is to maximise the realisation of human preferences. Humble machines initially are uncertain about what those preferences are. Learning about human preferences is human behaviour itself as a source of information.

Allowing human-AI interaction in good collaboration, there should be a balance between the level of autonomy, the overall human control, and thus confidence in the system, as suggested by the automation-control matrix (see Fig. 8.3).

Exploring how various tasks impact automation, recent work has distinguished four task dimensions along the automation preferences, namely process consequence; social consequence, familiarity, and complexity (He et al., 2023a, 2023b). Process consequence reflects how users perceive the cost of failure when an AI agent commits a mistake. Social consequence is associated with the user's perception of risks when allowing the agent to represent them to others. Familiarity correlates with the user's knowledge of the system and/or the task. Complexity was defined as the overall difficulty or effort required for a user to complete a task.

The authors claimed the importance of these dimensions to disentangle the when, why, how strategy in delegating control between users and conversational task assistants (He et al., 2023a, 2023b). The when, what, why approach is not new, however. "WHO" human or system should perform "WHAT" task is in the foundation of any system development, and thus has been broadly discussed in literature concerned with automation and control (for an overview, see Vagia et al., 2016). It was noted at the very beginning the importance of "WHEN" control is necessary to be applied (Endsley & Kaber, 1999; Endsley & Kiris, 1995). The authors initially suggested five levels of control, namely none, decision support, consensual AI, monitored AI, and full automation (Endsley & Kiris, 1995). Later updating their own work, they distinguished ten levels of control, namely manual control, action support, batch processing, shared control, decision support, blended decision making, rigid system, automated decision making, supervisory control, and full automation (Endsley & Kaber, 1999). For details on various taxonomies concerning control and AI governance, see Chap. 11, Table 11.9 (Bialkova, 2024f)

Note, however, that users' preferences along certain dimensions are dynamic and may vary over time. Such dynamics allow for the adaptation of task control and thus assure efficient automation processing. We make a distinction along the task performance flow, i.e., acquisition, analysis, decision, and action. The current distinction is based on a literature audit and earlier work on automation for independent functions defining information acquisition, information analysis, decision selection, and action implementation (for an overview see Parasuraman et al., 2000). Another study took similar approach, acknowledging the observe, orient, decide, and act task functions (Proud et al., 2003). For each function, the authors described eight levels of control. While for Levels 1–2, the human is primary and the computer is secondary; for Levels 6–8, the computer operates independently of the human and the human has decreasing access to information and a descaled capability of control. For intermediate Levels 3–5, the computer operates with human interaction.

We must also point out hereby that human performance flows from attention to action. Recent work from our laboratory exploring multisensory experiences with virtual reality (VR) and augmented reality (AR) applications suggested a four-stage process framework, encompassing attention, sensation, perception, and action (Bialkova, 2022c, 2023d). Attention is defined as the process mediating perceptual selectivity for further action (Allport, 1987; Yantis, 2000) and could be goal-direct or stimulus-driven. To have an impact on decision making, attended information needs to be decoded and provided meaning to, a process we refer to as perception. Once the decoded information is connected to prior knowledge and working memory contents, it is made sense of and thus could play a role in decision making. Working memory is defined as a system with a limited capacity for temporary maintenance and manipulation of information (e.g., Baddeley, 1986; Bialkova & Oberauer, 2010; Cowan, 2005; Oberauer, 2002, 2009; Oberuer and Bialkova, 2009).

One may argue whether the performance flow is a straight line and so simple from attention to action. Before taking action, however a decision is made regarding which direction to go. This decision is guided by upper-level executive control operations (Bialkova, 2008; Logan, 1985, 2003; Norman & Shallice, 1986, 2000; Schneider & Shiffrin, 1977; Shiffrin & Schneider, 1977). Based on the classical psychology literature, as described above, we suggest hereby a model on human performance flow (Fig. 8.4).

The reason we suggest such a detailed model is to establish fundaments to build around a conceptual model for autonomous AI agency mirroring human thoughts and behaviour. With respect to AI agent performance flow, we envisage the following core components: acquisition, analysis, decoding/ extracting, decision, and action implementation (see Fig. 8.5). Acquisition can be either top-down (task-oriented) or bottom-up (AI acquiring information in free will). Control operates as a dynamic function and may vary in time, in line with the task performed, and the AI performance flow itself. Given that topic of control is crucial from technical, UX, as well as ethical and legislative perspectives, we dedicate further discussion to control, in terms of AI governance and how to govern AI (see Chap. 11, Bialkova, 2024f).

We also suggest the enhancement of agent characteristics, by mirroring human behaviour from perception to action (see Fig. 8.6). An augmented AI agent is expected to be able to acquire and analyse information coming from various sensors, respectively reflecting various modalities, e.g., visual, auditory, tactile, somatic, and hopefully in the future olfactory and gustatory. Decoding and extracting of information in fact reflect perception, as discussed above in classical behavioural theories. Learning

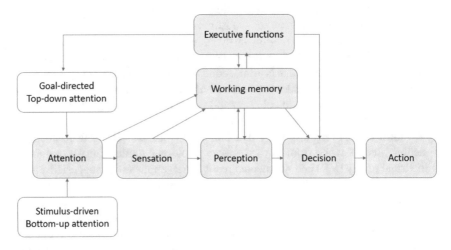

Fig. 8.4 Human performance flow from attention to action

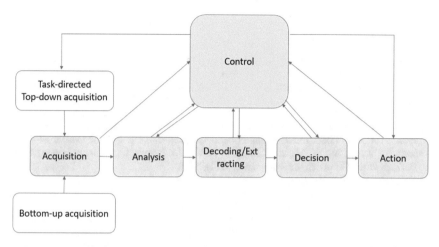

Fig. 8.5 AI performance flow from acquisition to action

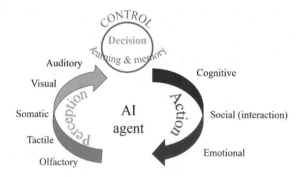

Fig. 8.6 Augmented AI agent

and memory functions are also typical for an AI agent. Superintelligent systems are capable of performing tasks with high memory load and extreme speed, which is a great advantage for elevating the performance capacity and decision efficacy. Decision-making process could be either autonomous (internal) or controlled by human operator (external).

As has been seen in the empirical part (Chaps. 5 and 7, Bialkova, 2024c, 2024e) users expect that AI agent is able to perform cognitive tasks, to be enjoyable, as well as to (inter)act socially. Parameters enumerated above are crucial in rising AI agency and enhancing their application in everyday scenarios and business practices. In this respect, the current book brings valuable insights, to be implemented in the development of new generation augmented AI agents.

References

Alcañiz, M., Bigné, E., & Guixeres, J. (2019). Virtual reality in marketing: A framework, review, and research agenda. *Frontiers in Psychology, 10,* 1530.

Allport, A. (1987). Selection for action: Some behavioral and neurophysiological considerations of attention and action. In H. Heuer & A. F. Sanders (Eds.), *Perspectives on perception and action* (pp. 395–419). Erlbaum.

Antsaklis, P. J. (1998). Setting the stage: Some autonomous thoughts on autonomy. In *Proceedings of the 1998 IEEE ISIC/CIRA/ISAS Joint Conference, Gaithersburg, USA, September 14–17.*

Antsaklis, P. J., Passino, K. M., & Wang, S. J. (1990). An introduction to autonomous control systems. *IEEE Control Systems Magazine, 11*(4), 5–13.

Baddeley, A. D. (1986). *Working memory.* Clarendon Press.

Bialkova, S. (2021). Would you talk to me? The role of chatbots in marketing. In *ICORIA2021, June 26–28, in Bordeaux, France.*

Bialkova, S. (2022a). How may I help you? In *Chatbots implementation in marketing, European marketing academy conference, EMAC2022, May 24–27, in Budapest, Hungary.*

Bialkova, S. (2022b). *Interacting with chatbot: How to enhance functionality and enjoyment? AEMARK2022, 7–10 September 2022.* Valencia, Spain.

Bialkova, S. (2022c). From attention to action: Key drivers to augment VR experience for everyday consumer applications. In *Proceedings of 29th IEEE, conference on virtual reality and 3D user interfaces (VR), 8th workshop on everyday virtual reality, 12–16 March 2022, Christchurch, New Zealand*

Bialkova, S. (2023a). I want to talk to you: Chatbot marketing integration. *Advances in Advertising Research (Vol. XII,* pp. 23–36). https://doi.org/10.1007/978-3-658-40429-1_2

Bialkova, S. (2023b). AI-driven customer experience: Factors to consider. In *Philosophy of artificial intelligence and its place in society* (pp. 341–357). IGI Global.

Bialkova, S. (2023c). How to optimise interaction with chatbots? Key parameters emerging from actual application. *International Journal of Human-Computer Interaction.* https://doi.org/10.1080/10447318.2023.2219963

Bialkova, S. (2023d). Enhancing multisensory experience and brand value: Key determinants for extended, augmented, and virtual reality marketing applications. In A. Simeone, B. Weyers, S. Bialkova, & R. W. Lindeman (Eds.), *Everyday virtual and augmented reality. Human-computer interaction series* (pp. 181–195). Springer.

Bialkova, S. (2023e). I need your help: Key parameters guiding satisfaction with chatbots. In *European Marketing Academy Conference, EMAC2023, 23–26 May 2023, in Odense, Denmark.*

Bialkova, S. (2008). *Control mechanisms in task switching.* Ipskamp.

Bialkova, S. (2024a). Introduction to chatbot AI applications. In *The rise of AI user applications: Chatbots integration foundations and trends.* (Chapter 1). Springer. https://doi.org/10.1007/978-3-031-56471-0_1

Bialkova, S. (2024b). Core theories applied in chatbot context. In *The rise of AI user applications: Chatbots integration foundations and trends.* Springer (Chapter 3). https://doi.org/10.1007/978-3-031-56471-0_3

Bialkova, S. (2024c). Chatbot efficiency—Model testing. In *The rise of AI user applications: Chatbots integration foundations and trends.* Springer (Chapter 5). https://doi.org/10.1007/978-3-031-56471-0_5

Bialkova, S. (2024d). Anthropomorphism—What is crucial? In *The rise of AI user applications: Chatbots integration foundations and trends.* Springer (Chapter 6). https://doi.org/10.1007/978-3-031-56471-0_6

Bialkova, S. (2024e). Chatbot agency—model testing. In *The rise of AI user applications: Chatbots integration foundations and trends.* Springer (Chapter 7). https://doi.org/10.1007/978-3-031-56471-0_7

Bialkova, S. (2024f). Explainable AI. In *The rise of AI user applications: Chatbots integration foundations and trends.* Springer (Chapter 11). https://doi.org/10.1007/978-3-031-56471-0_11

Bialkova, S., & te Paske, S. (2021). Campaign participation, spreading e-WOM, purchase: How to optimise CSR effectiveness via Social media? *European Journal of Management and Business Economics, 31*(1), 108–126.

Bialkova, S. E., & Oberauer, K. (2010). Direct access to working memory contents. *Experimental Psychology, 57*(5), 383–389.

Blut, M., Wang, C., Wünderlich, N., & Brock, C. (2021). Understanding anthropomorphism in service provision: A meta-analysis of physical robots, chatbots, and other AI. *Journal of the Academy of Marketing Science, 49*, 632–658.

Cassell, J. (2000). Embodied conversational interface agents. *Communication of the ACM, 43*(4), 70–78.

Cassell, J., & Bickmore, T. W. (2000). External manifestations of trustworthiness in the interface. *Communication of the ACM, 43*(12), 50–56.

Chattaraman, V., Kwon, W.-S., & Gilbert, J. E. (2012). Virtual agents in retail web sites: Benefits of simulated social interaction for older users. *Computers in Human Behavior, 28*(6), 2055–2066.

Choi, Y. (2021). A study of employee acceptance of artificial intelligence technology. *European Journal of Management and Business Economics, 30*, 318–330.

Cowan, N. (2005). *Working memory capacity.* Psychology Press.

DeLone, W. H., & McLean, E. R. (2003). The DeLone and McLean model of information systems success: A ten-year update. *Journal of Management Information System, 19*(4), 9–30.

Derrick, D. C., Jenkins, J. L., & Nunamaker, J., Jr. (2011). Design principles for special purpose, embodied, conversational intelligence with environmental sensors (SPECIES) agents. *AIS Transactions on Human-Computer Interaction, 3*(2), 62–81.

Diebold, J. (1952). Automation. In *The advent of the automatic factory.* D. Van Nostrand Company, INC.

Endsley, M. R., & Kaber, D. B. (1999). Level of automation effects on performance, situation awareness and workload in a dynamic control task. *Ergonomics, 42*(3), 462–492.

Endsley, M. R., & Kiris, E. O. (1995). The out-of-the-loop performance problem and level of control in automation. *Human Factors, 37*(2), 381–439.

Flavián, C., Pérez-Rueda, A., Belanche, D., & Casaló, L. V. (2021). Intention to use analytical artificial intelligence (AI) in services—The effect of technology readiness and awareness. *Journal of Service Management, 33*(2), 293–320.

He, J., Piorkowski, D., Muller, M., Brimijoin, K., Houde, S., & Weisz, J. (2023a). Rebalancing worker initiative and AI initiative in future work: Four task dimensions. In *Proceedings of the 2nd annual meeting of the symposium on human-computer interaction for work (CHIWORK'23)* (Article 3, pp. 1–16). Association for Computing Machinery.

He, J., Piorkowski, D., Muller, M. J., Brimijoin, K., Houde, S., & Weisz, J. D. (2023b). *Understanding how task dimensions impact automation preferences with a conversational task assistant.* AutomationXP@CHI.

Krämer, N. C., Bente, G., Eschenburg, F., & Troitzsch, H. (2009). Embodied conversational agents: Research prospects for social psychology and an exemplary study. *Social Psychology, 40*(1), 26–36.

Landim, A. R. D. B., Pereira, A. M., Vieira, T., Costa, E. B., Moura, J. A. Wanick, B. V., & Bazaki, E. (2022). Chatbot design approaches for fashion E-commerce: An interdisciplinary review. *International Journal of Fashion Design, Technology and Education, 15*(2), 200–210.

Liao, M., & Sundar, S. S. (2022). When e-commerce personalization systems show and tell: Investigating the relative persuasive appeal of content-based versus collaborative filtering. *Journal of Advertising, 51*(2), 256–267.

Lin, J. S., & Wu, L. (2023). Examining the psychological process of developing consumer-brand relationships through strategic use of social media brand chatbots. *Computers in Human Behavior, 140*, 107488.

Liu, B., & Sundar, S. S. (2018). Should machines express sympathy and empathy? Experiments with a health advice chatbot. *Cyberpsychology, Behavior and Social Networking, 21*(10), 625–636.

Logan, G. D. (1985). Executive control of thought and action. *Acta Psychologica, 60*, 193–210.

Logan, G. D. (2003). Executive control of thought and action: In search of wild homunculus. *Current Directions in Psychological Science, 12*, 45–48.

Luo, X., Tong, S., Fang, Z., & Qu, Z. (2019). Frontiers: Machines vs. humans: The impact of artificial intelligence chatbot disclosure on customer purchases. *Marketing Science, 11*, 1–11.

Nass, C., Steuer, J., & Tauber, E. R. (1994). Computers are social actors. In: *Proceedings of the SIGCHI Conference on Human Factors in Computing Systems. April 24–28, 1994, in Boston, USA.*

Norman, D. A., & Shallice, T. (1986). Attention to action: Willed and automatic control of behavior. In R. J. Davidson, G. E. Schwartz, & D. Shapiro (Eds.), *Consciousness and self-regulation* (Vol. 4, pp. 1–18). Plenum.

Norman, D. A., & Shallice, T. (2000). Attention to action: Willed and automatic control of behavior. In M. S. Gazzaniga (Ed.), Cognitive neuroscience. A reader (pp. 325–402). Blackwell Publishing.

Oberauer, K. (2009). Design for a working memory. In B. H. Ross (Ed.), The psychology of learning and motivation, pp. 45–100.

Oberauer, K. (2002). Access to information in working memory: Exploring the focus of attention. *Journal of Experimental Psychology: Learning, Memory, and Cognition, 28*(3), 411–421.

Oberauer, K., & Bialkova, S. (2009). Accessing information in working memory: Can the focus of attention grasp two elements at the same time? *Journal of Experimental Psychology: General, 138*(1), 64–87.

Parasuraman, R., Sheridan, T.B., and Wickens, C.D. (2000). A model for types and levels of human interaction with automation. *IEEE Transactions on Systems, Man, and Cybernetics. Part A, Systems and Humans: A Publication of the IEEE Systems, Man, and Cybernetics Society, 30*(3), 286–297.

Pereira, T., Limberger, P. F., Minasi, S. M., & Buhalis, D. (2022). New insights into consumers' intention to continue using chatbots in the tourism context. *Journal of Quality Assurance in Hospitality & Tourism.*

Pillai, R., & Sivathanu, B. (2020). Adoption of AI-based chatbots for hospitality and tourism. *International Journal of Contemporary Hospitality Management, 32*(10), 3199–3226.

Proud, R. W., Hart, J. J., & Mrozinski, R. B. (2003). Methods for determining the level of autonomy to design into a human spaceflight vehicle: a function specific approach (No. JSC-CN-8129).

Russell, S. (2019). *Human compatible: Artificial intelligence and the problem of control.* Viking.

Russell, S., & Norvig, P. (2022). *Artificial intelligence: A modern approach* (4th ed.). Pearson.

Schneider, W., & Shiffrin, R. M. (1977). Controlled and automatic human information processing: I. Detection, search, and attention. *Psychological Review, 84*(1), 1–66.

Schwede, M., Mozafari, N., Hammerschmidt, M., & von Schnakenburg, N. (2022). Can chatbots be persuasive? How to boost the effectiveness of chatbot recommendations for increasing purchase intention. In *Proceedings of the Hawaii international conference on system sciences*

Sheridan, T. B., & Verplank, W. L. (1978). *Human and computer control of undersea teleoperators.* MIT. Department of Mechanical Engineering.

Shiffrin, R. M., & Schneider, W. (1977). Controlled and automatic human information processing: II. Perceptual learning, automatic attending, and a general theory. *Psychological Review, 84*(2), 127–190.

Trivedi, J. (2019). Examining the customer experience of using banking chatbots and its impact on brand love: The moderating role of perceived risk. *Journal of Internet Commerce, 18*(1), 91–111.

Vagia, M., Transeth, A. A., & Fjerdingen, S. A. (2016). A literature review on the levels of automation during the years. What are the different taxonomies that have been proposed? *Applied ergonomics, 53*(Pt A), 190–202.

Wahde, M., & Virgolin, M. (2023). DAISY: An implementation of five core principles for transparent and accountable conversational AI. *International Journal of Human-Computer Interaction, 39*(9), 1856–1873.

Yantis, S. (2000). Goal-directed and stimulus-driven determinants of attentional control. In S. Monsell & J. Driver (Eds.), *Control of cognitive processes: Attention and performance XVIII.* MIT.

Youn, S., & Jin, S. V. (2021). "In A.I. We trust?" The effects of parasocial interaction and technopian versus luddite ideological views on chatbot-based customer relationship management in the emerging 'feeling economy'. *Computers in Human Behavior, 119*, 106721.

Chapter 9
AI Transforming Business and Everyday Life

Abstract The aim of this chapter is to discuss the benefits of AI systems that foster fundamental business transformation. The effects emerging from the literature audit and substantiated in the model testing hereby demonstrate the power of AI systems to equip companies with the tools needed to manage their relationships with customers in an economically feasible manner. In the literature brought to the table, we see a profound discussion on the expected development of AI systems, and the possibility of replacing humans in the near future. Large language model (LLM) incorporating machine learning (ML), deep learning (DL), and natural language processing (NLP) techniques can aid in training on how to collect and handle large amounts of data. Managing such data quickly, correctly, and securely, could generate market intelligence to boost investments and revenues, which any company wants to achieve. AI may encourage more accurate, distinctive, and scalable marketing, personalised businesses (plans) tailored to specific user demands. Having access to a vast array of customer data, AI can refine browsing history and generate personalised strategies for better targeting, resonating with individual(s) demands. In such a way, it is possible to differentiate not only between customers, but also between companies, by offering a unique selling point, USP. Elevating chatbot capacity with the characteristics as emerging hereby to be crucial in AI efficiency and agency, is a prerequisite for delivering the desired USP, to create experience that brings customers to a journey beyond the traditional market space. However, there are some challenges, such as the risk, privacy, and ethics, that need further attention. Moreover, the bias, believability, and authenticity of information exchange invite further exploration. Although, recently developed and implemented AI systems may generate high volume and diverse content. It turns out this content could be fabricated and not necessarily reflect real facts and data. This is a serious issue worth explanation, given the impact it may have on scaling up business and shaping everyday life, as discussed in detail below.

9.1   Implication for Marketing Practices—Benefits

Having received an enormous amount of venture capital investment, AI is inevitably transforming business and everyday life. The accelerated advancement of AI, and the broad scope of tasks and activities it can perform, opened new avenues for marketing practices, and exiting opportunities for business developments. Lifting AI capacity with the characteristics as emerging hereby to be crucial in chatbot efficiency and agency, is beneficial for delivering the desired USP (unique selling point).

Elevated AI capacity could facilitate brand management and enhance satisfaction, encouraging the creation of experiences that bring customers to a journey beyond the traditional marketing space. These are crucial methods for building predictive models to support companies in their bid to optimise marketing investment and maximise revenues.

Not surprisingly then, marketers are increasingly implementing algorithms that mirror human cognition. AI applications mimicking human functioning are already recognised as business advantage of marketing practices. Academics have also been inspired to study how AI may revolutionise the way in which the business is done, respectively, looking at the services provided (Belanche et al., 2019, 2020; Chung et al., 2020; Flavián et al., 2021; Huang & Rust, 2018a, 2018b) brand management (Kumar et al., 2019; Teixeira & Remondes, 2023; Tirunillai & Tellis, 2014), advertising (Bakpayev et al., 2022; Deng et al., 2019; Lou et al., 2022), communication (Lee & Cho, 2020), sales processes (Bigné, 2023; Marianai et al., 2023), HR (Kim et al., 2021), and modelling (Mustak et al., 2021). Note also that chatbots and AI systems in general may be either organisation or end-user choices. In this respect, the need for explainable AI (XAI) systems was well acknowledged. Figure 9.1 presents the business-consumer XAI pyramid (but see also Chap. 8, Bialkova, 2024d for details on task assigned by different stakeholders with respect to AI). Therefore, various AI-enabled technologies such as robots (e.g., Belanche et al., 2019; Park et al., 2021), chatbots (e.g., Bialkova, 2023a, 2023b, 2023c; Brill et al., 2019), virtual agents (e.g., Miao et al., 2022; Ben Mimoun et al., 2017) with different levels of automation (Vagia et al., 2016), autonomy (He et al., 2023a), and control (He et al., 2023b) have been considered. Algorithmic trading software speeds up transactions and financial market operations received significant attention (See Table 1.2, Chap. 1, Bialkova, 2024a). Price shaping algorithms (Chen et al., 2016) not only analyse, but also directly guide consumers toward specific products, offers, and services. Social media bots and news-ranking algorithms (Ferrara et al., 2016) can spread specific content, targeting particular audiences, and thus, totally changing peoples' opinion. Note, however, that AI agency can shape human behaviour and societal outcomes in intended as well as in unintended ways (see Table 9.1).

Despite the substantial body of literature, as listed above, scientists are continuously looking to improve the way AI is implemented and used. In this respect, the current work provides valuable assets to better understand the AI systems currently used on the market and what is needed to further improve this technology. We strongly recommend that researchers from different domains (HCI, UX, XAI, marketing,

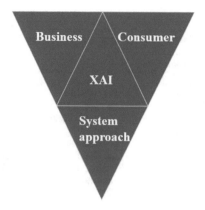

Fig. 9.1 Business-consumer XAI pyramid

psychology) join efforts in order to design AI systems that appropriately meet the rising consumer demand for high quality, functional, and enjoyable interaction.

For example, data mining approach is more frequently used in reshaping brand strategies. Companies adopt big data analytics to better understand their customers and to differentiate offerings from competitors. Enabling marketers to track key performance dimensions over time provides tools for dynamic mapping of competitive brand positions on those dimensions over time (Tirunillai & Tellis, 2014).

Moreover, converting the user generated content, UGC into structured data could be very insightful for firm performance and shaping new marketing/management strategies in the competitive landscape. Associated with UGC, the electronic word of mouth (eWOM) has received significant attention. Attitudes toward a product or service could change along with eWOM. Techniques such as data mining demonstrated to empower the text analysis, i.e., text mining (for an overview, see Tang & Guo, 2015). Furthermore, linguistic parameters generated via data mining were found to be reliable predictors of consumer attitudes and thus the spread of eWOM. The authors claimed that text mining can explain additional variance in consumers' attitudes above and beyond the star rating (many brands use to capture the consumer review rate).

Machine learning has also been demonstrated to be a reliable technique to navigate brands in properly reacting to eWOM and UGC. In providing better and quicker insights into comments and reactions, ML has been applied in sentiment analyses and review references on various digital platforms, i.e., websites (Ballestar et al., 2019), Twitter (Bigné et al., 2021; Ghiassi & Lee, 2018), Instagram (Chan & Yang, 2023), Facebook (Tiwari & Sinha, 2020), and YouTube (Severyn et al., 2016).

AI is gradually establishing algorithmic decision makers as key organisational actors. ML has been claimed to help human decision making from management and the economy to medical support (Kleinberg et al., 2018).

Table 9.1   AI transformational effect

Business	AI for business transform performance	System approach	Consumer
Automation	AI-enabled	Autonomous agents	Acquisition, retention, and
Automated personalised	systems	Biometrics	expansion
targeting	AI-based	Chatbot	Analyse data to identify
Advertising	customisation	Computer vision	safety or quality problems
Access to data	Big data	CAPI	Attitudes formation and
Audience engagement	analytics	Data mining	change
Brand management	Data	Intelligent agents	Automate personalised
Brand/firm performance	classification	Internet of things, IoT	targeting
Data-value creation and	Data forecasting	Hardware	CLV—customer lifetime
extraction	Decision support	ML	value
Competitive advantage	Causal	NLP	Customer relationship
Capabilities increase	interpretation	Neural networks	management
Effective business	Content analysis	Real-time translate	Customer experience
decisions	Classification	Recommender systems	Customer sentiments
Informed decisions in	Expert system	Software	Forecast predict
real time	Feature	Soft computing fuzzy	improvement
Internal operation	extraction	logic	HAIC-human-AI
Interaction with	Knowledge	Speech recognition	interaction
customers	management	Service robots	Human-AI communication
Improving market	Modelling	Text mining	HCAI—human-centred AI
performance	problem	Voice assistance	identify customer key
Industry/Organisations	Provide better/	Wearables	needs
Individual/customer	improved		Loyalty and trust
Market growth	models		Navigate customer journey
Offering	Navigate/		Predict what a particular
competitiveness	Predict/Forecast		customer is likely to buy
Operational efficacy	Prediction		Satisfaction enhancement
Organisational agility	Prescriptive		Understanding customers
Predict what users will	analysis		better
do (on website/app)	Retrieval		
Product development	Optimisation		
Product discrimination	SEO (search		
Pricing	engine		
Profitability	optimisation)		
Refine browsing history	Sentiment		
Review Analysis	analysis		
Revenue increase			
Salesforce			
Service enhanced			
support			
Segmentation			
Society/market			
Strategic marketing			
Supply chain			
Targeting and			
positioning Improved			
Tailored offerings/			
operations to various			
target groups			
Vendors facilitation			

The application of deep neural networks in the context of high and low involvement industries has been reported to significantly impact the techniques in managing the brand-consumer dynamics (Yang et al., 2022), to predict conversion (Ma & Sun, 2020). Employing millions of social media users' brand engagement data, Yang et al. (2022) have built a brand-user network and then compressed the network into a lower dimensional space using a deep autoencoder technique. The researchers captured latent relationships among thousands of brands and across many categories. Earlier work analysing approximately 130,000 customers' evaluations concerning airline services also applied neural networks (Leminen et al., 2018). The authors claimed that by detailing customer satisfaction, consumer insights might predict the intention to reuse particular services.

Conversion API (CAPI—conversions application programming interface) technology was designed and implemented to improve the accuracy of tracking conversions, and thus advertising effectiveness. CAPIs may help detect what and how leads to higher costs, inaccurate testing models, and poorer customer experiences. The idea is to improve advertising campaigns and their impact on consumers, and thus to increase revenues.

The greatest transformational impact is expected on existing business models, improvements in operational efficiency, increases in revenue, strengthening of offerings' competitiveness, and enhancing customer experience, as reported by another study investigating the potential of AI for business, by interviewing organisation leaders (Brock & von Wangenheim, 2019). Table 9.1 provides an overview of AI transformational effect for business and consumers by incorporating various system approaches and performance strategies. Note, however, implementing AI applications aiming superintelligence goes with various challenges and risks. We discuss these in detail in the subsequent section.

9.2 Challenges

Technical development and economic pressure predetermine the continuing progress in AI capability. A question arises hereby whether these AI systems take into account the real needs humans and society have. In the pursuit of creating and developing superintelligence, researchers should not forget to fully reflect human values. Furthermore, there is a need to re/consider the broad and unattended consequences that AI could exhibit, as well as the possible downstream effects for individuals and the society as a whole. Poor or uncertain commercial returns are often considered the primary reason for not adopting AI, especially for small and midsize companies (Kumar et al., 2019).

Furthermore, there is a legitimate reason to seriously consider AI risks. Although it was acknowledged a long time ago that a person working in partnership with a machine and information resources is "better" than that same person working unassisted (Friedman, 2009) there is a need to look closely at this relationship. As postulated by the "fundamental theorem" of bioinformatics, informatics is more about people than technology, and thus, in order for the theorem to hold, resources must be informative in addition to being correct. Put differently, we need to determine a (**Human + AI system**) that works well, find solutions, enjoy interactions. It seems this is a design question, and thus, optimal design should be found. Understanding the behaviour of AI systems is essential not only for the human ability to control AI actions, but also to minimise potential harm caused by uncontrolled behaviour. Figure 9.2 provides a summary of the key challenges, and the details are presented below, respectively reflecting: technicality; UX and design; management; ethics; policy and legislation. As has been seen, the term "control" is addressed in all of the tree branches. In particular, the balance between autonomous agency and supervised control is under question. Transparency is also recognised in all of the tree branches. Fairness appears in technical, UX, and ethical branches. Reliability and safety appear in both UX and legislation branches. Trust is addressed by UX, ethics, and legislation branches.

9.2.1 Technical

Despite the high discrimination power of AI-based predictive models (i.e., deep learning neural networks), the low interpretability of their black box representation is still a challenge. Neural networks have proven to possess superior ability at discovering hidden patterns in data. However, biases and endogeneities tend to be more likely pronounced and thus to be picked up by the model (De Bruyn et al., 2020), especially when the data are incomplete or when there is a mismatch between the training data and the cases encountered at the test time (Lakkaraju et al., 2016). Bias can also reflect manual data labelling by humans, i.e., the performance of various text and image classification algorithms is predetermined by the way dataset is selected, trained, and optimises accuracy on specific features and representations. As a result, the behaviour demonstrated by the algorithm will be substantially shaken. Therefore, value trade-offs between competing and incompatible notions of bias, and/or between human versus machine biases were suggested (Rahwan et al., 2019), as possible solutions to overcome biases.

Although observable data and available source code, an AI system may possess insufficient predictive power over its outputs. Predictions may lack precision, due to a major challenge for machine learning approaches – feature selection, which is often domain dependent. Agency behaviour may deviate from the expected one as a result of interactions with other agents and systems. Anticipating agency behaviour and analysing data insights could also be impaired by changing contexts/environments as a result of the algorithm itself.

It was noted that natural language is difficult to analyse objectively, mainly because of its high dimensionality such as the number of coordinates needed to locate objects in multidimensional space, and large samples.

Despite the excellent capability to model statistical co-occurrences, deep neural network (DNN) and natural language processing (NLP) models might lack a real

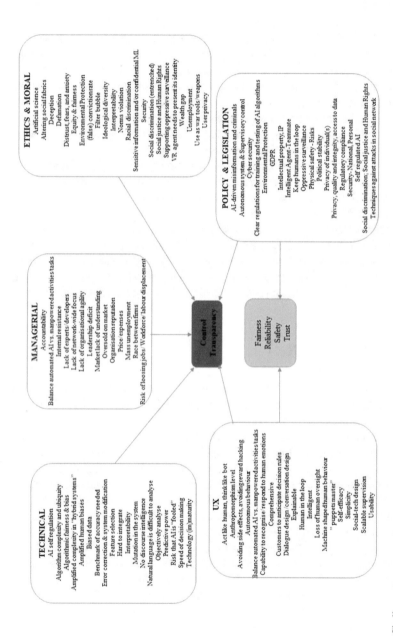

Fig. 9.2 Challenge tree

intelligent understanding of discourse (Bender et al., 2021; Wahde & Virgolin, 2023). Furthermore, some of the attributes, and thus, the performances of algorithms may be difficult or even impossible to be analysed formally. The complex properties of the algorithms and the environments in which they operate have been highlighted as possible reasons for (in)adequate analysis (Rahwan et al., 2019). AI may generate illegible predictions with high complexity, even with well-described analytical solutions and mathematical formulas. The complexity of AI agency is relatively high at the moment, and there is even a tendency to expand complex systems which could preclude the correct estimation of the algorithm effect.

Revealing what extra properties emerge when interacting AI agents are capable of generating is a key challenge. Interaction between simple agents and communication among intelligent machines could foster complex behaviour, and as a result, a deviation from what is expected and the common sense. "Fights" between bots have even been reported (Tsvetkova et al., 2017). The researchers investigated the extent to which bots undid each other's edits, reflecting "fights" characterised by long-lasting history and reciprocity.

A "mutation" in the algorithm may also born particular behaviour, and thus, AI may exhibit a very different evolutionary path. The current book, therefore, alarms the need for serious reconsideration of the way AI systems are designed, especially given the UX and XAI. Table 9.2 provides a summary of key challenges with respect to technicality, user experience (UX), design, and human-centred AI (HCAI).

9.2.2   UX, Design, HCAI

Although created by humans, AI systems may not necessarily face the same limitations as human performance experiences. In contrast, machine superiority and new capabilities may emerge, especially in assembling collective AI agencies that may lead to entirely new collective behaviour, and possibly collective intelligence. This behaviour may exhibit memory-triggering patterns when digital footprints are generated. There is a need to look for an optimal socio-technical design. In the infancy of technology, the level of agent intelligence was a direct function of human intelligence and how it was programmed/designed, i.e., decision support systems. Currently, we are witnessing decision-making systems that possess broad intelligence and demonstrate superhuman capabilities.

However, while humans may profit from AI assistance and learn from this new (collective) behaviour, technological advancement could bring some challenges.

For example, a lack of human scrutiny may cause failures in usability, reliability, safety, fairness, and other AI challenges (Liao & Varshney, 2021). The authors further acknowledged the need to create explainable systems, as understanding how AI functions could be the turning point for users to trust, adopt, and use technology in the future. Although AI has been recognised as a tool for opening opportunities for humans and computers to work better together, it may be the case that computers

Table 9.2 Challenges with respect to technicality, UX, HCAI

Aspect	Challenge	References
Technical	*AI may create a system that self-regulates *Algorithm complexity and ubiquity *Algorithmic fairness & bias *Amplified complexity in "hybrid systems" composed of many machines and humans interacting and manifesting collective behaviour *Benchmark of accuracy, e.g., in document classification, facial recognition, object detection *Biased data *Error correction and system modification *Feature selection, which is often domain-dependent *Hard to integrate *Human bias (amplified in data) *Interpretability *Mutation in the system *Not any real intelligent understanding of discourse, despite excellent capability to model statistical co-occurrences with DNN *Natural language is difficult to analyse objectively (due to its high dimensionality such as number of coordinates needed to locate objects in multidimensional space, and large samples) *Objectively analyse *Predictive power *Risk that AI is "fooled" into altering decision outcomes, i.e., through the manipulation of the data it uses as input or through its design *Speed of decision making *Technology (im)maturity *Transparency	Amodei et al. (2016) Bender et al. (2021) Chan et al. (2019) Davenport and Ronaki (2018) De Bruyn et al. (2020) Fiok et al. (2021) He et al. (2023a, 2023b) Jahanbakhsh et al. (2023) Lakkaraju et al. (2016) Libai et al. (2020) Lipton (2018) Rahwan et al. (2019) Shrestha et al. (2019) Wahde and Virgolin (2023)
UX, design, HCAI	*Act like human, think like bot *Anthropomorphism level *Autonomous behaviour *Avoiding side effects, avoiding reward hacking *Balance between automated by AI versus manpowered activities/tasks *Capability to recognise, emulate, and respond appropriately to human emotions *Clarity and consistency *Comprehensiveness *Controllable *Customers to anticipate or to reverse the engineer firms' decision rules *Dialogue design/conversation design *Empathy and engagement *Explainability *Human in the loop *Intelligence *Lack of human scrutiny may lead to failures in usability, reliability, safety, fairness, etc *Loss of human oversight *Machine-shaped human behaviour *"Puppets master" *Self-efficacy and control *Safe exploration, distributional shift *Scalable supervision *Simplicity *Social-technical design *Transparency *Trust	EU Commission (2019, 2020) Amodei et al. (2016) De Bruyn et al. (2020) Ferrara et al. (2016) Huang et al. (2019) Liao and Varshney (2021) Libai et al. (2020) Rahwan et al. (2019) Wu et al. (2022)

overtake humans (we pay special attention to AI governance in Chap. 11, Bialkova, 2024e).

Despite the benefits a high level of automation could bring (He et al., 2023a, 2023b) and the amount of autonomy available to be retained in an AI-dominated world (Russell, 2019), it was argued that humans should still have a high level of overall control and confidence in the system (Li & Hilligese, 2021). Moreover, when a human is immersed in the inner loop, effective human/computer dialogue is expected to occur, which is a prerequisite for success.

Dialogue design, however, is one of the biggest challenges, despite the numerous designs suggested for chatbot and AI system communication. Effective dialogue allows a computer to explain itself in terms of what a human can understand. AI itself understanding human intent and mental state is a prerequisite for efficient dialogue (Li & Hilliges, 2021). The core questions that arise in dialogue design are closely related to whether user needs are met, i.e., is it user focused. Thus, engagement emerged as an essential principle in dialogue design, in almost any paper dealing with the issue (Ghandeharioun et al., 2019; Moore et al., 2023; Vázquez et al., 2023). Empathy was also pointed out as a crucial element in dialogue design (Ghandeharioun et al., 2019; Vázquez et al., 2023). Several other parameters emerged in various studies, e.g., clarity and accuracy (Vázquez et al., 2023), simplicity (Berg, 2015), consistency (Ghandeharioun et al., 2019), context awareness (Ghandeharioun et al., 2019; Moore et al., 2023), errors handling (Vázquez et al., 2023), and feedback (Moore et al., 2023). Note that the above-mentioned principles nicely cohere with the outcomes of our empirical part (Chaps. 5 and 7, Bialkova, 2024b, 2024c) exploring the key feature a chatbot should demonstrate, to be accepted by users.

Furthermore, users should be given a clear description of how a conversational system reaches a particular conclusion, i.e., explainability. Perhaps upon request, details on how the conversational system works could be provided, thus opening the opportunity to identify and correct errors if necessary (Wahde & Virgolin, 2023). The possibility for modification and extension of the system is also expected.

Experts should reconsider which activities could go in a fully automated manner and which require manpower. Thus, a balance between automated AI versus manpowered activities/tasks needs to be achieved. Some researchers even suggested that prior to any optimisation, humans, and computers need to come to an agreement on the type of optimisation envisaged, and how and what will be done (Li & Hilligese, 2021).

In the same vein, it is important to define the temporal point(s) that are crucial for making decisions by humans versus bots. Several papers acknowledged the risk of losing human oversight (Rahwan et al., 2019). This is especially relevant when AI systems operate in a tiny time scale, and thus, algorithmic decisions may respond faster than humans, may possibly decide and react promptly. A question to consider, therefore, concerns the autonomy of AI agency, i.e., the functional ability of some AI systems to generate outputs such as "decisions" with limited or no human intervention.

Closely related to this challenge is the operational context and who needs explanation of what task is performed and how. Recently, four operational contexts have been noted (Maxwell & Duma, 2023), namely, Design and testing of the system (data science team); Human-IN-the-loop (human user before using the system), Human-on-the-loop (human user while decisions are taken or algorithmic outputs are created), Ex-post challenge (explanation given after a decision is made to person affected by the decision). Note that human-in-the-loop terminology was suggested in an earlier work (for details, see Zheng et al., 2017). We should also mention that customers already try to anticipate or to reverse the engineer firms' decision rules (Libai et al., 2020). However, regulation is needed to explicitly guarantee that the user is kept in the loop.

Problem related to accidents in machine learning systems may also emerge. Associated with unintended and harmful behaviour as a result of poor design of real-world AI system accidents, risks were categorised in five major practical research problems (Amodei et al., 2016). These problems reflect whether the objective function is wrong, i.e., "avoiding side effects" or "avoiding reward hacking", or whether the objective function is too expensive to be frequently analysed, i.e., "scalable supervision". "Safe exploration" and "distributional shift" were also acknowledged as undesirable performance during the learning process. The researchers also suggested possible solutions to overcome these pitfalls (for an overview, see Amodei et al., 2016).

9.2.3   Management (and Control)

A continuous update of search engines and algorithmic optimisation is recommended if organisations want to engage end users, to sustain marked dynamics, and to stay ahead of competitors. Aiming at enhancing competitive advantage, however, firms may sharpen the race between each other leading to monopolies in the market (Libai et al., 2020). Furthermore, in their attempt to overtake competitor brands, firms may not only target the prediction of customer behaviour, but also, we argue that they employ AI to govern end-user performance without deliberate will (see Table 9.3, for an overview of managerial challenges).

Extra challenges emerge, namely organisational agility, security risks, and lack of leadership, as mentioned by business leaders perceiving development with respect to AI projects (Brock & von Wangenheim, 2019).

Furthermore, AI could be seen as a threat to job market, and workforce/labour displacement. Although AI is tremendously reshaping the service market by constituting a major source of innovation, performing various tasks may increase unemployment (Huang & Rust, 2018a, 2018b). Currently, we are witnessing the substitution of manpower by machines not only in physical tasks, but also in various intellectual and financial tasks. Generative AI has also been incorporated into creative industries and arts, considered in the past to have the lowest potential for automation, and previously considered to be at least endangered by AI.

Therefore, there is a need for a balance between the nature of tasks and the type of activities automated by AI versus those performed by humans. Given that AI mirrors human behaviour, it is worth paying further attention to the level of

Table 9.3 Challenges with respect to management

Aspect	Challenge	References
Managerial/marketing	*Accountability, including auditability, minimisation and reporting of negative impact, trade-offs and redress *Balance between automated by AI versus manpowered activities/tasks *Internal resistance *Lack of experts/developers *Lack of network-wide focus *Lack of organisational agility *Leadership deficit *Market lack of understanding *Oversold on market *Organisation reputation *Price/expenses *Race between firms trying to predict customer behaviour *Risk of losing jobs (AI substituting manpower *Producing mass unemployment *Workforce/labour displacement	Brock and von Wangenheim (2019) Davenport and Ronaki (2018) EU AIHLEG (2019) Huang and Rust (2018a, 2018b) Libai et al. (2020) Ord (2020)

agent autonomy and control. As well acknowledged in the psychology literature, human performance is directed by two control mechanisms: (1) top-down, reflecting executive, goal-directed, endogenous, conscious control; and (2) bottom-up, also defined as automatic, stimulus-driven, exogenous, subconscious (for an overview see Bialkova, 2008). However, the question is whether AI agents could be controlled by humans (i.e., top-down, goal-directed), or whether they become autonomous and take decisions ignoring human control. This is not only a managerial question, but also concerns technical development, ethics and legislation.

Experts already noted some requirements for the person performing the control, i.e., being knowledgeable of the operational characteristics and limitations of the algorithm; to engage in deliberative control thought; and to have the authority and physical ability to intervene in the system and change the decisions made (Maxwell, 2023). Other experts even predict that AI may create numerous undetected endogeneity issues beyond human control (De Bruyn et al., 2020), given that AI models increasingly interact with each other, and generate data on their own. AI may create a system that self-regulates, which is not just managerial (Libai et al., 2020), but we may argue to require new regulations and legislation. We dedicate special attention to AI governance and control in Chap. 11, Bialkova, 2024e.

The complexity of the challenge at stake is further amplified by the fact that "hybrid systems" composed of large number of machines, also incorporate human interaction and collective behaviour. However, there is a lack of network-wide focus encompassing the entire network as a level of analysis.

Furthermore, given the power of reinforcement learning to train agents in the long term, this may be reflected in learning a short-term strategy. AI may acquire new behaviour through its own experience, past knowledge, actions, and feedback. This may introduce some risks, especially if the behaviour is not desirable, not common sense, or dangerous for the individuals and society. Moreover, algorithms are trained over historic datasets and react to a limited variety of foreseen scenarios and contexts (Rahwan et al., 2019). Reasonably then the question arises as to what their response will be to unforeseen cases and situations they have not been trained for.

To adequately manage fast-changing AI models, there is a need to close management not only of brand/product life cycle, but also to govern the AI life cycle. Such governance may preclude risks, predict AI performance, and thus appropriately navigate machines and human behaviour. New rules, managerial strategies, responsibilities, and even new roles may be required to face the AI dynamics. Good collaboration between managers and AI experts is needed to improve the existing IT governance and control. It may also be the case that AI experts learn some marketing and consumer tactics, while business managers need to learn some IT and data science basics. In this respect, the current book offers fundamental understandings. We further suggest some tips and tricks for empowering management and encouraging business growth through AI systems integration (see Table 9.5).

Although aiming to improve human welfare and wellbeing, AI systems may sometimes create some risks for humans. A broader consideration of AI systems and reflection on ethical and moral issues are therefore needed.

9.3 Ethics and Legislation

9.3.1 Ethical and Moral Issues

The first question arising is whether it is possible to initiate "artificial science", i.e., knowledge about artificial objects and phenomena (in terms of Rahwan et al., 2019). We further wonder whether the content generated by AI is always true (the philosophy view what is true). Recently there were several illustrations of how ChatGPT generated texts do not correspond to real objects and facts. For example, researchers have been cited as authors of particular text/journal articles, but a close audit shows that such papers have never been published. This is a serious issue from ethical perspective, but also scientific integrity point of view.

Furthermore, there may be the case that the AI system creators have not been able to foresee all the effects (either positive or negative) that the AI agent will exhibit and thus affect the individual and society. Nudged toward particular behaviour, people are supposed to profit from the implementation of AI systems. Note, however, that nudging human behaviour through particular algorithms may have some downsides, leading to risks and costs. A critical concern, therefore, is the way AI scales up individuals' effect into impact for society as a whole. Despite the possibilities computational social science opens for collecting and analysing data at a scale was recognised a decade ago (Lazer et al., 2009), revealing patterns of individual and group behaviours calls further inspection.

The way machine learning algorithms work should be transparent. Transparency was acknowledged as a crucial factor by experts from the entire spectrum. While computer scientists examined how a system reaches decisions by looking at the mathematical models and technicalities (i.e., Fiok et al., 2021; Lipton, 2018; Wahde & Virgolin, 2023), psychologists (Park et al., 2021) and marketing practitioners (Libai et al., 2020; Mustak et al., 2021) have acknowledged the ethical aspects of transparent decisions. Scientists, however, are univocal in that only transparency regarding XAI system performance can assure desired results and correct relationships in the way organisations and individuals are affected. Alternatively, there is a risk for tactical and strategic mistakes, especially if managers are not aware of the mechanisms underlying how decisions are taken and actions are executed.

Moreover, the question arises whether AI could preclude social discrimination, or whether there is a greater disparity between social classes. In the same vein, could AI help diminish the wealth gap, or will allow only a few companies/individuals to accumulate further wealth is worth attention.

For example, a survey among EU citizens revealed that 90% of respondents thought that AI could breach fundamental rights and 87% thought that the use of AI may lead to discriminatory outcomes (European Commission, 2019).

Therefore, a critical question is whether the capabilities developed by AI are quality based and trustworthy. Risk and Trust emerged as crucial components in our literature audit as well. Companies need to establish multiple partnerships with external entities to foster trust and maintain sustainable relationships with clients. Consumers are very sensitive when communicating with chatbots and AI systems. This is an emergent call to rethink value exchange and thus how to enhance trust in new high-end AI aids.

For example, social bots and VR agents need to present their identity. Imagine that you communicate with an AI agent whose physical features are absolutely identical to those of really existing humans. However, the behaviour of VR agent may often deviate from that of the original human. Thus, human beings should always be informed (i.e., a validation technique could be assigned), so that they can know whether they are directly interacting with another human being or a machine.

Capitalising the impact that AI systems could have on shaping human social relationships and forming collective action, social bots are more and frequently used. AI-generated content may be used to manipulate or deceive individuals or society as a whole. Recently, there were couple of cases where the faces and voices of celebrities were used for fake advertisements. Famous journalists were modelled via AI techniques to spread false news via video channels. Social bots have been used to shake election in several countries across the globe. Politicians' identity has also been "stolen" and employed to spread propaganda. These are only part of the examples of

Table 9.4 Challenges with respect to ethics and legislation

Aspect	Challenge	References
Ethical moral	*Artificial science—knowledge about artificial objects and phenomena *Altering social fabrics *Deception *Defamation *Distrust, fears, and anxiety that users may have about AI systems *Equity and fairness *Environmental protection *Fairness and diversity *Fairness, accountability, and transparency *(false) conviction rate *Filter bubble *Ideological diversity *Interpretability *Norms violation *Racial discrimination *Scenarios dealing with sensitive information and/or confidential ML models *Security *Social discrimination (entrenched) *Social justice and human rights *Supporting oppressive surveillance *Transparency *Trust/privacy *VR agents need to present their identity *producing mass unemployment *Used as war tools/weapons *User privacy *Wealth gap—could AI help diminish wealth gap? Or will allow only few companies/individuals to accumulate further wealth?	Arrieta et al. (2020) Bigné (2023) EU AIHLEG (2019) Mustak et al. (2021) Ord (2020) Przegalinska et al. (2019) Rahwan et al. (2019) Rigaki and Garcia (2023) Shneiderman (2022) Shrestha et al. (2019)
Policy and legislation	*AI-driven misinformation and criminals *AI may create a system that self-regulates *Autonomous system & Supervisory control *Control *Cyber security *Digital sovereignty *Develop commonly accepted requirements regarding the training and testing of AI algorithms, possibly in combination with some form of warranty *Environmental protection *Fake personas/masked identity *GDPR *Intellectual property, IP *Intelligent agent—teammate and tele-operated device *Keep humans in the loop *National security *Oppressive surveillance *Personal/individual privacy *Physical safety *Political stability/accountability *Policing *Privacy, quality and integrity, access to data *Regulatory compliance *Reliable, safe, trustworthy systems *Security risks *Social discrimination *Social justice and human rights *Surveillance *Techniques to effectively deal with attacks in social network *Transparency *Trading rules(violation)	EU AIHLEG (2019) Ferrara et al. (2016) Haenlein and Kaplan (2019) Libai et al. (2020) Maxwell and Duma (2023) Maxwell (2023) Ord (2020) Zheng et al. (2017)

how AI could be employed improperly and thus generate risks for human individuals and society as a whole.

Further concerns reflect whether and how AI may alter the social fabric in more fundamental ways. These include, but are not limited to how politicians, governments, or NGOs could employ AI agencies to change the nature of civic participation, political accountability, economic feasibility, transparency in decisions made, and democracy. Uncertainty about the degree to which AI agency can influence policing, surveillance, and warfare, is also a high risk requesting serious consideration (see Table 9.4 for details). The above-discussed issues further challenge the policy and legislation.

9.3.2 Policy and Legislation

Regulatory bodies should consider reciprocal civil and criminal penalties that should encourage the prevention of malfunctioning AI launches. For example, creating fake personas or masking true identities may not only destroy a company/stakeholder reputation, but definitely open legal challenges. Thus, developing commonly accepted requirements regarding the training and testing of AI algorithms, possibly in combination with some form of warranty is urgently needed.

These regulations closely reflect the need to adopt adequate detection, training, and prevention (Haenlein & Kaplan, 2019), techniques to effectively deal with attacks in social networks (Ferrara et al., 2016). Similarly, selectively propagating specific information (such that the user is navigated to see) resulting from personalised searches, recommendation systems, and algorithmic curation may lead to intellectual isolation, known as a "filter bubble".

Note also that highly recommended and very fashionable "personalisation", in fact opens the question of whether all customers are treated equality and in a fair manner. Experts have already inspired debate whether users should only receive content that is "personalised" for them or whether they should be given the right to browse through and select content on their choice (Jahanbakhsh et al., 2023). Prioritising products, offers, and services via e-commerce could be seen as a sign of diversity and differences in the way various customers are approached. This is a serious question inviting further reflection and possible legislative measures to equally manage specific customer needs and to handle the fairness of the brand-consumer relationship.

A recent report on combining legal and human–computer interaction (HCI) approaches in the aim to achieve meaningful algorithmic explainability (Maxwell and Duma, 2023) suggested five purposes of XAI related to legal requirements, namely: contestability, empowering and redressing information asymmetries, control over system performance, evaluation of individual algorithmic results, and ensuring public administration transparency.

Further concerns are alarming for policy measures to preclude malicious actions that subvert markets, i.e. related to misinformation or direct market manipulation and violation of trading rules. A lack of specific regulations concerning agency efficiency, functionality, and autonomy may impair not only end users, but also the performance of the entire organisation and the society as a whole.

Interactions between simple agents can foster higher-order relationships and architectural properties that are difficult or even impossible to be characterised by simplistic representations. These high-order architectures may further generate more sophisticated AI agency, complex behaviour, and interactions, thus unlocking high risks. Whether and how the behaviour of a particular AI evolves over time in the same or different contexts, and which environmental factors lead to the expression of specific behaviours by machines need close regulation.

A "mutation" in the system may also reflect perturbation of the evolutionary trajectory. Whether small errors in algorithms or bugs in the data they use could promote wide effects in the society, should be further considered. For example, if the above scenarios are realised by AI systems operating at schools, hospitals, social care centres, imagine whether and how those will alter human development and quality of life?

Moreover, machines could communicate between each other and thus reshape their behaviour interchangeably. AI agents using simple algorithms for local inter-actions can possibly produce unpredictable behaviour once aggregated into a large collective. In other words, synthetic inputs could force AI systems to produce unexpected and undesired outputs. Such attacks should be precluded, and possibly regulated, so that machine behaviour is not studied in isolation, but rather researchers have to look for better ways to disentangle complex predator–prey dynamics, which are not easily understood so far. There is a need to set requirements for high-risk AI, standardisation, conformity assessment, and biometric identification systems. This is very important to prevent further obstacles to cross-border AI single market and to guarantee digital sovereignty.

The EU AI Act (2023) is the first step toward such a regulatory mechanism. With the rise of AI, it is crucial to build trust in consumers, and the EU AI Act is expected to facilitate such processing. The frequent risk of misinformation emerging on online social spaces, stolen identity, and avatar personality encouraged the GDPR requirement for "meaningful information about the logic involved". To remain compliant with laws such as GDPR, it is crucial to assign specific rules and regulations regarding how data associated with individuals are stored, processed, and managed. To maintain the privacy protections required by the GDPR is only one of the many compulsory elements. There is a need for deep investigation so that solutions for businesses and end users who are affected by automated decision-making systems must be provided. Although various AI algorithms are implemented by the system creators, incorporating technical details on human-centred design does not necessarily transform a chatbot into a successful real-world AI application. Furthermore, how to tackle privacy and security is still an open question, among other challenges that may lead to risks in regard to AI application.

The European AI Act (2023), a Regulatory Framework defined four levels of risk in AI:

Fig. 9.3 Pyramid of risks

- Unacceptable risk
- High risk
- Limited risk
- Minimal or no risk.

AI practices generating unacceptable risks are prohibited. Regulations are needed for high risks' AI systems. Limited risks systems should be transparent, while for minimal or no risk system no obligation is assigned. Figure 9.3 illustrates the pyramid of risks (based on the EU AI Act, 2023).

In the case of low or minimal risk, AI applications could be launched to the market. The AI act proposal, regulatory framework (2023) allows the free use of minimal-risk AI. This includes applications such as AI-enabled video games or spam filters. The vast majority of AI systems currently used in the EU fall into this category.

A note of caution should be made hereby, explainable AI (XAI) systems need to be transparent (for detailed overview, see Chap. 11, Bialkova, 2024e). Thus, EU regulations and in general AI-related legislation, should take into account the XAI principles, and assign these when assessing AI challenges at all level of the risk pyramid.

To evaluate the level of risk a four-stage procedure was suggested from development, conformity assessment, registration in EU database, to actual launch of the system on the market. In case of substantial changes in AI system life cycle, there is a need to return to stage 2 (conformity assessment). For details of the stages in risk evaluation see the EU AI Act (2023).

Despite the warning calls in creating responsible AI systems, the lack of action, or limited measures are very likely to reflect the challenges enumerated in the current chapter. As seen, responsible AI requires, technology, UX, managerial and business experience, moral, ethical as well as legislative solutions (see Table 9.5, for key takeaways). However, many questions remain open and invite further inspection.

Furthermore, while AI experts may lack business and consumer insights, marketing practitioners may lack the technical skills to disentangle complex algorithms that may possibly forecast behaviour, ignoring bias, and appropriately governing AI. Therefore, an integrative approach and joint effort by experts from various domains are needed. The current chapter and book hopefully provide such an

Table 9.5 Key takeaways on how AI can enhance business growth

Tips	Tricks
• Revenue generation, marketing growth in the digital age • Value creation and extraction improved • Attracting, acquiring, and retaining customers through data/information exchange, enhanced by AI approaches • Near-human customer contact, real time • Managing adequately big data is a prerequisite for successful business • Very modest, marginal costs for various touch points along the experiential journey • Appropriate predictions and navigation to what consumers desire to have • Treat all stakeholders in safe, transparent, and fair manner • Life-cycle governance • Increase accountability • Facilitate go/no-go decisions	• Focus on responsible AI basics • Guarantee safe, transparent, and reliable AI doing what is expected to do • AI support for business-critical decision making • Minimise bias by data, algorithms, and models • Maximise benefits • Impact evaluation • Continuous consumer/user insights • AI life-cycle assessment may capture potential algorithmic and model gaps and thus preclude risks

integrative overview, and useful insights to help in sorting out some of the challenges society faces in regard to AI implementation and to use it wisely.

References

Amodei, D., Olah, C., Steinhardt, J., Christiano, P. F., Schulman, J., & Mané, D. (2016). *Concrete problems in AI safety.* ArXiv, abs/1606.06565.

Arrieta, A. B., Díaz-Rodríguez, N., del Ser, J., Bennetot, A., et al. (2020). Explainable artificial intelligence (XAI): Concepts, taxonomies, opportunities and challenges toward responsible AI. *Information Fusion, 58*, 82–115.

Bakpayev, M., Baek, T. H., van Esch, P., & Yoon, S. (2022). Programmatic creative: AI can think but it cannot feel. *Australasian Marketing Journal, 30*(1), 90–95.

Ballestar, M. T., Grau-Carles, P., & Sainz, J. (2019). Predicting customer quality in e-commerce social networks: A machine learning approach. *Review of Managerial Science, 13*, 589–603.

Belanche, D., Casaló, L. V., & Flavián, C. (2019). Artificial intelligence in FinTech: Understanding robo-advisors adoption among customers. *Industrial Management & Data Systems, 119*(7), 1411–1430.

Belanche, D., Casaló, L. V., Flavián, C., & Schepers, J. (2020). Service robot implementation: A theoretical framework and research agenda. *The Service Industries Journal, 40*(3–4), 203–225.

Bender, E. M., Gebru, T., McMillan-Major, A., & Shmitchell, S. (2021). On the dangers of stochastic parrots: Can language models be too big? In *Proceedings of the 2021 ACM conference on fairness, accountability, and transparency (FAccT' 21)* (pp. 610–623). Association for Computing Machinery, New York.

Ben Mimoun, M. S., Poncin, I., & Garnier, M. (2017). Animated conversational agents and e-consumer productivity: The roles of agents and individual characteristics. *Information & Management, 54*(5), 545–559.

Berg, M. M. (2015). NADIA: A simplified approach towards the development of natural dialogue systems. In: C. Biemann, S. Handschuh, A. Freitas, F. Meziane, & E. Métais (Eds.), *Natural language processing and information systems. NLDB 2015. Lecture notes in computer science* (Vol. 9103). Springer.

Bialkova, S. (2008). *Control mechanisms in task switching.* Ipskamp.

Bialkova, S. (2023a). I want to talk to you: Chatbot Marketing Integration. *Advances in Advertising Research, XII,* 23–36. https://doi.org/10.1007/978-3-658-40429-1_2.

Bialkova, S. (2023b). AI-driven customer experience: Factors to consider. In *Philosophy of artificial intelligence and its place in society* (pp. 341–357). IGI Global.

Bialkova, S. (2023c). How to optimise interaction with chatbots? Key parameters emerging from actual application. *International Journal of Human-Computer Interaction.* https://doi.org/10.1080/10447318.2023.2219963

Bialkova, S. (2024a). Introduction to chatbot AI applications. In *The rise of AI user applications: Chatbots integration foundations and trends.* (Chapter 1). Springer. https://doi.org/10.1007/978-3-031-56471-0_1

Bialkova, S. (2024b). Chatbot efficiency—Model testing. In *The rise of AI user applications: Chatbots integration foundations and trends.* Springer (Chapter 5). https://doi.org/10.1007/978-3-031-56471-0_5

Bialkova, S. (2024c). Chatbot agency—Model testing. In *The rise of AI user applications: Chatbots integration foundations and trends.* Springer (Chapter 7). https://doi.org/10.1007/978-3-031-56471-0_7

Bialkova, S. (2024d). AI connecting business and consumers. In *The rise of AI user applications: Chatbots integration foundations and trends.* Springer (Chapter 8). https://doi.org/10.1007/978-3-031-56471-0_8

Bialkova, S. (2024e). Explainable AI. In *The rise of AI user applications: Chatbots integration foundations and trends.* Springer (Chapter 11). https://doi.org/10.1007/978-3-031-56471-0_11

Bigné, E. (2023). Artificial intelligence in tourism. In L. Moutinho et al. (Eds.), *Philosophy of artificial intelligence and its place in society* (pp. 98–115). IGI Global.

Bigné, E., Nicolau, J. L., & William, E. (2021). Advance booking across channels: The effects on dynamic pricing. *Tourism Management, 86,* 104341.

Brill, T., Munoz, L., & Miller, R. J. (2019). Siri, Alexa, and other digital assistants: A study of customer satisfaction with artificial intelligence applications. *Journal of Marketing Management, 35*(15–16), 1401–1436.

Brock, J.K.-U., & von Wangenheim, F. (2019). Demystifying AI: What digital transformation leaders can teach you about realistic artificial intelligence. *California Management Review, 61*(4), 110–134.

Chan, C. P., & Yang, J. H. (2023). Instagram text sentiment analysis combining machine learning and NLP. *ACM Transactions on Asian and Low-Resource Language Information Processing.*

Chan, D., Rao, R., Huang, F., & Canny, J. F. (2019). GPU accelerated t-distributed stochastic neighbor embedding. *Journal of Parallel and Distributed Computing, 131,* 1–13.

Chen, L., Mislove, A., & Wilson, C. (2016). An empirical analysis of algorithmic pricing on amazon marketplace. In *Proceedings of the 25th international conference on World Wide Web.*

Chung, M., Ko, E., Joung, H., & Kim, S. J. (2020). Chatbot e-service and customer satisfaction regarding luxury brands. *Journal of Business Research, 117,* 587–595.

Davenport, T. H., & Ronanki, R. (2018). Artificial intelligence for the real world. *Harvard Business Review, 96*(1), 108–116.

De Bruyn, A., Viswanathan, V., Beh, Y. S., Brock, J. K., & von Wangenheim, F. (2020). Artificial Intelligence and Marketing: Pitfalls and opportunities. *Journal of Interactive Marketing, 51,* 91–105.

Deng, S., Tan, C. W., Wang, W., & Pan, Y. (2019). Smart generation system of personalized advertising copy and its application to advertising practice and research. *Journal of Advertising, 48*(4), 356–365.

European Commission. (2020). *White paper on artificial intelligence. A European approach to excellence and trust.* Commission-white-paper-artificial-intelligence-feb2020_en.pdf (europa.eu). https://commission.europa.eu/system/files/2020-02/commission-white-paper-art ificial-intelligence-feb2020_en.pdf. Accessed 25 Jan 2024.

European Commission. (2019). *Communication: Building trust in human centric artificial intelligence.* Shaping Europe's digital future (europa.eu). https://digital-strategy.ec.europa.eu/en/lib rary/communication-building-trust-human-centric-artificial-intelligence. Accessed 25 Jan 2024

European Commission AI Act. (2023). *AI Act | Shaping Europe's digital future (europa.eu).* https:// digital-strategy.ec.europa.eu/en/policies/regulatory-framework-ai. Accessed 25 Jan 2024.

European Commission—AI HLEG. (2019). *Ethics guidelines for trustworthy AI.* Ethics Guidelines for AI (europa.eu). https://www.europarl.europa.eu/cmsdata/196377/AI%20HLEG_Eth ics%20Guidelines%20for%20Trustworthy%20AI.pdf. Accessed 25 Jan 2024.

Ferrara, E., Varol, O., Davis, C. A., Menczer, F., & Flammini, A. (2016). The rise of social bots. *Communications of the ACM, 59,* 96–104.

Fiok, K., Farahani, F. V., Karwowski, W., & Ahram, T. (2021). Explainable artificial intelligence for education and training. *The Journal of Defense Modeling and Simulation, 19*(2), 133–144.

Flavián, C., Pérez-Rueda, A., Belanche, D., & Casaló, L. V. (2021). Intention to use analytical artificial intelligence (AI) in services–the effect of technology readiness and awareness. *Journal of Service Management, 33*(2), 293–320.

Friedman, C. P. (2009). A "Fundamental Theorem" of Biomedical Informatics. *Journal of the American Medical Informatics Association, 16*(2), 169–170.

Ghandeharioun, A., Shen, J. H., Jaques, N., Ferguson, C., Jones, N., Lapedriza, A., & Picard, R. (2019). Approximating interactive human evaluation with self-play for open-domain dialog systems. *Advances in Neural Information Processing Systems, 32,* 13665–13676.

Ghiassi, M., & Lee, S. (2018). A domain transferable lexicon set for twitter sentiment analysis using a supervised machine learning approach. *Expert Systems with Applications, 106,* 197–216.

Haenlein, M., & Kaplan, A. (2019). A brief history of artificial intelligence: On the past, present, and future of artificial intelligence. *California Management Review, 61*(4), 5–14.

He, J., Piorkowski, D., Muller, M., Brimijoin, K., Houde, S., & Weisz, J. (2023a). Rebalancing worker initiative and ai initiative in future work: Four task dimensions. In *Proceedings of the 2nd annual meeting of the symposium on human-computer interaction for work (CHIWORK '23)* (Article 3, pp. 1–16). Association for Computing Machinery, New York, NY.

He, J., Piorkowski, D., Muller, M. J., Brimijoin, K., Houde, S., & Weisz, J. D. (2023b). *Understanding how task dimensions impact automation preferences with a conversational task assistant.* AutomationXP@CHI.

Huang, M. H., & Rust, R. T. (2018a). Artificial intelligence in service. *Journal of Service Research, 21*(2), 155–172.

Huang, M. H., & Rust, R. T. (2018b). Artificial intelligence in service. *Journal of Service Research, 21*(2), 155–172.

Huang, M. H., Rust, R., & Maksimovic, V. (2019). The feeling economy: Managing in the next generation of artificial intelligence (AI). *California Management Review, 61*(4), 43–65.

Jahanbakhsh, F., Katsis, Y., Wang, D., Popa, L., & Muller, M. (2023). Exploring the use of personalized AI for identifying misinformation on social media. In *Proceedings of the 2023 CHI conference on human factors in computing systems (CHI'23)* (Article 105, pp. 1–27).

Kim, S., Wang, Y., & Boon, C. (2021). Sixty years of research on technology and human resource management: Looking back and looking forward. *Human Resource Management, 60*(1), 229–247.

Kleinberg, J., Lakkaraju, H., Leskovec, J., Ludwig, J., & Mullainathan, S. (2018). Human decisions and machine predictions. *Quarterly Journal of Economics, 133*(1), 237–293.

Kumar, V., Rajan, B., Venkatesan, R., & Lecinski, J. (2019). Understanding the role of artificial intelligence in personalized engagement marketing. *California Management Review, 61*(4), 135–155.

Lakkaraju, H., Kamar, E., Caruana, R., & Horvitz, E. (2016). Identifying unknown unknowns in the open world: Representations and policies for guided exploration. In *AAAI conference on artificial intelligence*.

Lazer, D., Pentland, A., Adamic, L., Aral, S., Barabási, A.-L., Brewer, D., Christakis, N., Contractor, N., Fowler, J., Gutmann, M., Jebara, T., King, G., Macy, M., Roy, D., & Van Alstyne, M. (2009). Computational social science. *Science, 323*, 721–723.

Lee, H., & Cho, C. H. (2020). Uses and gratifications of smart speakers: Modelling the effectiveness of smart speaker advertising. *International Journal of Advertising, 39*(7), 1150–1171.

Leminen, S., Rajahonka, M., Westerlund, M., & Wendelin, R. (2018). The future of the internet of things: Toward heterarchical ecosystems and service business models. *Journal of Business & Industrial Marketing, 33*(6), 749–767.

Li, Y., & Hilliges, O. (2021). *Artificial intelligence for human computer interaction: A modern approach, book Preface*. Springer.

Liao, Q. V., & Varshney, K. R. (2021). *Human-centered explainable AI (XAI): From algorithms to user experiences*. ArXiv, abs/2110.10790.

Libai, B., Bart, Y., Gensler, S., Hofacker, C. F., Kaplan, A., Kötterheinrich, K., & Kroll, E. B. (2020). Brave new world? On AI and the management of customer relationships. *Journal of Interactive Marketing, 51*, 44–56.

Lipton, Z. C. (2018). The mythos of model interpretability: In machine learning, the concept of interpretability is both important and slippery. *Queue, 16*(3), 31–57.

Lou, C., Kang, H., & Tse, C. H. (2022). Bots vs. humans: How schema congruity, contingency-based interactivity, and sympathy influence consumer perceptions and patronage intentions. *International Journal of Advertising, 41*(4), 655–684.

Ma, L., & Sun, B. (2020). Machine learning and AI in marketing—Connecting computing power to human insights. *International Journal of Research in Marketing, 37*(3), 481–504.

Mariani, M., Hashemi, N. M., & Wirtz, J. (2023). Artificial intelligence empowered conversational agents: A systematic literature review and research agenda. *Journal of Business Research, 161*, 113838.

Maxwell, W., & Dumas, B. (2023). Meaningful XAI based on user-centric design methodology. In *Combining legal and human-computer interaction (HCI_ approaches to achieve meaningful algorithmic explainability*. Centre on Regulation in Europe (CERRE).

Maxwell, W. (2023). Meaningful human control to detect algorithmic errors. In J. Eynard & C. Castets-Renard (Eds.), *Artificial intelligence law: Between sectoral rules and comprehensive regime—Comparative law perspectives* (forthcoming).

Miao, F., Kozlenkova, I. V., Wang, H., Xie, T., & Palmatier, R. W. (2022). An emerging theory of avatar marketing. *Journal of Marketing, 86*(1), 67–90.

Moore, R. J., An, S., & Ren, S. J. (2023). The IBM natural conversation framework: A new paradigm for conversational UX design. *Human-Computer Interaction, 38*(3–4), 168–193.

Mustak, M., Salminen, J., Ple, L., & Wirtz, J. (2021). Artificial intelligence in marketing: Topic modeling, scientometric analysis, and research agenda. *Journal of Business Research, 124*, 389–404.

Ord, T. (2020). *The precipice: Existential risk and the future of humanity*. Hachette Book Group, Inc.

Park, S. S., Tung, C. D., & Lee, H. (2021). The adoption of AI service robots: A comparison between credence and experience service settings. *Psychology & Marketing, 38*, 691–703.

Przegalinska, A. K., Ciechanowski, L., Stróz, A., Gloor, P. A., & Mazurek, G. (2019). In bot we trust: A new methodology of chatbot performance measures. *Business Horizons, 62*(6), 785–797.

Rahwan, I., Cebrian, M., Obradovich, N., Bongard, J. C., et al. (2019). Machine behaviour. *Nature, 568*, 477–486.

Rigaki, M., & García, S. (2023). A survey of privacy attacks in machine learning. *ACM Computing Surveys, 56*, 1–34.

Russell, S. (2019). *Human compatible: Artificial intelligence and the problem of control*. Viking.

Severyn, A., Moschitti, A., Uryupina, O., Plank, B., & Filippova, K. (2016). Multi-lingual opinion mining on YouTube. *Information Processing Management, 52*, 46–60.

Shneiderman. B. (2022). *Human-centered AI*. Oxford Academic.

Shrestha, Y. R., Ben-Menahem, S. M., & von Krogh, G. (2019). Organizational decision-making structures in the age of artificial intelligence. *California Management Review, 61*, 66–83.

Tang, C., & Guo, L. (2015). Digging for gold with a simple tool: Validating text mining in studying electronic word-of-mouth (eWOM) communication. *Marketing Letters, 26*, 67–80.

Teixeira, S., & Remondes, J. (2023). *The use of artificial intelligence in digital marketing: Competitive strategies and tactics*. IGI Global. ISBN13: 9781668493243.

Tirunillai, S., & Tellis, G. J. (2014). Mining marketing meaning from online chatter: strategic brand analysis of big data using latent Dirichlet allocation. *Journal of Marketing Research, 51*(4), 463–479.

Tiwari, S., & Sinha, A. (2020). Sentiment analysis of facebook data using machine learning. *International Journal of Innovative Research in Applied Sciences and Engineering, 4*, 2456–8910.

Tsvetkova, M., García-Gavilanes, R., Floridi, L., & Yasseri, T. (2017). Even good bots fight: The case of Wikipedia. *PLoS ONE, 12*(2), e0171774.

Vagia, M., Transeth, A. A., & Fjerdingen, S. A. (2016). A literature review on the levels of automation during the years. What are the different taxonomies that have been proposed? *Applied Ergonomics, 53*(Pt A), 190–202.

Vázquez, A., López Zorrilla, A., Olaso, J. M., Torres, M. L. (2023). Dialogue management and language generation for a robust conversational virtual coach: Validation and user study. *Sensors, 23*(3) (Article 1423).

Wahde, M., & Virgolin, M. (2023). DAISY: An implementation of five core principles for transparent and accountable conversational AI. *International Journal of Human-Computer Interaction, 39*(9), 1856–1873.

Wu, X., Xiao, L., Sun, Y., Zhang, J., Ma, T., & He, L. (2022). A survey of human-in-the-loop for machine learning. *Future Generation Computer Systems, 135*, 364–381.

Yang, Y., Zhang, K., & Kannan, P. K. (2022). Identifying market structure: A deep network representation learning of social engagement. *Journal of Marketing, 86*(4), 37–56.

Zheng, N., Liu, Z., Ren, P., Ma, Y., Chen, S., Yu, S., Xue, J., Chen, B., & Wang, F. (2017). Hybrid-augmented intelligence: collaboration and cognition. *Frontiers Information Technology & Electronic Engineering, 18*, 153–179.

Chapter 10
Data Management

Abstract The speed and accuracy of data management are essential advantages offered by AI systems. A further advantage could be if the data are transformed to insightful solutions facilitating business performance and end-user applications. The current chapter addresses how to possibly generate such solutions, translating user needs into explainable data architectures. Understanding how to generate, train, test, and optimise AI-generated behaviour is also in the focus hereby. Machine behaviour could be navigated by exposing AI systems to specific training data. While substantial human effort was needed to annotate, characterise and interpret information, the enhancement of autonomous capabilities could mark a new era in data management. In this respect, classification algorithms for text, voice, and images are trained to optimise accuracy on a specific set of human-labelled datasets. Most importantly, the selection, labelling, and management of a particular dataset and the chosen features can reshape not only the behaviour of an AI system. Rather, the user behaviour could be modified by the way the system is trained. However, data management may experience some bias, but this is a call to rethink AI systems, in order to preclude biased responses. We further recommend remediation of the AI systems currently available on the market. As seen from the outcomes of the field studies reported hereby, informativeness, accuracy, and competence are crucial parameters determining proper system functioning, and thus its adoption by users. Therefore, by fine-tuning algorithms and data architectures, an effective approach for data management is expected to be created to appropriately meet the user expectations and business demands for transformational AI solutions.

10.1 Core Aspects and Techniques

Marketing practices try to substitute various processes that previously required human cognitive abilities with innovative AI tools, using computer software and algorithms, focusing at advancing the performance of different tasks. Not surprisingly, companies are investigating in AI applications, aiming at facilitating various marketing-related activities, such as strategic planning, content research and creation, personalisation and profiling, customer relationship management, and customer journey optimisation.

Improved data management via AI advancement helps organisations to minimise expenses, enables brands to reach new clients, and facilitates companies to stay ahead of competitors. AI aims at revolutionising the way the audience is reached, within the right time and the proper message.

We have to also point out that the evolution of related research is reflected in the evolution of AI applications and the way data are managed. At the infancy of technology development, simple rules were used by early algorithmic programs (Rahwan et al., 2019) in order to navigate behaviour for example, in trading, buyers' and/or sellers' performance (for an overview of algorithmic trading, see Kissell, 2020).

In the era of user-centric marketing, brand strategies are more and more oriented toward offering personalised journeys, rather than broad audience segmentation. Understanding customers is crucial in predicting their future (purchase) behaviour. Analysing big data could be well used for in-depth investigations of consumer performance, in terms of attention, perception, and action, both offline and online. Online, following a customer's performance in real time is even more powerful. Data mining agents may learn which individuals to possibly target in advertising campaigns and/or social media. In such a way AI techniques could not only analyse, but also navigate customer performance at any single moment in time.

Therefore, one of the main objectives when dealing with large amount of data in the pursuit of extracting customer insights is to turn unstructured data (in various forms, i.e., text, images, audio, and video) into structured clusters. Diverse techniques are respectively employed, such as image recognition, speech recognition, and search engine optimisation. The data processing methods used differ according to the area type, task, and operational quantitative results. For example, data preprocessing, data annotation, and iterative labelling are acknowledged as core data processes, while computer vision (CV), natural language processing (NLP), and speech processing (SP) are enumerated as area types (for an extended overview, see Wu et al., 2022).

Despite the increased adoption of big data analytics and smart algorithms, generating strategic value, especially from isolated and unfocused actions, turns out to be much more difficult. Although there were numerous calls for clear guidelines on how to value data toward insightful decisions, related research is not univocal. There is a need for systems that harness the volume, variety, and velocity of available customer data to generate valuable insights enabling a guidance for data management, decision integration, and investment.

To achieve a sustainable competitive advantage from big data, however, the need for agility in combining rich data across the organisation has been recognised (Brock & von Wangenheim, 2019; Chen et al., 2012). Deployment of analytics that sense and respond to customers in a dynamic environment was also noted (Kitchens et al., 2018). It was explicitly argued that big data power does not preclude the need for vision or human insight (McAfee & Brynjolfsson, 2012). Other way round, managing data is possible when only measuring info properly. There is a huge amount of data, such as UGC, reviews, user responses, and other unstructured data available outside organisational boundaries. Therefore, the need for identification, collection, and integration of data across functional silos both within and outside the organisation was acknowledged (Kitchens et al., 2018). These, however, turn into key challenges in achieving the agility of organisation(s).

While standard analytical procedures demonstrate computational inadequacy (Liu et al., 2016), AI techniques show several advantages (De Bruyn et al., 2020; Kannan et al., 2023; Yang et al., 2022). AI is supposed to not structure the huge amount of data generated by consumers, but rather to provide insights about both, cognitive (i.e., reasoning, decision making) and emotional (i.e., sentiment analysis) aspects. In such a way, understanding consumers need and demands, AI could project future behaviour (Ma & Sun, 2020; Yang et al., 2022). Moreover, it is possible to suggest innovation opportunities for brands, products, and services. Shaking the way data are managed with new technology, a reconsideration of the marketing mix (product/ service, price, promotion, and place) was brought to the table (Kannan & Li, 2017).

Machine learning, ML, techniques (for an extensive overview, see Arrieta et al., 2020) are expected to provide better cognitive insights, in comparison with those available from traditional analytics (Davenport & Ronanki, 2018). The amount, intensity, and details of the data supplied are greater through ML approaches. Models are typically trained on only a partial subset of the data, and on this base improvement in the model is predicted. Training and iterations are expected to evolve over time, providing improved categorisations and predictions when implemented on new datasets. The ML approach is suggested as being flexible in incorporating a wide variety of data in tabular, graphical, and text format and is capable of offering versatile ensemble-like performance across a wide portfolio of customer analytics tasks (Kitchens et al., 2018). As key aspects of improving a large language model (LLM), computer power, the number of trainable parameters, i.e., the size of the model and data quality were enumerated. Various techniques are suggested for specific tasks and application contexts. Employing advanced customer analytics, data clustering, and the creation of infrastructure are enabled, aiming at focused, agile, and dynamic maintenance of brand-consumer relationships. See Table 10.1, for a summary of data management techniques with respect to their application in marketing practices.

ML and, in particular, multilayer perceptron (MLP) artificial neural networks (ANNs) have been applied to explore marketing performance in response to consumer behaviour via cashback websites (Ballestar et al., 2019). The number of registration transactions and the number of purchase transactions were the two predictors reported to be with the highest relative importance to the referrer on the cashback website. Another model, which uses only the recency, frequency, monetary value (RFM) of purchases, and probabilistic predictions of individual customer churn, was also suggested (Kitchens et al., 2018). Moreover, given the ability of various AI applications to track cookies, search histories, and other activity data, predictive analytics have the power to recommend customised pricing, in real time. Hereby, however, the question about ethics arises. Whether the search engine optimisation (SEO) techniques respect morality and legislation is an issue worth further reflection. Ethical dilemmas should be solved, as well as appropriate regulations are needed before launching new generation AI systems.

Table 10.1 Data management techniques and their marketing applications

Methods	Application	References
Data mining (various methods in different papers)	Advertising brand mapping eWOM, UGC (blogs, forums, online review) Individual predictions	Liu et al. (2016) Netzer et al. (2012) Ribeiro et al. (2016) Tang and Guo (2015) Tirunillai and Tellis (2014) Zhang et al. (2018b)
Decision support Fuzzy logic	Estimate guest loyalty	Lau et al. (2015)
Machine learning (various methods in different papers)	Ads efficiency/optimisation Loyalty, cashback websites Price formation Twitter Translate (NLP) Voice recognition (text to speech) Websites exploration	Ballestar et al. (2019) Ghiassi and Lee (2018) Misra et al. (2019) Schwartz et al. (2017)
Deep learning	LLM in various customer analytics tasks For predicting customer behaviour	Kitchens et al. (2018) Yang et al. (2022)
Multilayer perceptron (MLP) artificial neural network (ANN)	Customer-brand relationship Forecast customer quality perception, satisfaction Registration and purchase transactions	Ballestar et al. (2019) Haryanto et al. (2015)
Neural network	Brand personality Customer engagement feedback, attitudes, or perceptions, eWOM Product development Relationship, loyalty, sentiment analysis	Ansari and Riasi (2016) Chong et al. (2016) Haryanto et al. (2015) LeCun et al. (2015) Leminen et al. (2018) Thieme et al. (2000) Yang et al. (2022)

Emerging as core insights extracted via artificial neural networks (ANNs), emotional authenticity, brand partnerships, brand salience, and brand personality mediated by brand relationships enhanced the brand loyalty (Haryanto et al., 2015). It was shown that when detailing customer satisfaction, consumer insights might predict the intentions to reuse particular services. For example, analysing approximately 130,000 customers' evaluations, a neural network was applied in the context of airline services to predict behaviour (Leminen et al., 2018). A recent paper provided very promising results applying deep neural networks, for both, high (automotive) and low (food and beverage) involvement products (Yang et al., 2022).

Computational strategies based on adaptive heuristics or explicit maximisation of expected utility are employed by more sophisticated agents. Reinforcement learning

(Sutton & Barto, 2018) algorithms are considered even more sophisticated, demonstrating behaviour characterised by particular attributes as a function of the representations and context evaluation (e.g., Deng et al., 2017). Furthermore, AI behaviour is generated according to how the features of the environment are perceived, including the resolution and accuracy of object detection and systems classification.

We have to point out hereby that data management techniques could vary by purpose and type of analytical procedure used, i.e., descriptive, diagnostic, predictive, suggestive/prescriptive. Table 10.2 provides a summary of core techniques employed with respect to analytics used and their applications in marketing practices.

How to effectively utilise the enormous amount of text information was well demonstrated in earlier work exploring electronic word of mouth communication, eWOM (Bialkova, 2021; Tang & Guo, 2015). Linguistic parameters generated by text analysis were claimed to be predictive indicators of eWOM communicators' attitudes toward a product or service. Furthermore, specified text analysis indicators can explain additional variation in the attitudes of consumers spreading eWOM. Going above and beyond the star rating, such information is especially relevant for obtaining deeper insight into consumer opinion.

Table 10.2 Data management techniques by analytical procedure

Analytics	Application	References
Descriptive Search and summary of historical data in order to identify patterns or meaning	Validating prior investments Understand current performance Summary statistics and tests Dashboards Visualisation	Berman and Israeli (2020) Yang et al. (2022)
Diagnostic Identify trends and behaviour pattern(s) Determine the causes of trends and correlations between variables	Market basket analysis Product market dynamic change Customer insights Trends in eWOM, UGC Identify fraud/fake info	Bialkova (2021) Wedel and Kannan (2016)
Predictive Predicting future outcomes, based on previous data uncover relationships and patterns within large volumes of data that can be used to predict behaviour and events	Recency, frequency, and monetary value (RFM) of purchase AI algorithms predict products aligning with customer/user interests Customer engagement customised pricing, real-time offerings eWOM spread	Ballestar et al. (2019) Haryanto et al. (2015) Kitchens et al. (2018) Ribeiro et al. (2016) Tang and Guo (2015) Yang et al. (2022)
Suggestive/prescriptive Optimisation of models and methods	Review analysis eWOM Implementing Data mining	Zhang et al., (2018a)

Despite of enormous number of examples of text mining techniques (as seen from literature audit and reported above), data management instruments and methods are also widely applied with respect to other modalities, such as auditory (e.g., speech recognition; phonetic recognition), visual (e.g., face recognition, image recognition, eye gaze), and tactile (e.g., kinematics estimator, grasp stability). Table 10.3 provides an overview of the core techniques used with respect to modality.

For audio modalities, DNN and signal processing were well documented, a while ago (for an overview, see Hinton et al., 2012). Visuals (text and image) have also received significant attention (Netzer et al., 2012; Simonyan et al., 2013). Table 10.4 summarises the key technologies used for modelling visual and audio modalities, recognised as the most developed AI systems. Although eye gaze is extremely informative concerning consumer attention and choice (Bialkova et al., 2020), ML techniques are still needed to navigate the attention of AI agent properly. Advancement of technology will possibly allow such navigation, as well as the inclusion of other modalities, i.e., olfaction, gustatory, and somatosensory, hopefully in the near future.

Table 10.3 Techniques used as a function of application modality

Modality	Architecture	Capability
Auditory Voice Speech	ML, deep learning, DNN	Recommendation systems Personal assistant Speech recognition (text to voice and vice versa) Voice recognition Phonetic recognition
Visual Text Semantics	NNT deep learning, NLP	Translation, classification
Visual Eye gaze Face	Convolutional Neural Networks (CNN), Deep learning, Opinion mining	Computer vision Tracking Image recognition
Visual Images Video	CNN, Graph mining	Big data analytics Predictive analytics Graphical models graphic user interface
Touch	Deep learning, Neural networks	Kinematics estimator Estimated position/touch location Grasp stability Slip detection
Memory Reasoning	Computation modelling, ML, deep learning, neural networks, Reinforcement learning	Cognitive computing Expert systems

Table 10.4 Methods for modelling audio and visual modalities

Visuals		Audio
Text	Pictorial/images	Voice
• Computational linguistics • Content and text analysis • Document representation • Enterprise search system • Information retrieval • Information extraction • Multilingual analysis • Opinion mining • Query processing • Question-answering systems • Relevance feedback • Search engines • Sentiment/affect analysis • Statistical NLP • Text visualisation • Topic models • User models • Web stylometric analysis	• Graph mining • Face recognition • Opinion mining • Information retrieval • Information extraction • Sentiment/affect analysis	• DNN • HMM • GMM • Signal processing

10.2 Demystifying the Process

Despite the good amount and variety of methods, a need emerges for simplified rules, explainable codes that facilitate the performance of specific architectures and training models, to demystify the "black boxes" gap. The functioning of various processes should be interpretable rather than knowing what is at the input and the output stage. In order to extract valuable insights that could provide actionable guidance for data management, decision integration of systems that harness the volume, variety, and velocity of available customer data is required.

Data Volume and Dimensions

Volume relates to the sheer amount of data that are generated in a given context. Data appear in different formats and types, creating a great variability. The speed of data generation and frequency of data changes determine the velocity, which requires real-time analysis and decision making. The high dimensionality and data volume size add another layer of complexity to understanding AI behaviour. Creating a value-justified data infrastructure is a prerequisite for agile deployment of advanced analytics (Kitchens et al., 2018).

Furthermore, the data are characterised by veracity, reflecting quality, context, and accuracy.

Data Quality, Accuracy, and Integrity

Data sources are often unstructured, noisy (McAfee & Brynjolfsson, 2012), and thus, they are difficult to integrate into a coherent architecture that can provide focused consumer insights and values. Furthermore, incomplete data or a mismatch between training data and the cases confronted at the test stage may cause discrepancies (Lakkaraju et al., 2016). Therefore, the type of data collected, appropriate quantitative measures, and prioritising integration efforts are crucial for deriving correct assumptions and value propositions.

Data Access, Availability, and Collection

High-performing AI algorithms demand training on extensive datasets (e.g., Huang & Rust, 2018), which often goes at the price of high costs and resource demands (Davenport & Ronanki, 2018; Kaperonis, 2024). The way the data are collected predetermines the success or failure of the model training and thus the correctness of the prediction. These imperfections have led to the need for adapting reporting mechanisms for datasets and models. A reasonable question arises as to who may or may not own the data. Similarly, who may or may not want to share information about their models is a core problem worth attention. Recent research has also pointed out the necessity of data independence (Wahde & Virgolin, 2023). This is a serious issue given the data ownership.

Data Ownership and Privacy

Often the data with which a system is trained are property of a particular brand, company, or organisation. The same holds for the source code and model structure for the most frequently used algorithms in various societal activities and initiatives. Not surpassingly then, source code and model structure are overwhelmingly packed with industrial secrecy and legal protection of intellectual property. The inputs and outputs are the only parameters that are publicly available about AI systems, in many scenarios. Consumer models use the services that the model owner provides usually via programming codes or user interface.

Scalable AI identification technology such as facial recognition and other involuntary methods of identification using biometric data (i.e., fingerprints, personality assessment through microexpressions, and automatic voice recognition) enable personal discovery with high precision and efficiency. However, the question about the ownership of these data, especially in public places, is still relevant and getting higher importance. Automatic identification opens new risks and raises strong concerns of an ethical and legal nature, given the unpredictable and undesired outcomes that AI may have on individuals and society, especially when used uncontrolled. We already mentioned in Chap. 9 (Bialkova, 2024b) the need for regulations to preclude problems such as stolen identity, fake news propaganda, and adversary attacks (i.e., membership inference, reconstruction, property inference, and model extraction).

Although increasing investigations, researchers are still facing challenges, given that various attacks are applicable only to specific sets of assumptions, or to a small training dataset, number of classes or participants. Therefore, a reasonable concern arises about accuracy of models and their predictive power.

Predictive Power

Any customer analytics approach aims at providing actionable and valuable insights, and therefore incorporates a variety of rich, relationship-oriented constructs. The question hereby is whether an AI system can predict with accuracy and precision the variety in customer behaviour in challenging environments, untrained contexts, and scenarios. A crucial factor thus is the demonstrated ability to drive significant value. Accuracy defined as extent to which the model accurately predicts unseen instances could be enhanced by producing significantly more accurate trees (Guidotti et al., 2018).

While computer scientists have focussed on mathematical algorithms and models behind the architecture, in the marketing literature, prediction reflects anticipated future customer behaviour based on historical data. Predictions may lack precision, due to poor feature selection (which is often domain dependent). This is a major challenge for the machine learning approaches, as acknowledged by several authors (for a review see Arrieta et al., 2020).

Concerning the market side, predictive power was associated with the capability of big data analytics to drive strategic value. In particular, evaluations based on added business value relative to the costs of data acquisition, management, integration, and real-time feature construction were noted (Kitchens et al., 2018). The researchers further distinguished between churn prediction, conversion prediction, and customer lifetime value (CLV). The churn prediction application is associated with the firm's focus on the customers, and it should be seen as investment and continued marketing efforts (i.e., how to retain customers). The conversion prediction reflects the identification of customers who are very likely to respond to individual communications, i.e., via e-mails, or promotions. However, reduced messaging fatigue (do not overwhelm with communications) and expanded customer reach (prevent attrition) are expected. The CLV prediction accounts for identifying customers who could successfully be expanded through participation in a premium loyalty program, i.e., how to keep loyal brand ambassadors.

The authors also acknowledged the need for a principled, flexible, versatile predictive model. The capability of theory-driven predictions following certain principles and rules to disentangle the various aspects of relationship-oriented data was associated with principled prediction. Flexibility reflects the possibility to accommodate complex and a wide variety of data in constructs of various formats and structures. Versatility reflects the variety of customer analytics initiatives and applications.

Furthermore, predictive power was argued to depend on the model/algorithmic fairness.

Algorithmic Fairness

It reflects *statistical parity* (meaning that an equal proportion of defendants are detained in each race group); *conditional statistical parity* (associated with controlling for a limited set of "legitimate" risk factors, an equal proportion of defendants detained within each race group); and *predictive equality* (i.e., the accuracy of decisions is equal across race groups, as measured by false positive rate) as suggested by Corbett-Davies and colleagues (2017). To achieve algorithmic fairness the researchers argued two-stage processing, namely a formal criterion of fairness should be defined first, and then a decision rule should be developed to satisfy that measure, either exactly or approximately (Corbett-Davies et al., 2017; but see also Verma & Rubin, 2018). A trade-off between statistical parity and accuracy was further suggested as possible solution to fairness issue (Zhao & Gordon, 2022). Group versus individual fairness also received attention (Ray et al., 2023) in the attempt of scientists to disentangle the challenges related to appropriate algorithmic functioning.

10.3   Harmful Behaviours in Algorithmic Systems

Inspection of algorithmic systems for biased, discriminatory, or otherwise harmful behaviour is already in the focus of many research initiatives. Auditing different algorithms, methods, and designs is suggested. An early taxonomy summarised key audit aspects, namely: (1) code audits, (2) non-invasive user audits, (3) scraping audits, (4) sock puppet audits, and (5) crowdsourced/collaborative audits (for an overview, see Sandvig et al., 2014). Some of the methods enumerated in the taxonomy have demonstrated shortages, and in particular, from the user perspective, i.e., how people discover and make sense of algorithmic (harmful) behaviour (DeVos et al., 2022). A revisit of theory and methods is invited, especially given that some approaches are uncapable of detecting problematic issues when deployed in real-life scenarios that ordinary users of algorithmic systems are able to quickly recognise. In the following, we provide details on major algorithmic deviations that may impact performance, as well as possible solutions (and for a summary, see Table 10.5). Figure 10.1 provides an illustration of the Solutions tree to address harmful behaviour.

Adversary may attempt to evade a deployed system at test time by carefully manipulating attack samples (Biggio et al., 2013), trying to extract information about the training data or to extract the model itself (for a review see Rigaki & García, 2023). The authors identified four types of attacks, namely: membership inference, reconstruction, property inference, and model extraction, which appeared either on centralised learning or on distributed learning.

Following common safety protocols, researchers have suggested proactive protection mechanisms that should anticipate and prevent the adversarial impact (Biggio et al., 2013, but see also Song et al., 2019). The detection of potential vulnerabilities of learning before they are exploited by an adversary, the investigation of the impact of the corresponding attacks, and the devising of appropriate countermeasures were enumerated as core steps to oppose attacks that significantly impair classifier's performance. Differential privacy (associated with the extraction of useful information about the population as a whole, but not learning about the individual); regularisation (ML techniques reducing overfitting and lifting model performance

Table 10.5 Problematic behaviour and possible solutions

Problem	Implication context	Solution
Adversary (evasion attacks)	Evasion of deployed system at test time, Extracting information about the training data or extracting the model itself	*To identify potential vulnerabilities before being attacked; *To investigate the impact of the corresponding attacks, i.e., evaluating classifier security; *To devise appropriate countermeasures (Biggio et al., 2013)
Accuracy	Model predictions for unseen instances	*Using both, the oracle guide and the original data produce significantly more accurate trees (Guidotti et al., 2018)
Bias	Perception of Trust Believability of data/ prediction/outcomes	*Value trade-offs between competing and incompatible notions of bias (Corbett-Davies et al., 2017; Rahwan et al., 2019; Verma & Rubin, 2018) *Value trade-offs between human versus machine biases (Rahwan et al., 2019) *Trade-off between statistical parity and accuracy (Zhao & Gordon, 2022) *Auditing an LM for biases by a priori understanding of what categories might be salient (Bender et al., 2021) *Use of new dataset
Fairness	Users affected by model decisions, regulatory entities/agencies	*Formal criterion of fairness and a decision rule should be developed to satisfy that measure (Corbett-Davies et al., 2017) *Trade-off between statistical parity and accuracy (Zhao & Gordon, 2022) *Group versus individual fairness (Ray et al., 2023)
Performance deviation	Benchmark required	*Benchmarks to be coupled with metrics to quantify performance on standardised tasks
Low Interpretability	Commonly assessed using logical and/or mathematical proofs	*Visualisation of Convolutional Neural Networks (CNN), *Diagnosis of CNN representations, * Disentanglement of 'the mixture of patterns' encoded in each filter of CNNs, *Building explainable models, and *Semantic-level middle-to-end learning via human–computer interaction (Zhang & Zhu, 2018)

(continued)

Table 10.5   (continued)

Problem	Implication context	Solution
Misinformation	False inputs Fake data	*Define who has to decide what is misinformation (i.e., centralised or democratised assessment) *Detecting the level of automation used in the recognition of false content *Identify what is done to the content detected as misinformation *Fact checking algorithms (Jahanbakhsh et al., 2023)
Privacy leak	Leak of data or model due to attacks in system architecture	*Differential privacy *Regularisation *Prediction vector tampering (Rigaki & García, 2023)

generalisation); and prediction vector tampering (restriction of the output or predictions of a model) were also reported as defensive strategies against attacks (Rigaki & García, 2023).

Misinformation is closely related to how further decisions are taken and thus how AI systems operate. For example, data might be incorrect, due to false inputs or misinformation. Several cases of false data and newsfeeds have been reported from social media and various digital channels. Recent work, therefore, suggested approaches to detect and deal with misinformation (Jahanbakhsh et al., 2023). The core techniques encompass the identification of who has to decide what is misinformation (i.e., centralised or democratised assessment), detecting the level of automation used in the recognition of false content, and determining what is done to the content detected as error prone; these are part of the strategies used to deal with misinformation. Fact checking and machine learning algorithms have been employed to fight against misinformation. In such a way it is hoped to enable users to specify a set of trusted sources, to assess content while their assessments are organised as structured metadata, as well as to use filters blocking misinformation and working only with trustworthy sources.

Bias is broadly defined as a systematic error with respect to the ground truth, as opposed to a random error. Biases could have different causes and origins.

Algorithmic bias often appears as a result of the training process, especially when working with skewed data (Barocas & Selbst, 2016). For example, if a particular group is underrepresented in the training process, the generated model is less accurate. Algorithms may become biased by the same issues if the original model is biased anyhow (Beutel et al., 2017). Being a serious problem, bias attracted researchers' efforts in developing techniques to "de-bias" ML algorithms and models.

Human bias could also be replicated, given the capacity of AI systems to generate decisions based on algorithms and models designed by human engineers. Thus, leveraging endogenous relationships in the data, spurious correlation employment may often follow human bias (De Bruyn et al., 2020).

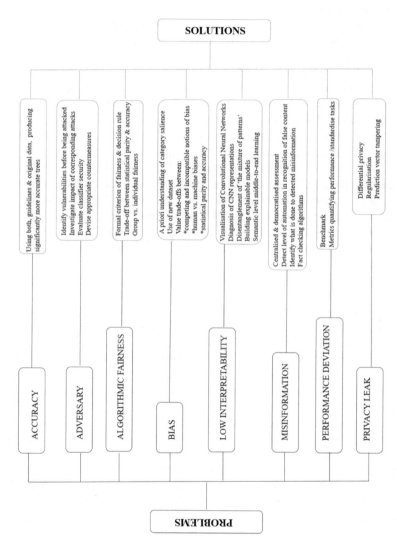

Fig. 10.1 Solutions tree to face problematic behaviour

Historically common bias. Biased models may propagate stereotypes and problematic associations for humans as well as for language models, LMs (Bender et al., 2021). LMs may not only propagate and amplify problematic associations, but also generate more and abusive language, which could be included in the next iteration of large-scale training data collection.

Bias may have huge and negative impact on end users and businesses when AI makes decisions based on historical datasets, which may be characterised by historically common biases. If businesses lack the technical tools to forecast how highly complex algorithms may perform as circumstances change, this could lead to many negative outcomes. A plausible solution could be the use of new datasets. Taken together, these findings show that AI continuously evolves its own decision making based on new data. However, governance is required and protection should be considered. **To ensure that AI appropriately supports** business-critical decision making, it is very important to decrease AI bias through the use of data, algorithms, and models so that all stakeholders are treated in a transparent and fair manner.

Auditing an LM for biases by a priori understanding of what categories might be salient (Bender et al., 2021) was mentioned as a possible solution. Value trade-offs between competing and incompatible notions of bias (Corbett-Davies et al., 2017; Rahwan et al., 2019; Verma & Rubin, 2018), as well as value trade-offs between human versus machine biases (Rahwan et al., 2019), and trade-offs between statistical parity and accuracy (Zhao & Gordon, 2022) are also pointed out as potential solutions to preclude biases.

Benchmark should be established with metrics to quantify performance on standardised tasks (Rahwan et al., 2019). In such a way better, faster, and more robust algorithms are expected to be generated, and thus leading to improvement of AI system performance. A further optimisation of the system performance could be envisaged when parallel to algorithmic maximisation, broader indicators are taken into account, analogous to the human behaviour indicators investigated by psychology and consumer scientists. In this respect, we believe that the current book provides important lessons and useful insights with the taxonomy suggested of agency efficiency.

Low interpretability is associated with the passive properties of a learning model and is assessed with mathematical proofs (Fiok et al., 2021). Although AI predictive models (i.e., deep neural networks) have exhibited superior performance in various tasks, their interpretability is always a challenge. Characterised by high discrimination power, deep neural networks still have low interpretability of their black box representation. Several bottlenecks of deep learning, such as learning from a few annotations, learning via human–computer communications at the semantic level, and semantically debugging network representations have been acknowledged (Zhang & Zhu, 2018). As possible solutions to face the above challenges, the authors suggested five research directions for interpretable/disentangled representations, i.e., visualisation of Convolutional Neural Networks (CNN), diagnosis of CNN representations, disentanglement of "the mixture of patterns" encoded in each filter of CNNs, building explainable models, and semantic-level middle-to-end learning via human–computer interaction (for detailed overview, see Zhang & Zhu, 2018).

Exploring explainable models such as interpretable CNNs (Zhang et al., 2018b), capsule networks (Sabour et al., 2017), interpretable RCNNs (Wu et al., 2017), and InfoGANs (Chen et al., 2016) have emerged as promising research directions to demystify the black box in neural networks.

Privacy leak of the data and model information is mainly due to the way the AI system is constructed. For example, support vector machines (SVMs), where the support vectors are the data points from the training dataset are easy to attack. Linear classifiers are relatively easy to retrieve and can reverse the way their parameters operate. Considering the large number of parameters the neural networks operate, simple attacks are less feasible, however not impossible at the training of data or the model itself (for an overview, see Rigaki & García, 2023). The authors further suggested defence mechanisms to protect privacy, such as differential privacy (extracting useful information about population as a whole, without learning about single individual); regularisation (techniques in ML aiming to reduce overfitting and to increase model generalisation performance); prediction vector tampering (i.e., restriction of the output to the top k classes or predictions of a model). It was also pointed out that despite the relatively good theoretical explanation of why leaks happen, there is a need to know how these theoretical notions are applied in real system settings. There are areas, learning tasks and datasets, that have been largely ignored and thus inviting further exploration.

Personalisation must be performed while respecting privacy (Kaperonis, 2024). Privacy concerns in targeting by advertising techniques were acknowledged a while ago (Datta et al., 2014). The authors reported that setting specific features when tracing users' browsing behaviour may in fact generate choices leading to discriminatory ads.

To address privacy concerns while considering the complexity of user demand, market management and XAI experts should cooperate. Regulatory bodies have already taken several steps toward setting rules to respect individual privacy (e.g., EU AI Act, 2023). Some of the key technology giants are also working toward respecting privacy and restricting data leaks.

While data management currently employing AI techniques is often focused on getting insights to benefit companies, there is a need to orient the focus toward the consumers. Elevating consumer enjoyment when interacting with AI systems turns to be a prerequisite for consumer satisfaction. As reported hereby (Chap. 5, Bialkova, 2024a) enjoyment and functionality are crucial parameters determining quality perception of AI systems used by consumers. Put differently, a user-centric approach is strongly recommended to increase the benefits consumers see. These, however, should not go at the expenses of AI performance. Fairness, accountability and transparency should be achieved. Security and safety should be guaranteed.

Note also a lack of network-wide focus, and therefore, analysing the entire network is required. This deficit calls for further investigation on how collaborative, systemic aspects of AI should be managed.

10.4   Managerial Solutions

Transparency. Data transparency and, in general, transparency of AI performance (i.e., how decisions are derived) were acknowledged to be crucial to how AI systems are perceived. In contrast, a lack of transparency about the reasoning behind AI decisions would reduce trust and may rise reservations toward AI system use (Jahanbakhsh et al., 2023). Many scholars, therefore, have reported the need for transparent data, algorithms, and models.

For example, a dialogue manager was suggested to be responsible for determining the user's intent and deriving the necessary information required for the response (Wahde & Virgolin, 2023). In such a way, the processing typically associated with access to the agent's knowledge base, algorithmic modelling, and formulation of the output would provide transparency in a human understandable manner. Therefore, opposing the massive, distributed conglomerate of operations on which the "black box" systems rely on, the transparent operations demonstrate human interpretable behaviour, by achieving high precision at low recall costs. The authors suggested interpretability, inherent capability to explain, independent data, interactive learning, and inquisitiveness (the agent eagerness to learn), as five principles of accountable and transparent conversational agents (Wahde & Virgolin, 2023).

Transparency is often associated with interpretability.

Interpretability is reflecting the capability of explainable AI in providing methods and techniques in such a way that is understood by humans (irrespective of whether being experts or end users). This means that predictions, classifications, decision making, and recommendations for actions should be interpretable. There are a number of definitions what interpretability should involve. The core aspects encompass (1) the intention behind the system; (2) the data sources used; and (3) how the inputs are related to the outputs of the model (e.g., Arrieta et al., 2020; De Bruyn et al., 2020; Guidotti et al., 2018).

Acknowledging the increased interaction of AI models with one another, and the data generation and classifications on their own, these may lack interpretability and even to create undetected endogeneity issues going beyond the human control (De Bruyn et al., 2020). The authors further noted the possibility of human bias replication, given the superior ability of AI systems to generate human based models and decision patterns, leveraging endogenous relationships in the data. We touched upon these points when discussing possible challenges in data management (see Table 10.5).

Interpretable, explainable, and fair AI systems should assure reliable performance. The reliability of AI systems could be improved through the use of technical practices such as audit trails (i.e., tools for reviewing and analysing failures, errors, and near misses), benchmark tests (i.e., verification and validation of algorithms and models), continuous review (of data quality and bias testing, for example). Reliability, especially automation reliability is fundamental to design strategies (Vagia et al., 2016). It is a base to build confidence, as well as to maintain sustainable relationships with stakeholders affected by AI decisions (Shneiderman, 2020, 2022).

To facilitate data management and to assure pertinent performance of algorithms and models, relevant regulations are required. **Ethics and Legislation** have already been addressed in detail for AI systems (see Chap. 9, Bialkova, 2024b). In particular, we should mention the AI liability directive (2019) and the EU AI Act (2023). Furthermore, given the increasing autonomy of AI systems, a clear distinction should be made regarding AI governance versus governing AI. Such a distinction is discussed in detail in Chap. 11, Bialkova, 2024c, which dedicates special attention to explainable AI, XAI.

References

Ansari, A., & Riasi, A. (2016). Modelling and evaluating customer loyalty using neural networks: Evidence from startup insurance companies. *Future Business Journal, 2*(1), 15–30.

Arrieta, A. B., Díaz-Rodríguez, N., del Ser, J., Bennetot, A., et al. (2020). Explainable Artificial Intelligence (XAI): Concepts, taxonomies, opportunities and challenges toward responsible AI. *Information Fusion, 58*, 82–115.

Ballestar, M. T., Grau-Carles, P., & Sainz, J. (2019). Predicting customer quality in e-commerce social networks: A machine learning approach. *Review of Managerial Science, 13*, 589–603.

Barocas, S., & Selbst, A. D. (2016). Big data's disparate impact. *California Law Review, 104*, 671–732.

Bender, E. M., Gebru, T., McMillan-Major, A., & Shmitchell, S. (2021). On the dangers of stochastic parrots: Can language models be too big? In *Proceedings of the 2021 ACM Conference on Fairness, Accountability, and Transparency (FAccT '21)* (pp. 610–623). Association for Computing Machinery.

Berman, R., & Israeli, A. (2020). The value of descriptive analytics: Evidence from online retailers. *Marketing Science, 41*, 1074–1096.

Beutel, A., Chen, J., Zhao, Z., & Chi, E. H. (2017). Data decisions and theoretical implications when adversarially learning fair representations. arXiv:abs/1707.00075.

Bialkova, S. (2021). How user generated content impacts ad effectiveness: Lessons from tourism industry. In *European Marketing Academy Conference, EMAC2022*, May 25–28, Madrid, Spain.

Bialkova, S. (2024a). *Chatbot efficiency—Model testing*. The rise of AI user applications: Chatbots integration foundations and trends. (Chapter 5). Springer. https://doi.org/10.1007/978-3-031-56471-0_5

Bialkova, S. (2024b). *AI transforming business and everyday life*. The rise of AI user applications: Chatbots integration foundations and trends. (Chapter 9). Springer. https://doi.org/10.1007/978-3-031-56471-0_9

Bialkova, S. (2024c). *Explainable AI*. The rise of AI user applications: Chatbots integration foundations and trends. (Chapter 11). Springer. https://doi.org/10.1007/978-3-031-56471-0_11

Bialkova, S., Grunert, K. G., & Trijp, H. V. (2020). From desktop to supermarket shelf: Eye-tracking exploration on consumer attention and choice. *Food Quality and Preference, 81*, 103839.

Biggio, B., Corona, I., Maiorca, D., et al. (2013). Evasion attacks against machine learning at test time. In H. Blockeel, K. Kersting, S. Nijssen, & F. Železný (Eds.), *Machine learning and knowledge discovery in databases. ECML PKDD 2013*. Lecture Notes in Computer Science (Vol. 8190, pp. 387–402). Springer.

Brock, J.K.-U., & von Wangenheim, F. (2019). Demystifying AI: What digital transformation leaders can teach you about realistic artificial intelligence. *California Management Review, 61*(4), 110–134.

Chen, H., Chiang, R. H., & Storey, V. C. (2012). Business intelligence and analytics: From big data to big impact. *MIS Quarterly, 36*(4), 1165–1188.

Chen, X., Duan, Y., Houthooft, R., Schulman, J., Sutskever, I., & Abbeel, P. (2016). InfoGAN: Interpretable representation learning by information maximizing Generative Adversarial Nets. Advances in Neural Information Processing Systems. Presented at the Neural Information Processing Systems (NIPS), Barcelona, Spain.

Chong, A. Y. L., Li, B., Ngai, E. W., Ch'ng, E., & Lee, F. (2016). Predicting online product sales via online reviews, sentiments, and promotion strategies. *International Journal of Operations & Production Management, 36*(4), 358–383.

Corbett-Davies, S., Pierson, E., Feller, A., Goel, S., & Huq, A. Z. (2017). Algorithmic decision making and the cost of fairness. In *Proceedings of the 23rd ACM SIGKDD International Conference on Knowledge Discovery and Data Mining.*

Datta, A., Tschantz, M. C., & Datta, A. (2014). Automated experiments on ad privacy settings. *Proceedings on Privacy Enhancing Technologies, 2015*, 112–192.

Davenport, T. H., & Ronanki, R. (2018). Artificial intelligence for the real world. *Harvard Business Review, 96*(1), 108–116.

De Bruyn, A., Viswanathan, V., Beh, Y. S., Brock, J. K., & von Wangenheim, F. (2020). Artificial intelligence and marketing: Pitfalls and opportunities. *Journal of Interactive Marketing, 51*, 91–105.

Deng, Y., Bao, F., Kong, Y., Ren, Z., & Dai, Q. (2017). Deep direct reinforcement learning for financial signal representation and trading. *IEEE Transactions on Neural Networks and Learning Systems, 28*, 653–664.

DeVos, A., Dhabalia, A., Shen, H., Holstein, K., & Eslami, M. (2022). Toward user-driven algorithm auditing: Investigating users' strategies for uncovering harmful algorithmic behavior. In *Proceedings of the 2022 CHI Conference on Human Factors in Computing Systems (CHI '22)*. ACM, Article 626.

European Commission. (2019). Communication: Building Trust in Human Centric Artificial Intelligence | Shaping Europe's digital future (europa.eu). https://digital-strategy.ec.europa.eu/en/library/communication-building-trust-human-centric-artificial-intelligence. Accessed January 20, 2024.

European Commission AI Act. (2023). AI Act | Shaping Europe's digital future (europa.eu). https://digital-strategy.ec.europa.eu/en/policies/regulatory-framework-ai. Accessed January 25, 2024.

Fiok, K., Farahani, F. V., Karwowski, W., & Ahram, T. (2021). Explainable artificial intelligence for education and training. *The Journal of Defense Modeling and Simulation, 19*(2), 133–144.

Ghiassi, M., & Lee, S. (2018). A domain transferable lexicon set for Twitter sentiment analysis using a supervised machine learning approach. *Expert Systems with Applications, 106*, 197–216.

Guidotti, R., Monreale, A., Ruggieri, S., Turini, F., Giannotti, F., & Pedreschi, D. (2018). A survey of methods for explaining black box models. *ACM Computing Surveys, 51*(5), Article 93.

Haryanto, J. O., Silva, M., & Moutinho, L. (2015). Neural network approach to understanding the children's market. *European Journal of Marketing, 49*(3/4), 372–397.

Hinton, G., Deng, L., Yu, D., Dahl, G. E., et al. (2012). Deep neural networks for acoustic modeling in speech recognition. *Signal Processing Magazine, IEEE, 29*(6), 82–97.

Huang, M. H., & Rust, R. T. (2018). Artificial intelligence in service. *Journal of Service Research, 21*(2), 155–172.

Jahanbakhsh, F., Katsis, Y., Wang, D., Popa, L., & Muller, M. (2023). Exploring the use of personalized AI for identifying misinformation on social media. In *Proceedings of the 2023 CHI Conference on Human Factors in Computing Systems (CHI '23)* (Article 105, pp. 1–27).

Kannan, P. K., & Li, H. (2017). Digital marketing: A framework, review and research agenda. *International Journal of Research in Marketing, 34*(1), 22–45.

Kannan, P. K., Yang, Y., & Zhang, K. (2023). Unlocking deeper insights into customer engagement through AI-powered analysis of social media. *Data Management and Business Review, 3*(1 & 2).

Kaperonis, S. (2024). How artificial intelligence (AI) is transforming the user experience in digital marketing. In S. Teixeira, & J. Remondes (Eds.), *The use of artificial intelligence in digital marketing: Competitive strategies and tactics* (pp. 117–141). IGI Global.

Kissell, R. (2020). *Algorithmic trading methods: Applications using advanced statistics, optimization, and machine learning techniques* (2nd ed.). Academic.

Kitchens, B., Dobolyi, D., Li, J., & Abbasi, A. (2018). Advanced customer analytics: Strategic value through integration of relationship-oriented big data. *Journal of Management Information Systems, 35*(2), 540–574.

Lakkaraju, H., Kamar, E., Caruana, R., & Horvitz, E. (2016). Identifying unknown unknowns in the open world: Representations and policies for guided exploration. In *AAAI Conference on Artificial Intelligence*.

Lau, H. C. W., Nakandala, D., Zhao, L., & Lai, I. K. W. (2015). Using fuzzy logic approach in estimating individual guest loyalty level for international tourist hotels. *International Journal of Services Technology and Management, 21*(1), 127–145.

LeCun, Y., Bengio, Y., & Hinton, G. E. (2015). Deep learning. *Nature, 521*, 436–444.

Leminen, S., Rajahonka, M., Westerlund, M., & Wendelin, R. (2018). The future of the Internet of Things: Toward heterarchical ecosystems and service business models. *Journal of Business & Industrial Marketing, 33*(6), 749–767.

Liu, X., Singh, P. V., & Srinivasan, K. (2016). A structured analysis of unstructured big data by leveraging cloud computing. *Marketing Science, 35*(3), 363–388.

Ma, L., & Sun, B. (2020). Machine learning and AI in marketing—Connecting computing power to human insights. *International Journal of Research in Marketing, 37*(3), 481–504.

McAfee, A. P., & Brynjolfsson, E. (2012). Big data: The management revolution. *Harvard Business Review, 9*(10), 60–68.

Misra, M., Schwartz, E. M., & Abernethy, J. (2019). Dynamic online pricing with incomplete information using multiarmed bandit experiments. *Marketing Science, 38*(2), 226–252.

Netzer, O., Feldman, R., Goldenberg, J., & Fresko, M. (2012). Mine your own business: Market-structure surveillance through text mining. *Marketing Science, 31*, 521–543.

Rahwan, I., Cebrian, M., Obradovich, N., Bongard, J. C., Bonnefon, J. F., Breazeal, C., Crandall, J. W., Christakis, N. A., Couzin, I. D., Jackson, M. O., Jennings, N. R. (2019). Machine behaviour. *Nature, 568*, 477–486.

Ray, A., Padmanabhan, B., & Bouayad, L. (2023). Systemic fairness. arXiv e-prints, arXiv-2304.

Ribeiro, M. T., Singh, S., & Guestrin, C. (2016). "Why should I trust you?": Explaining the predictions of any classifier. In *Proceedings of the 22nd ACM SIGKDD International Conference on Knowledge Discovery and Data Mining* (pp. 1135–1144).

Rigaki, M., & García, S. (2023). A survey of privacy attacks in machine learning. *ACM Computing Surveys, 56*(4), Article 101, 1–34.

Sabour, S., Frosst, N., & Hinton, G. E. (2017). Dynamic routing between capsules. In *Advances in Neural Information Processing Systems 30, NIPS 2017* (pp. 3859–3869).

Sandvig, C., Hamilton, K., Karahalios, K., & Langbort, C. (2014). Auditing algorithms: Research methods for detecting discrimination on Internet platforms. In *64th Annual Meeting of the International Communication Association* Seattle, WA, USA, May 22, 2014.

Schwartz, E. M., Bradlow, E. T., & Fader, P. S. (2017). Customer acquisition via display advertising using multi-armed bandit experiments. *Marketing Science, 36*(4), 500–522.

Shneiderman, B. (2020). Human-centered artificial intelligence: Reliable, safe & trustworthy. *International Journal of Human-Computer Interaction, 36*, 495–504.

Shneiderman, B. (2022). *Human-centered AI*. Oxford University Press.

Simonyan, K., Vedaldi, A., & Zisserman, A. (2013). Deep inside convolutional networks: Visualising image classification models and saliency maps. arXiv:1312.6034.

Song, L., Shokri, R., & Mittal, P. (2019). Privacy risks of securing machine learning models against adversarial examples. In *Proceedings of the 2019 ACM SIGSAC Conference on Computer and Communications Security*.

Sutton, R. S., & Barto, A. G. (2018). *Reinforcement learning: An introduction* (2nd ed.). The MIT Press.

Tang, C., & Guo, L. (2015). Digging for gold with a simple tool: Validating text mining in studying electronic word-of-mouth (eWOM) communication. *Marketing Letters, 26*, 67–80.

Thieme, R. J., Song, M., & Calantone, R. J. (2000). Artificial neural network decision support systems for new product development project selection. *Journal of Marketing Research, 37*(4), 499–507.

Tirunillai, S., & Tellis, G. J. (2014). Mining marketing meaning from online chatter: Strategic brand analysis of big data using latent Dirichlet allocation. *Journal of Marketing Research, 51*(4), 463–479.

Vagia, M., Transeth, A. A., & Fjerdingen, S. A. (2016). A literature review on the levels of automation during the years. What are the different taxonomies that have been proposed? *Applied Ergonomics, 53*(Pt A), 190–202.

Verma, S., & Rubin, J. S. (2018). Fairness definitions explained. In *2018 IEEE/ACM International Workshop on Software Fairness (FairWare)* (pp. 1–7).

Wahde, M., & Virgolin, M. (2023). DAISY: An implementation of five core principles for transparent and accountable conversational AI. *International Journal of Human-Computer Interaction, 39*(9), 1856–1873.

Wedel, M., & Kannan, P. (2016). Marketing analytics for data-rich environments. *Journal of Marketing, 80*, 121–197.

Wu, T., Li, X., Song, X., Sun, W., Dong, L., & Li, B. (2017). Interpretable R-CNN. arXiv:1711.05226.

Wu, X., Xiao, L., Sun, Y., Zhang, J., Ma, T., & He, L. (2022). A survey of human-in-the-loop for machine learning. *Future Generation Computer Systems, 135*, 364–381.

Yang, Y., Zhang, K., & Kannan, P. K. (2022). Identifying market structure: A deep network representation learning of social engagement. *Journal of Marketing, 86*(4), 37–56.

Zhang, H., Rao, H., & Feng, J. (2018a). Product innovation based on online review data mining: A case study of Huawei phones. *Electronic Commerce Research, 18*(1), 3–22.

Zhang, Q., Wu, Y. N., & Zhu, S. C. (2018). Interpretable convolutional neural networks. In *2018 IEEE/CVF Conference on Computer Vision and Pattern Recognition*, Salt Lake City, UT, USA, 2018 (pp. 8827–8836).

Zhang, Q., & Zhu, S. C. (2018). Visual interpretability for deep learning: A survey. *Frontiers of Information Technology & Electronic Engineering, 19*, 27–39.

Zhao, H., & Gordon, G. J. (2022). Inherent tradeoffs in learning fair representations. *Journal of Machine Learning Research, 23*(57), 1–26.

Chapter 11
Explainable AI (XAI)

Abstract The new generation of AI technology should enable creation of explainable systems that users can understand. Although the behaviour and thus the output of AI systems might be affected by various factors, such as algorithms, architecture, training, and data, the ultimate goal is to guarantee a transparent and human-centred approach. In this respect, the characteristics as emerging hereby to be crucial in chatbot efficiency and agency should be applied to lifting AI capacity. The present chapter further discusses the continuous improvement of explainable AI (XAI) and the possibility of enhancing software testing approaches. It is important to manage machine behaviour so that human–computer interaction (HCI) design is delivered through informed human-centred solutions. The distinctive constellation of cognitive, emotional, and social aspects suggested by the current work is a prerequisite for providing the desired human–AI interaction. Moreover, offering the right unique selling points (USPs) will facilitate the design of experience bringing customers to a journey beyond the traditional market space in extraordinary life activities.

11.1 XAI Goals

Although AI agents can perform various tasks at high speed and with super intelligence, this does not necessarily mean that they are efficient, functional, and useful, and that they provide satisfactory performance, which was reported by our respondents evaluating the experience they have with chatbots currently available on the market. Furthermore, with the rise of AI applications, we witness a continuous advancement in development of systems that are autonomous in perception, reasoning, decision making and action. The machines, however, may not be able to explain the decisions and actions they take to stakeholders (human experts and end users). For humans may be a challenge to govern AI, and in the near future, to properly deal with AI governance. Therefore, it is more than ever needed to understand how computational agents perceive, decide, and act in their own, real time in the real world.

© The Author(s), under exclusive license to Springer Nature Switzerland AG 2024 187
S. Bialkova, *The Rise of AI User Applications*,
https://doi.org/10.1007/978-3-031-56471-0_11

Having deep insights into how AI systems work, and in particular, understanding the performance of human-centred explainable AI (HCXAI), is crucial in determining the benefits, costs and trade-offs of these systems. Despite the broad terminology used among the scientific community, the interpretability and explainability of AI are the most commonly employed terms. To provide oversights of the potential, as well as the downstream consequences born by the ubiquitous use of AI in society, is a key task of scholars. The current book aimed at advising such an overview blending expertise from various domains, from AI, UX, computer and cognitive sciences, psychology and consumer behaviour, to marketing. To disentangle complex phenomena, especially the "black box" in AI behaviour when introduced in everyday context applications, we offer a multidisciplinary perspective.

At the infancy of technology, some forms of logical interference and human-like symbolism generated intervention steps as a basis for explanation. However, these often have been found to be incapable of facing complexity of real-life scenarios. The implementation of internal representations (such as support vector machines, random forests, probabilistic models, and neural networks) marked a new era in AI development, elevating the system efficiency, but at the same time descaling opacity and explainability.

Therefore, the core goals of explainable AI (XAI) are to understand and appropriately manage the AI generation and performance (see Table 11.1 for a classification of XAI with respect to deep learning, DL).

The ability of a computer to explain itself in terms of how a human can understand was hypothesised to reflect the understanding of human intent and mental state and is a prerequisite for effective dialogue (Li & Hilliges, 2021). Researchers further noted that a lack of human scrutiny may cause failures in usability, reliability, safety,

Table 11.1 XAI algorithms classification in deep learning (with some examples of applications)

Deep learning processing	Deep network representations	Producing systems	Hybrid transparent and black box
Linear proxy models—LIME	Role of layers—SVM	Attention networks—SAN, COCO	Neural-symbolic systems—CRILP, SHRUTI, CoFrNet
Decision trees—CRED, RxREN	Role of individual units—CNN	Representation disentanglement—InfoGAN	Knowledge base, KB-enhanced systems—HeLiS, HorusAI, KBANN
Automatic rule extraction—deepRED, FERNN	Representation vector—CAV	Explanation generation—visual and textual, MCB	Deep formulation—DKFs, DVBFs, DkNN
Salience mapping—CAM, deepLift, LRP			Relational reasoning—sort-of-CLEVER
			Case base reasoning—SYRUS, PERSUADER

fairness, and other AI challenges (Liao & Varshney, 2021). Designing explainable AI that provides understanding of how the system functions was recognised as a bottleneck guiding user trust and adoption of AI.

Stakeholders (human experts and end users) need to know the rationales behind the system reasoning and decision making. Concerning the impact of AI actions, end users would like to well understand how the system behaves, its strengths and weaknesses, and how to possibly preclude pitfalls. The same holds for experts interested in system design, implementation, and improvement. They would like to know the mechanisms behind decision, action, and control, and thus to appropriately navigate future system development. Not surprisingly, several academic scholars as well as key market players have invested in XAI approaches (for reviews, see Dodge et al., 2021; Gunning et al., 2021; Hu et al., 2021; Ribeiro et al., 2016).

Data analytics and autonomy were mentioned by experts as the most intriguing problems XAI faces. We have already paid notable attention to data management (Chap. 10, Bialkova, 2024f) and autonomy (Chap. 9, Bialkova, 2024e). Hereby, the idea is to provide a summary of the core properties and goals of XAI and an improved explainability toolbox, aiming at the very needed holistic understanding.

Explainability, interpretability, and transparency are the most frequently mentioned as key AI goals, as emerging from the literature audit. We elaborate on these in detail below and provide a summary in Table 11.2.

Explainability reflects the ability of AI to offer explainable models (1) with high accuracy and performance; (2) by enabling humans to understand, to trust, and to (3) appropriately manage the AI. Explicitly explaining decisions to humans answering the questions of what, why, and how happened (Arrieta et al., 2020; Miller, 2019) may facilitate interpretation. Although often the terms explainability and interpretability are used as equal and interchangeable, some authors make distinction assigning respectively passive vs. dynamic model characteristics to the above terms. While explainability is associated with the action taken by the model/system to explain its performance, interpretability reflects passive features of making sense to humans (Arrieta et al., 2020). It was argued that a high level of perceived explainability has a strong impact on trust and the perceived usefulness of the system (Hamm et al., 2023). To improve explicability, however, a design reconsideration of the intelligent system is invited (Herm et al., 2022).

Interpretability reflects the ability to explain or provide meaning in understandable terms to a human (Doshi-Velez & Kim, 2018; Guidotti et al., 2018). One of the core goals is to secure more useful information from the model (Lipton, 2018). Interpretability helps to detect, and consequently, correct from bias in the training dataset (Arrieta et al., 2020). Various methods have been identified with respect to the type of interpretable explanator, i.e., decision tree, decision rules, feature importance, saliency mask, sensitivity analysis, partial dependence plot, prototype selection, and activation maximisation (Guidotti et al., 2018). Furthermore, understandable models have also been named transparent (Lipton, 2018).

Transparency: We define this term hereby as follows: A human should "see through" the AI decision and action. Moreover, human should be in continuous and direct control of AI performance. Some of the transparency objectives encompass

Table 11.2 XAI core principles

XAI goals	Definition	Objectives	Relevant references (XAI)
Explainability	Ability to offer explainable models with high accuracy and performance. Enabling humans to understand, trust and to appropriately manage AI	• Which is the best way to provide explanation?	Arrieta et al. (2020) Angelov et al. (2021) Gunning et al. (2021)
Interpretability	Ability to explain or to provide the meaning in understandable terms to a human	• How useful is the information extracted from the model? • Which are the problems requiring interpretation?	Arrieta et al. (2020) Doshi-Velez and Kim (2018) Fiok et al. (2021) Gilpin et al. (2018) Guidotti et al. (2018) Lipton (2018) Montavon et al. (2018)
Transparency	Human should "see through" the AI decision and action	• Does AI produce a unique solution? • Does the algorithm converge? • What each parameter represents? • How complex/simple is the model?	Arrieta et al. (2020) Angelov et al. (2021) Gilpin et al. (2018) Lipton (2018)
Understandability	Functional understanding of the model, and what it predicts	• What the model has learnt?	Montavon et al. (2018)

understanding of the algorithms, as well as what each parameter represents (Lipton, 2018). The author further noted the model complexity as possible way to estimate transparency. The existence of simulatable models, decomposable models and algorithmically transparent models was argued. Therefore, transparency has different degrees depending on the level of model interpretability. Although transparency was recognised as a key feature of explainable models, in reality, ML models may lack sufficient transparency (for an overview, see Arrieta et al., 2020; Fig. 6). Therefore, earlier work noted the need for high system transparency, allowing understanding of decisions to be made.

Understandability reflects functional understanding of the model, and what it predicts, without necessity to explain the internal structure of the model or algorithmic functioning and data processing (Montavon et al., 2018). The authors focused on interpreting the outputs of a DNN and explaining individual predictions.

HUMAN Performance

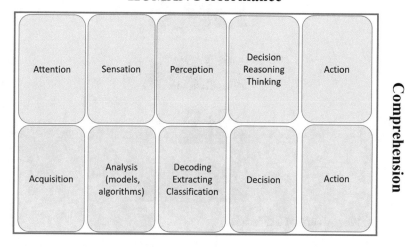

Fig. 11.1 Explainability matrix

We advise the core XAI objectives to be addressed at each stage of the AI performance from acquisition, analysis, decoding, and decision to action. The performance flow was described in detail in Chap. 8, Bialkova, 2024d. The explainability matrix offers an illustration of the performance flow (see Fig. 11.1).

In line with earlier work, we have to also note the three aspects of XAI approaches, namely the training process, model representation, and explainable interface (Gunning et al., 2021). Model representations encompassed three techniques, i.e., interpretable models (aiming at developing machine learning, ML techniques that provide inherent explanations that are easy to understand), deep explanations (encompassing deep learning and hybrid deep learning in addition to prediction), and model induction techniques (generating explanations from less transparent, black box models). The explanation interface is supposed to connect the user to the model and most importantly to offer understanding and interaction with the system. We suggest one extra aspect of XAI, i.e., to carefully consider the datasets employed. As seen in Chap. 10, Bialkova, 2024f, working with the right data is crucial for model efficiency and proper AI functioning. Figure 11.2 illustrates the core elements of XAI architecture.

Although the call to take into account user knowledge, tasks, and concepts of operation has been acknowledged, it seems that there is a lack of properly communicating of these. Therefore, there is urgent need to involve different stakeholders to appropriately manage communication and information flow. Currently, we suggest that developers, users and other stakeholders, i.e., businesses, policymakers, and regulators communicate during the process rather than after the AI system is launched into

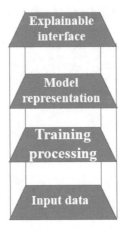

Fig. 11.2 Elements of XAI architecture

the market. Only such interactions may appropriately address the need to better understand and manage AI. In this respect, it is important to point out that technical, UX, managerial, and policy aspects should be taken into account. In Chap. 9, Bialkova, 2024e (e.g., see Fig. 9.2), we presented potential challenges and how these could be addressed. Therefore, the current work contributes to better understand of how AI systems function and to advance science in disentangling obstacles XAI faces.

Furthermore, we present hereby, a holistic framework encompassing all the elements that XAI should possess to be successful and to distinguish itself with explanation effectiveness. The technical measures are developed based on a literature audit (see Table 11.3), and the experience measures (see Table 11.4) are based on the empirical work performed in our laboratory and discussed in detail in Part II of the current book.

Table 11.3 Measures to assess explanation effectiveness: Technical aspects

Functionality measures	Learning performance measure	Explanation effectiveness measure
Content (rationales, cause-effect consequence) Speed of generating/ comprehend explanation Modality (visual, auditory, tactile etc.) Query/exploration types (natural languages; multiple choice) User–AI interaction	Prediction accuracy of the model in its given domain to accomplish a task Ability to detect and correct for bias (datasets and algorithms)	Explanation satisfaction Explanation goodness Model understanding Trust assessment User–AI task performance

Table 11.4 Measures to access explanation effectiveness: Experience aspects

Utilitarian	Hedonic	Output
Accuracy	Comprehension	Attitudes
Correctness	Enjoyment	Satisfaction
Credibility	Interactivity	Trust
Ease of use		Use
Functionality		Recommendation
Informativeness		
Precision		
Quality		
Skilfulness		

The approach we suggest provides quantitative tools for assessing the design of AI systems at different stages, from idea, prototyping, to being ready for launch to the market.

Although advanced machine learning (ML) and deep learning (DL) algorithms have outperformed humans in various tasks and applications, their implication in real-life situations is precluded due to their poor interpretability and explainability. Put differently, how the formal objectives of ML/DL algorithms match the costs of their deployment (Lipton, 2018) alter the demand for interpretability and explainability. In any case, the explainability is a function of XAI properties.

11.2   XAI Properties

Based on the literature audit, we present in detail the core properties emerging to be crucial for XAI. Table 11.5 provides the taxonomy of XAI properties. Figure 11.3 offers an illustration of responsible XAI. The fundaments of XAI are explainability, interpretability and understandability (as discussed in the previous section). Transparency is the bottleneck assuring that XAI goals are met through well-functioning properties (as discussed in details below).

Accountability including auditability, minimisation and reporting of negative impact, trade-offs, and redress (EU AI HLEG, 2019) was addressed by few works (Arrieta et al., 2020; Gilpin et al., 2018; Yazdanpanah et al., 2023).

Accuracy reflects the extent to which the model accurately predicts unseen instances (Guidotti et al., 2018), and it is measured by the accuracy score. Accuracy score is determined by the number of correct answers divided by the total number of questions (Huysmans et al., 2011). Speed and confidence in providing answers are closely related to accuracy.

Fidelity provides a measure of the ability of an interpretable model to accurately imitate the behaviour of a black box predictor, on the test dataset (Guidotti et al., 2018). Fidelity is also measured with an accuracy score, but with respect to the prediction of the black box. It reflects the percentage of matches over the size of the dataset.

Table 11.5 Taxonomy of XAI properties (in alphabetical order)

XAI property	Definition	Queries	Relevant references (XAI)
Accuracy	Extent to which the model accurately predicts unseen instances. It is measured by the accuracy score. The percentage of matches over the size of the test dataset	• To which extent the model accurately predicts unseen instances?	Arnold et al. (2019) Gilpin et al. (2018) Guidotti et al. (2018) Huysmans et al. (2011) Zhao and Gordon (2022)
Accountability	Including auditability, minimisation and reporting of negative impact, trade-offs, and redress	• Does the system assure auditability? • Is it possible to assess for risks and AI impact? • Are there mechanisms to detect potential trade-offs? • How to possibly redress in case of any harm or adverse occurrence?	Arrieta et al. (2020) Gilpin et al. (2018) EU AI HLEG (2019) Yazdanpanah et al. (2023)
Causality	Controlled changes in the input due to a perturbation affect in the model behaviour; will occur in the real system	• Does the explanation rule(s) provide causal or logical connections?	Doshi-Velez and Kim (2018) Goudet et al. (2018) Guidotti et al. (2018)
Compliance	Functioning in line with all applicable laws and regulations	• Does the model comply with regulations/legislation in force?	Arrieta et al. (2020) EU AI HLEG (2019)
Comprehensibility	Ability of a learning algorithm to represent its learned knowledge in a human understandable fashion	• When a model or explanation is comprehensible? • Which data record is more comprehensive?	Arrieta et al. (2020) Guidotti et al. (2018)
Fidelity	Reflects the capability of interpretable model in mimicking the behaviour of a black box	• To which extent the model is able to accurately imitate a black box predictor?	Guidotti et al. (2018)

(continued)

Table 11.5 (continued)

XAI property	Definition	Queries	Relevant references (XAI)
Fairness	Known as the accuracy parity. Fairness presents model capacity to reach explainability without favouritism/discrimination	• What is the model capacity to reach explainability without favouritism/discrimination?	Arnold et al. (2019) Arrieta et al. (2020) Corbett-Davies et al. (2017) Hardt et al. (2016) Heidari et al. (2018) Kim et al. (2018) Liao and Varshney (2021) Lipton (2018) Sharma et al. (2020) Zhao and Gordon (2022)
Generalisability	Implementation of portable models that do not require special training regimes or restrictions	• Could a purely reverse engineering procedure be followed? • Could the model/approach be used to open another black box?	Guidotti et al. (2018)
Interactivity	Ability of a model to be interactive with the user	• To what extent the model could interact with the user?	Arrieta et al. (2020) Liao and Varshney (2021) Neerincx et al. (2018)
Informativeness	Extracting information about the inner relations of a model Model providing knowledge via outputs to human decision-makers	• Does the model provide information able to relate the user's decision to the solution given? • Is there understanding/knowledge what the model does?	Arrieta et al. (2020) Lipton (2018)

(continued)

Table 11.5 (continued)

XAI property	Definition	Queries	Relevant references (XAI)
Privacy	Protecting sensitive information in the data	• Is sensitive information/data protected?	Arrieta et al. (2020) Doshi-Velez and Kim (2018) Guidotti et al. (2018) Liao and Varshney (2021)
Reliability/ robustness	Ability to maintain certain levels of performance independently from small variations of the parameters or of the input data. Assuring that algorithms reach certain levels of performance in the face of parameter or input variation	• Is the mode able to perform irrespective of variation in the dataset/parameters?	Doshi-Velez and Kim (2018) Guidotti et al. (2018) Sharma et al. (2020) Shneiderman (2020, 2022)

(continued)

Table 11.5 (continued)

XAI property	Definition	Queries	Relevant references (XAI)
Safety & Security	System being protected from danger; safeguarding against potential risks	• Have you set security/safety standards? • Are there security constraints? • To what extent the system is robust against adversarial attacks? • Could the system detect attacks? • What are the defending mechanisms?	Arnold et al. (2019) Arrieta et al. (2020) EU AI HLEG (2019) Liao and Varshney (2021) Shneiderman (2022)
Trustworthiness	Have the confidence of human users that a model will perform well	• Do users trust the system? • Do user trust the decision? • How confident they are in using it?	Arnold et al. (2019) Doshi-Velez and Kim (2018) EU AI HLEG (2019) Gilpin et al. (2018) Liao and Varshney (2021) Lipton (2018) Mehrotra et al. (2023) Shneiderman (2022) Yazdanpanah et al. (2023)

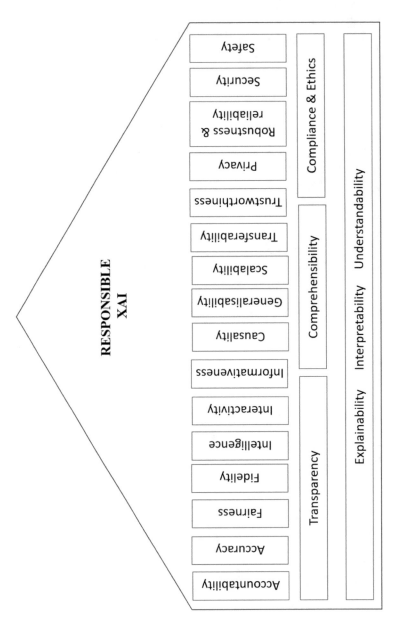

Fig. 11.3 House of responsible XAI

Fairness presents model capacity to reach explainability without favouritism/ discrimination. We have discussed in detail algorithmic fairness in Chap. 10, Bialkova, 2024f. Hereby, we point out how important fairness is in terms of XAI. Not surprisingly then, fairness was addressed by majority of the papers investigating XAI behaviour (Arnold et al., 2019; Arrieta et al., 2020; Corbett-Davies et al., 2017; Hardt et al., 2016; Heidari et al., 2018; Kim et al., 2018; Liao & Varshney, 2021; Lipton, 2018; Zhao & Gordon, 2022).

Causality reflects controlled changes in the input due to a perturbation affect in the model behaviour (Guidotti et al., 2018).

Generalisability is associated with the implementation of portable models that do not require special training regimes or restrictions (Guidotti et al., 2018). General- isability provides transfer of the model through various application scenarios and the use of the same model with different data. Thus, transferability is closely related to generalisability. Similarly, scalability opens opportunity to scale up of huge amount of input data with large input spaces (Guidotti et al., 2018).

Interactivity reflecting the ability of a model to be interactive with the user was addressed by several works in the XAI context (Arrieta et al., 2020; Liao & Varshney, 2021; Neerincx et al., 2018). In Chap. 2, Bialkova, 2024a, we also widely discussed it and addressed it in the empirical part (see Chap. 5, Bialkova, 2024b). As reported by our respondents, interactivity is loading on quality and ease of use perception, which further mediate user attitudes and satisfaction. We could therefore argue that interactive XAI would be better understood by users and thus accepted.

Informativeness associated with extracting of information about the inner rela- tions of a model was also mentioned by few papers as a core XAI parameter (Arrieta et al., 2020; Lipton, 2018). Model providing knowledge via outputs to human decision-makers turns to be crucial in elevating its comprehensibility. Informative- ness was addressed in detail in Chap. 2 (Theory), Bialkova, 2024a. We also tested empirically the impact it has on chatbot functionality, quality and ease of use percep- tion (see Chap. 7, Bialkova, 2024c). Our results clearly demonstrate the importance that AI system is informative, and this resonates with the way users perceive the agent performance.

Several researchers have noted that a lack of human-like behaviour in AI may cause failures not only in usability, but also in various parameters expected to char- acterise AI behaviour, such as reliability, safety, and fairness. Reliable, safe, and trustworthy AI were noted to be key tools for expanding human performance, while supporting human self-efficacy, mastery, and creativity (Shneiderman, 2022).

Reliability and robustness reflect the ability to maintain certain levels of perfor- mance independently from small variations of the parameters or of the input data (Guidotti et al., 2018). Reliable XAI should assure that algorithms reach certain levels of performance in the face of parameter or input variation (Doshi-Velez & Kim, 2018).

Safety and security of XAI were mentioned by several papers (Arrieta et al., 2020; Liao & Varshney, 2021; Shneiderman, 2022). System being protected from danger is a must (Arnold et al., 2019) and needs to safeguard itself against potential risks (EU AI HLEG, 2019). A secure system should have mechanisms to detect and defend against attacks such as adversarial. Data security and privacy are also very important, as we already discussed in detail in Chap. 10, Bialkova, 2024f.

Privacy of XAI reflects the protection of sensitive information, e.g., in the data, algorithms. Privacy was addressed by several XAI papers, in both technical (Arrieta et al., 2020; Doshi-Velez & Kim, 2018; Guidotti et al., 2018; Liao & Varshney, 2021), as well as ethical aspects (EU AI HLEG, 2019).

In order that a system works in a safe, secure and robust manner it should comply with rules.

Compliance is associated with functioning in line with all applicable laws and regulations (EU AI HLEG, 2019).

Trustworthiness reflects the confidence in humans or interacting parties (for a detailed overview on trust, see Chapter 2, Bialkova, 2024a. In the context of XAI, it is associated with the confidence human users have (e.g., Arrieta et al., 2020; Mehrotra et al., 2023) in the system/algorithm (Arnold et al., 2019) that a model will perform well (Lipton, 2018). Trust may be subjective and be associated with user understanding of the model. It may further arise because of well-designed independent oversight structures (Shneiderman, 2022) and is compulsory for autonomous agents (Yazdanpanah et al., 2023). It was argued that trustworthy AI should be lawful, ethical, and robust (EU AI HLEG, 2019).

Users may trust the system when they comprehend it well.

Comprehensibility reflects the ability of a learning algorithm to represent its learned knowledge in a human understandable fashion (Arrieta et al., 2020; Guidotti et al., 2018). One may, however, argue that this property is closely related to core XAI principles, i.e., explainability, interpretability, transparency, understandability. In fact, all of the properties discussed in the current section need to resonate with the core XAI goals should AI system be recognised as explainable and responsible (see Fig. 10.3).

Table 11.5 provides a summary of core XAI properties, including relevant queries, i.e., questions that need to be addressed concerning responsible XAI functioning.

The above parameters desirable for XAI nicely cohere with the core parameters emerging to be crucial in chatbot efficiency, as reported in Chaps. 5 and 7 hereby (Bialkova, 2024b, 2024c). Although desirable, this does not necessarily mean that these criteria are achieved. To test whether AI is explainable, we suggest an improved XAI toolbox. Table 11.6 provides the key tools to be implemented in measuring the degree of explainability, in relation to understanding, selection criteria, evaluation, and impact of XAI systems under consideration.

As part of the goals of the current book, we further suggest a toolkit that can help experts to measure whether XAI meets its performance objectives (see Table 11.7). Such must have features we believe are the key for answering challenging issues XAI faces today.

Table 11.6 Toolbox for assessing explainability

SELECTION criteria
- Why this specific system was employed in the particular task/context area?
- Is the AI system designed with interpretability in mind from the start?
- Does the system offer the desired understanding?
- Can you modify the system model/architecture over time?

UNDERSTANDING
- What the system model/architecture is?
- Is there understanding of the algorithms in training and testing stage?
- Does the system assure understanding of choice made and consequent outcomes?
- To what extent the decisions made by the AI system can be understood?
- To what extent the outcome generated by the AI system can be understood?

IMPACT
- To what degree the system decisions impact the end-user performance?
- To what degree do the system decisions affect the organisation's decision-making processes?
- Does the system implementation create value for the organisation/employees/the end user?

EVALUATION
- Are there simpler models that may provide better solutions for the problem in question?
- To what extent training and testing data can be analysed?
- Could the system interpretability be assessed continuously along the performance flow, i.e.,
  - at training
  - development
  - after decision, and
  - action execution?

Table 11.7 Toolkit for ensuring that XAI functions properly

Core guidelines	Key questions to answer
Human in the loop	• What is the human/user demand?
Contextual factors	• For what purpose/task the model is build? • What problem needs to be solved?
Techniques selected	• Is the model suitable for the task? • Does it serve the decision path? • What explanator technique is required? • What data are needed?

11.3 Governing AI Versus AI Governance

With the advance of AI and its extended application in everyday contexts, the limitations and risks in well-managed control and decision making are stronger pronounced. Explainable AI methods are very much needed to provide a feasible interpretation of what is happening in the so-called black box, as well as governing of AI is urgently required. Not surprisingly then, experts from various domains (i.e., UX developers, data science teams, human operators of the system, and regulatory bodies) were involved in the development of meaningful XAI based on user-centric design approaches.

To explain AI behaviour in various environments or specific contexts, it is important to understand what are the underlying mechanisms, functions of the AI system and causes of particular behaviour, so that they trigger the observed exhibition. AI behaviour is acknowledged to reflect the way in which environmental features are perceived, including the resolution and accuracy of object detection and systems classification. Blending various approaches hereby, we open avenues to answer broad questions such as: (1) how particular algorithms behave in specific environmental contexts, and (2) whether and how human interactions with these algorithms/AI systems will alter everyday life and societal impact.

Understanding AI and properly governing its performance requires us to answer several questions, as outlined in Table 11.8.

As already discussed in Chap. 9, Bialkova, 2024e, autonomy and control are crucial in AI performance. Previous work has largely explored and assigned different levels of control. For example, some of the earliest models suggested 5 levels of control, i.e., none, decision support, consensual AI, monitored AI, and full automation (Endsley & Kiris, 1995). On the basis of further research, the authors argued ten levels of control, encompassing manual control, action support, batch processing, shared control, decision support, blended decision making, rigid systems, automated decision making, supervisory control and full automation (Endsley & Kaber, 1999).

Furthermore, end users should be given the opportunity to reshape AI design. Some customers already try to anticipate or reverse the decision rules engineered by corporate AI experts. Therefore, we argue that keeping "humans in the loop" is a guarantee for successful human–AI interactions that adequately meet user demands, as well as provides opportunities for good governance of the system. See Table 11.9, for a summary of core taxonomies with respect to autonomy and control.

From a more contemporary view, incorporating regulatory mechanisms is suggested by the EU AI Act (2023) and the US NSTC report (2019). The US NSTC document proposes a three-component division between human and AI system roles,

Table 11.8 Toolbox on AI performance guidelines

1. Who is the end user/stakeholder?
2. What is the purpose/objectives of the AI employment?
3. Which tasks/activities will be performed and how?
4. What are the important factors to consider when designing (simpler) tasks?
5. What method-related factors are explored?
6. What kind of decision (data) are affected?
7. What the stakeholder affected by the AI decision and performance should know about the system functioning?
8. How to best explain the system architecture and functioning?
9. How an AI system works, making it possible to identify and correct errors?
10. How the system adapts, extends, or modifies if a change is necessary?
11. At what level the evaluation is performed?

Table 11.9 Level of control as suggested by various taxonomies

Riley (1989)	Endsley and Kiris (1995)	Draper (1995)	Endsley and Kaber (1999)	Parasuraman et al. (2000) (in line with Sheridan & Verplank, 1978)	Vagia et al. (2016)
1. None	1. None	1. Manual control	1. Manual control	1. No assistance	1. Manual control
2. Information fuser	2. Decision support	2. Manual control with Intelligent Assistance	2. Action support	2. Complete set of decision by computer	2. Decision proposal
3. Simple aid	3. Consensual AI	3. Shared Control	3. Batch processing	3. Narrow selection down to a few	3. Human decision select
4. Advisor	4. Monitored AI	4. Traded control	4. Shared control	4. Suggest one alternative	4. Computer decision select
5. Interactive advisor	5. Full automation	5. Supervisory control	5. Decision support	5. Execute suggestion if the human approves	5. Computer execution and human information
6. Adaptive advisor			6. Blended decision making	6. Allow human restricted time for veto before automatic execution	6. Computer execution and on call human information
7. Servant			7. Rigid system	7. Execute automatically	7. Computer execution and voluntarily information
8. Assistant			8. Automated decision making	8. Inform the human only if asked	8. Autonomous control
9. Associate			9. Supervisory control	9. Inform the human only if computer decides to	
10. Partner			10. Full automation	10. Act autonomously	
11. Supervisor					
12. Autonomous					

namely: AI performance (1) alongside the human; (2) complex monitoring functions; and (3) in lieu of a human (see Table 11.10 for details). The EU AI act (2023) did not explicitly define the responsibilities of AI. Such shortage is a warning call to adequately address the risks that AI systems may create (if their roles are not regulated on time). The EU Act suggests human oversights which is a step toward ensuring human involvement in high-risk AI applications.

The above regulatory documents are landmarks for the development of explainable AI systems. Improved interpretability and transparency, as part of these strategic document requirements, would definitely encourage development of more reliable systems and a better understanding of sophisticated AI models. Enabling auditing for regulatory requirements is another advantage of XAI implementation. For example, when the system works unexpectedly, XAI can be used to identify problems and help developers to ameliorate the system (performance).

Furthermore, regulations toward explainable systems would be beneficial for businesses, to apply the useful insights generated through AI performance, comprehending how these models achieve certain conclusions. Businesses may profit by faster adoption, taking advantage of the importance and speed of AI decisions. By incorporating life cycle governance, brands/organisations could adequately face the dynamics of accelerated AI system development and their integration into the market and everyday life. Appropriate governance may, however, go with some risks. Moreover, new roles, strategies, and responsibilities the business leaders may need to take up. See Table 11.11 for some tips in accelerating performance.

Employing pertinent AI applications and enhancing their capability, blended with efficient governance and control, definitely requires a collaboration between experts

Table 11.10 Level of AI responsibility and human oversight

EU AI Act, 2023	US NSTC report, 2019
(1) The output of the AI system needs to be validated by a human (2) Human intervention is ensured afterwards (3) Monitoring of the AI system ability to intervene in real time and deactivate	(1) AI performs functions alongside the human (2) AI performs functions when the human encounters high cognitive overload (3) AI performs functions in lieu of a human

Table 11.11 Tips how to accelerate performance

TIPS	TRICS
• Accelerate performance time • Engage with the audience • Focus on the user (not the bot/AI) • Interact naturally and accurately • Allow customers to deviate from the main flow • Increased content coverage • See and understand quickly • Easy manageable agents	• Generators, generative falls-back incorporation • Comprehensive visualisation • Use pre-build libraries, agents • Use module base flow

from various domains. In this respect, the current book hopefully provides the necessary knowledge, taxonomies, and advice needed to synchronise work between teams interested in developing XAI systems that function properly.

References

Angelov, P. P., Soares, E. A., Jiang, R., Arnold, N. I., & Atkinson, P. M. (2021). Explainable artificial intelligence: An analytical review. *WIley Interdisciplinary Reviews, 11*(5), e1424.

Arnold, M., Piorkowski, D., Reimer, D., Richards, J., Bellamy, R. K., Hind, M., Houde, S., Mehta, S., Mojsilović, A., Nair, R., Ramamurthy, K. N., & Olteanu, A. (2019). FactSheets: Increasing trust in AI services through supplier's declarations of conformity. *IBM Journal of Research and Development, 63*(4/5), paper 6, 1–13.

Arrieta, A. B., Díaz-Rodríguez, N., del Ser, J., Bennetot, A., et al. (2020). Explainable Artificial Intelligence (XAI): Concepts, taxonomies, opportunities and challenges toward responsible AI. *Information Fusion, 58*, 82–115.

Bialkova, S. (2024a). Audit of literature on chatbot applications. In *The rise of AI user applications: Chatbots integration foundations and trends.* (Chapter 2). Springer. https://doi.org/10.1007/978-3-031-56471-0_2

Bialkova, S. (2024b). Chatbot efficiency—Model testing. In *The rise of AI user applications: Chatbots integration foundations and trends.* (Chapter 5). Springer. https://doi.org/10.1007/978-3-031-56471-0_5

Bialkova, S. (2024c). Chatbot agency—Model testing. In *The rise of AI user applications: Chatbots integration foundations and trends.* (Chapter 7). Springer. https://doi.org/10.1007/978-3-031-56471-0_7

Bialkova, S. (2024d). AI connecting business and consumers. In *The rise of AI user applications: Chatbots integration foundations and trends.* (Chapter 8). Springer. https://doi.org/10.1007/978-3-031-56471-0_8

Bialkova, S. (2024e). AI transforming business and everyday life. In *The rise of AI user applications: Chatbots integration foundations and trends.* (Chapter 9). Springer. https://doi.org/10.1007/978-3-031-56471-0_9

Bialkova, S. (2024f). Data management. In *The rise of AI user applications: Chatbots integration foundations and trends.* (Chapter 10). Springer. https://doi.org/10.1007/978-3-031-56471-0_10

Corbett-Davies, S., Pierson, E., Feller, A., Goel, S., & Huq, A. Z. (2017). Algorithmic decision making and the cost of fairness. In *Proceedings of the 23rd ACM SIGKDD International Conference on Knowledge Discovery and Data Mining.*

Dodge, J., Anderson, A., Khanna, R., Irvine, J., Dikkala, R., Lam, K. H., Tabatabai, D., Ruangrotsakun, A., Shureih, Z., Kahng, M., & Fern, A. (2021). From "no clear winner" to an effective XAI process: An empirical journey. *Applied AI Letters, 2*(4), e36.

Doshi-Velez, F., & Kim, B. (2018). Considerations for evaluation and generalization in interpretable machine learning. In H. Escalante et al. (Eds.), *Explainable and interpretable models in computer vision and machine learning.* The Springer series on challenges in machine learning. Springer.

Draper, J. V. (1995). Teleoperators for advanced manufacturing: Applications and human factors challenges. *International Journal of Human Factors in Manufacturing, 5*, 53–85.

Endsley, M. R., & Kaber, D. B. (1999). Level of automation effects on performance, situation awareness and workload in a dynamic control task. *Ergonomics, 42*(3), 462–492.

Endsley, M. R., & Kiris, E. O. (1995). The out-of-the-loop performance problem and level of control in automation. *Human Factors, 37*(2), 381–439.

European Commission AI Act. (2023). AI Act | Shaping Europe's digital future (europa.eu). https://digital-strategy.ec.europa.eu/en/policies/regulatory-framework-ai. Accessed January 25, 2024.

European Commission—AI HLEG. (2019). Ethics guidelines for trustworthy AI, ethics guidelines for AI (europa.eu). https://www.europarl.europa.eu/cmsdata/196377/AI%20HLEG_Ethics%20Guidelines%20for%20Trustworthy%20AI.pdf. Accessed January 25, 2024.

Fiok, K., Farahani, F. V., Karwowski, W., & Ahram, T. (2021). Explainable artificial intelligence for education and training. *The Journal of Defense Modeling and Simulation, 19*(2), 133–144.

Gilpin, L. H., Bau, D., Yuan, B. Z., Specter, M. A., & Kagal, L. (2018). Explaining explanations: An overview of interpretability of machine learning. In *2018 IEEE 5th International Conference on Data Science and Advanced Analytics (DSAA)* (pp. 80–89).

Goudet, O., Kalainathan, D., Caillou, P., Guyon, I., Lopez-Paz, D., & Sebag, M. (2018). Learning functional causal models with generative neural networks. In H. Escalante et al. (Eds.), *Explainable and interpretable models in computer vision and machine learning*. The Springer series on challenges in machine learning. Springer.

Guidotti, R., Monreale, A., Ruggieri, S., Turini, F., Giannotti, F., & Pedreschi, D. (2018). A survey of methods for explaining black box models. *ACM Computing Surveys, 51*(5), Article 93.

Gunning, D., Vorm, E., Wang, J. Y., & Turek, M. (2021). DARPA's explainable AI (XAI) program: A retrospective. *Applied AI Letters, 2*(4), e61.

Hamm, P., Klesel, M., Coberger, P., & Wittmann, H. F. (2023). Explanation matters: An experimental study on explainable AI. *Electronic Markets, 33*, 1–21.

Hardt, M., Price, E., & Srebro, N. (2016). Equality of opportunity in supervised learning. In *Proceedings of Advances in Neural Information Processing Systems* (Vol. 29, paper 1654).

Heidari, H., Ferrari, C., Gummadi, K. P., & Krause, A. (2018). Fairness behind a veil of ignorance: A welfare analysis for automated decision making. In *Proceedings of Advances in Neural Information Processing Systems* (Vol. 31, paper 662).

Herm, L. V., Steinbach, T., Wanner, J., et al. (2022). A nascent design theory for explainable intelligent systems. *Electron Markets, 32*, 2185–2205.

Hu, B., Tunison, P., Vasu, B., Menon, N., Collins, R., & Hoogs, A. (2021). XAITK: The explainable AI toolkit. *Applied AI Letters, 2*(4), e40.

Huysmans, J., Dejaeger, K., Mues, C., Vanthienen, J., & Baesens, B. (2011). An empirical evaluation of the comprehensibility of decision table, tree and rule based predictive models. *Decision Support Systems, 51*, 141–154.

Kim, M., Reingold, O., & Rothblum, G. (2018). Fairness through computationally-bounded awareness. In *Proceedings of Advances in Neural Information Processing Systems* (Vol. 31, paper 2341, pp. 4842–4852).

Li, Y., & Hilliges, O. (2021). *Artificial intelligence for human computer interaction: A modern approach, book preface*. Springer.

Liao, Q. V., & Varshney, K. R. (2021). Human-centered explainable AI (XAI): From algorithms to user experiences. arXiv:abs/2110.10790.

Lipton, Z. C. (2018). The Mythos of Model Interpretability: In machine learning, the concept of interpretability is both important and slippery. *Queue, 16*(3), 31–57.

Mehrotra, S., Degachi, C., Vereschak, O., Jonker, C. M., & Tielman, M. L. (2023). *A systematic review on fostering appropriate trust in human-AI interaction*. ACM.

Miller, T. (2019). Explanation in artificial intelligence: Insights from the social sciences. *Artificial Intelligence, 267*, 1–38.

Montavon, G., Samek, W., & Müller, K. R. (2018). Methods for interpreting and understanding deep neural networks. *Digital Signal Processing, 73*, 1–15.

Neerincx, M. A., van der Waa, J., Kaptein, F., & van Diggelen, J. (2018). Using perceptual and cognitive explanations for enhanced human-agent team performance. In *Proceedings of International Conference on Engineering Psychology and Cognitive Ergonomics* (pp. 204–214). Springer.

Parasuraman, R., Sheridan, T. B., & Wickens, C. D. (2000). A model for types and levels of human interaction with automation. *IEEE Transactions on Systems, Man, and Cybernetics. Part A, Systems and Humans: A Publication of the IEEE Systems, Man, and Cybernetics Society, 30*(3), 286–297.

Ribeiro, M. T., Singh, S., & Guestrin, C. (2016). "Why should I trust you?": Explaining the predictions of any classifier. In *Proceedings of the 22nd ACM SIGKDD International Conference on Knowledge Discovery and Data Mining* (pp. 1135–1144).

Riley, V. A. (1989). A general model of mixed-initiative human-machine systems. *Proceedings of the Human Factors and Ergonomics Society Annual Meeting, 33*, 124–128.

Sharma, S., Henderson, J., & Ghosh, J. (2020). CERTIFAI: A common framework to provide explanations and analyse the fairness and robustness of black-box models. In *Proceedings of the AAAI/ACM Conference on AI, Ethics, and Society (AIES '20)* (pp. 166–172). Association for Computing Machinery.

Sheridan, T. B., & Verplank, W. L. (1978). *Human and computer control of undersea teleoperators.* Department of Mechanical Engineering, MIT.

Shneiderman. B. (2022). *Human-centered AI.* Oxford Academic.

Shneiderman, B. (2020). Human-centered artificial intelligence: Reliable, safe & trustworthy. *International Journal of Human-Computer Interaction, 36*, 495–504.

US NSTC report. (2019). The National Artificial Intelligence Research and Development Strategic Plan: 2019 update (nitrd.gov). https://www.nitrd.gov/pubs/National-AI-RD-Strategy-2019.pdf. Accessed January 20, 2024.

Vagia, M., Transeth, A. A., & Fjerdingen, S. A. (2016). A literature review on the levels of automation during the years. What are the different taxonomies that have been proposed? *Applied Ergonomics, 53*(Pt A), 190–202.

Yazdanpanah, V., Gerding, E. H., Stein, S., Jonker, C., et al. (2023). Reasoning about responsibility in autonomous systems: Challenges and opportunities. *AI & Society, 38*, 1453–1464.

Zhao, H., & Gordon, G. J. (2022). Inherent tradeoffs in learning fair representations. *Journal of Machine Learning Research, 23*(57), 1–26.

Chapter 12
Conclusions and Future Perspectives

The rise of artificial intelligence (AI) applications has inspired the scientific community to perform in-depth investigations and looking for explanations of the underlying mechanisms of AI behaviour. Becoming increasingly interested in the impact of AI systems may have on individuals and society, researchers from different disciplines pursue avenues for developing new, smarter, and superintelligent systems. Examining the state of the art, the current book provides an overview from the perspective of AI, UX, HCI, computer and cognitive sciences, psychology, consumer behaviour, and marketing in an attempt to provide the much-needed understanding of explainable AI (XAI).

The content of the book benefits AI explanations and AI explanation user studies, in the context of chatbots. It provides valuable advice on the factors determining the interaction between human users and AI. Such XAI could help developers to launch machine learning tools based on the type of human-centred interaction, opening new avenues for investigating and learning how to improve AI systems.

AI explanation-related topics as employed cross disciplines, a new framework, and the implementation of the new framework are suggested hereby. The book is important to readers in fields as enumerated above, i.e., from HCI to marketing. It will help not only AI developers, but it is hoped to be beneficial to various stakeholders (businesses, employees, and end users).

Although AI scientists can analyse and modify AI systems more easily in comparison to how investigation of any living system can be done, a note of caution should be made hereby. AI does not operate independently, but in the majority of cases, it co-exists with humans in complex hybrid environments. Thus, a multidisciplinary approach is invited to address the issues at stake. While computer and robotic scientists, commonly busy with exploring, designing and creating various AI systems are excellent mathematicians and engineers, they are not trained psychologists or behaviour scientists. A lacuna in their knowledge reflects the methodology in performing behavioural experiments, extracting insights from population-based statistics, deriving causal relationships from individuals' performance or assessing how collective behaviour observation impairs the transfer of psychology and social theories. In contrast, psychology and behavioural scientists are supposed to professionally apply the above, having the pertinent training and possessing relevant knowledge in behaviour methodology. However, they lack proficiency in system evaluation, and AI techniques to face particular mathematical and/or algorithmic problems arising when evaluating system underlying quality and architecture. Similarly, marketing and consumer studies of AI mainly take only an outside-in view. Usability and computer studies also focus on specific aspects determined by the nature of these disciplines.

Hereby, we explored the XAI from various perspectives and provided the much-needed understanding of the factors determining the efficiency of AI agency. Implementing these factors in the design of AI systems, we hope for designing not only engineering artefacts but also agents with particular behaviour patterns. By improving interpretability, i.e., XAI aiming at transparency, causality, privacy, fairness, trust, usability, and reliability (see Chap. 11), we expect to inspire relevant solutions.

The current book offers a cross-disciplinary approach, a profound audit and the very needed blending of theories across disciplines to understand the core mechanisms underlying human–AI interactions, as well as to enumerate the challenges faced by academic scholars and business practitioners. We have outlined key topics, crucial research questions, landmark practical cases, and academic studies, to offer understanding to the interdisciplinary nature of AI. We have provided a framework and a taxonomy organising the core concepts and theories addressing AI system behaviour. By presenting technical, UX, managerial, ethical, and legal challenges, we aim to inspire discussion and to provoke a move toward creating explainable AI systems.

Having sufficient capabilities to justify the term intelligence, AI systems are continuously revolutionising, enhancing their potential. A reasonable question therefore is: *how these capabilities will develop?*

As outlined, AI passes through mechanical, analytical to empathic capabilities, which are essential for recognising and understanding human emotions. Hereby, both cognitive and emotional aspects have emerged as fundamental in interacting with chatbots. Furthermore, social aspects seem to play a role in acknowledging AI systems as high quality and easy to use, adequately satisfying consumer demand. The question we address at the very beginning of the book is whether systems currently available at the market offer such quality. It is unclear whether the capabilities developed by AI are quality based and trustworthy. Moreover, although offering high speed and superintelligence, these systems may not necessarily be efficient, as reported by user evaluation. We have to note, therefore, several challenges emerged based on the literature audit, thus opening the floor for discussion and further exploration.

First, only a somewhat narrow focus has been placed by the research conducted thus far. Knowledge is dispersed across disciplines, calling for a joint effort of research from different domains to face the rising demand for explainable AI. The current book offers a multidisciplinary perspective and the initial steps toward such collaboration. We performed a profound literature audit across various disciplines and on this base propose taxonomies on core terms and theories applied with respect to AI and chatbot agency (see Chaps. 2 and 3).

Second, a thorough theoretical understanding of XAI is still lacking, which reflects the proposed AI architectures, AI behaviour as well as the user experience in real-life scenarios. High-precision laboratories experimental studies on factors that affect UX have provided useful insights thus far. However, in general, there is a deficit of knowledge and lack of work exploring the actual AI performance and user behaviour in realistic conditions and everyday contexts. These we addressed by asking consumer opinion after actual use of chatbots currently available on the market (for details, see Chaps. 5 and 7).

Third, there are various AI applications, popular algorithms and models for everyday scenarios, real-world deployment and implementation. However, there is a lack of systematic studies on real-life performance of AI systems. The knowledge scarcity of the actual AI impact on user experience in everyday scenarios invites further investigation. The current book addressed these gaps, by providing a close examination of consumer experience and evaluation after the actual use of AI chatbot agents, which are currently available on the market.

We propose the incorporation of applied experiments, randomised across conditions and samples, to enhance observational inference and strengthen the population-based descriptive statistics and methodologies. Often used as reliable measures in behavioural sciences, these should also play a central role in studying the machine behaviour, should one want to understand it. The outcomes of the current book, i.e., the empirical sections highlighted several aspects and core parameters for measuring human-centred AI, HCAI (see Chaps. 4 and 6). We further provide helpful guidelines to build appropriate research tools and protocols on how to explore AI performance and impact (see Chaps. 5 and 7).

In particular, functionality, emerging hereby as a core aspect of the way in which chatbot agency is perceived, has received significant attention in AI system development. We have to mention that functionality perception is critically shaped by the fit of AI behaviour to the environment and the appropriateness of agent performance for the task/action required. Focusing attention on how AI systems function may help to explain why some of these systems are rejected and declined over time, while others enjoy warm acceptance, and have opportunities for long life and expansion.

Successful functioning strongly correlates with how adequately the stakeholder demand is met. As reported in Chap. 5, functionality further reflects quality and ease of use perception. High-quality and easy to use systems are very likely to be adopted by end users, as well as to be transferred to new domains or contexts. Moreover, algorithm trading and AI system exchange became common practices between brand leaders and key players corporations, in order to speed up the profitability through the development and implementation of even more efficient AI. These dynamics are definitely driven by the success of the organisation, and its reputation and impact (see Chap. 8).

Fourth, how to build trustworthy AI is a crucial question addressed by the scientific community as well as regulatory bodies. The current book provides several suggestions for disentangling challenging issues related to elevating trust in AI systems (see Chap. 9). Moreover, future investigation is invited to address the development and evolution of AI itself. Experts from various domains should join efforts in "keeping humans in the loop", especially when monitoring how AI shapes (its) collective behaviour. There is still an open discussion on agents' autonomy (see Chap. 8) and whether AI algorithms should carry moral and ethical responsibility for their decisions and actions (see Chap. 9). These are vital questions concerning high and unacceptable risks by AI born scenarios.

Fifth, given the tendency to apply increasingly complex data, algorithms, and sophisticated machine learning methods, the mechanism underlying AI behaviour demands appropriate data management (as addressed in Chap. 10) and continued work on methodology interpretability and XAI (see Chap. 11).

There is an urgency to design a machine learning software which is fundamentally different from traditional software designed. While the traditional relies on programming, AI may need greater process of training. Researchers aim to build systems that can learn new things without requiring explicit programming. For example, artificial generative intelligence (AGI) and especially artificial super intelligence (ASI) have the ambitions of not only matching but also exceeding every aspect of human intelligence. This, however, opens avenues for further exploration given the challenges reflecting the full autonomy of AI systems. In Chap. 11, we have discussed in detail the need for governing AI before AI takes over and governs humans.

Sixth, currently, human stakeholders are ultimately responsible for any harm that AI deployment might generate. Given that AI is capable of managing a larger sociotechnical fabric, and thus amplifying its effects in an extremely short temporal window, in the near future, humans may be unable to control AI systems. Thus, it is time to seriously look and sharpen regulations. Although engineering AI behaviour is associated with what humans currently design and create, very soon, machines may be autonomous (for details, see Chap. 8) and take their own control (see Chap. 11). This is a warning call for increasing accuracy in terms of how AI architecture is designed, and how engineering choices are made. Factors such as the value of a learning rate, data acquisition, knowledge representations, training models, connecting agents, and cross-networking should be carefully inspected because they can predetermine the actual behaviour that algorithms may demonstrate (for details, see Chap. 10).

Seventh, it is important to continuously evaluate AI performance and its impact. Assessing how AI works and what its effect is on stakeholders (researchers, business, and end users) will be beneficial to improve the work done, to increase collaboration between teams engaged, to enhance customer experience and lifetime values. Assessment may also facilitate explainability and governance of AI. For example, assessing how algorithms and models work, could preclude pitfalls and help navigate their impact in the desired direction. Well-executed and timely performed AI system evaluations may capture risks, identify model gaps, face UX, and managerial needs. Increased accountability, facilitation, and speedup of go/no-go decisions are also expected through assessment of the end-to-end AI life cycle.

While the community is still in an exploratory mode regarding AI user applications, we hope the present book provides the necessary background to interested readers. We believe the current work will inspire researchers across disciplines to join efforts and to well collaborate on this very intriguing topic.

Thinking of XAI as a search for optimal design, we encourage you to start exploring. Enjoy the journey of discovery!

Dr Svetlana Bialkova

References

Bialkova, S. (2024a). Introduction to chatbot AI applications. In *The rise of AI user applications: Chatbots integration foundations and trends.* (Chapter 1). Springer. https://doi.org/10.1007/978-3-031-56471-0_1

Bialkova, S. (2024b). Audit of literature on chatbot applications. In *The rise of AI user applications: Chatbots integration foundations and trends.* (Chapter 2). Springer. https://doi.org/10.1007/978-3-031-56471-0_2

Bialkova, S. (2024c). Core theories applied in chatbot context. In *The rise of AI user applications: Chatbots integration foundations and trends.* (Chapter 3). Springer. https://doi.org/10.1007/978-3-031-56471-0_3

Bialkova, S. (2024d). Shaping chatbot efficiency-How to build better systems? In *The rise of AI user applications: Chatbots integration foundations and trends.* (Chapter 4). Springer. https://doi.org/10.1007/978-3-031-56471-0_4

Bialkova, S. (2024e). Chatbot efficiency—Model testing. In *The rise of AI user applications: Chatbots integration foundations and trends.* (Chapter 5). Springer. https://doi.org/10.1007/978-3-031-56471-0_5

Bialkova, S. (2024f). Anthropomorphism-What is crucial? In *The rise of AI user applications: Chatbots integration foundations and trends.* (Chapter 6). Springer. https://doi.org/10.1007/978-3-031-56471-0_6

Bialkova, S. (2024g). Chatbot agency—Model testing. In *The rise of AI user applications: Chatbots integration foundations and trends.* (Chapter 7). Springer. https://doi.org/10.1007/978-3-031-56471-0_7

Bialkova, S. (2024h). AI connecting business and consumers. In *The rise of AI user applications: Chatbots integration foundations and trends.* (Chapter 8). Springer. https://doi.org/10.1007/978-3-031-56471-0_8

Bialkova, S. (2024i). AI transforming business and everyday life. In *The rise of AI user applications: Chatbots integration foundations and trends.* (Chapter 9). Springer. https://doi.org/10.1007/978-3-031-56471-0_9

Bialkova, S. (2024j). Data management. In *The rise of AI user applications: Chatbots integration foundations and trends.* (Chapter 10). Springer. https://doi.org/10.1007/978-3-031-56471-0_10

Bialkova, S. (2024k). Explainable AI. In *The rise of AI user applications: Chatbots integration foundations and trends.* (Chapter 11). Springer. https://doi.org/10.1007/978-3-031-56471-0_11

Glossary

Acceptance adoption, and usage of a system (see also Technology Acceptance Model, TAM).

Accuracy The trueness and precision of the measurement method and result. Hereby, we define it as a precision of the system. It reflects the extent to which the model accurately predicts unseen instances and it is measured by the accuracy score.

Accuracy score Determined by the number of correct answers divided by the total number of questions. The percentage of matches over the size of the test dataset.

Accountability Including auditability, minimisation and reporting of negative impact, trade-offs and redress.

Adversary (evasive attacks) Evasion of deployed system at test time.

Algorithmic fairness Reflects *Statistical parity* (meaning that an equal proportion of defendants are detained in each race group); *Conditional statistical parity* (associated with controlling for a limited set of "legitimate" risk factors, an equal proportion of defendants are detained within each race group); *Predictive equality* means that the accuracy of decisions is equal across race groups, as measured by false positive rate.

Anthropomorphism From the Greek words anthropos (for man) and morphe (form/structure). It is associated with AI system having human-like behaviour, communication style, and interfaces.

Application Programming Interface (API) A set of rules that enable different applications to communicate with each other and exchange data and functionality easily and securely. Simplified software development and innovation by enabling applications to exchange data and functionality easily and securely.

Approximate matching of dynamic info (ADI) Classification technology based on similarities between two digital artifacts. It is used to find objects that resemble each other or to find objects that are contained in another object (see also Exact matching of dynamic info, EDI).

Artificial intelligence (AI) The intelligence of machines or software, as opposed to the intelligence of humans.

© The Editor(s) (if applicable) and The Author(s), under exclusive license to Springer Nature Switzerland AG 2024
S. Bialkova, *The Rise of AI User Applications*,
https://doi.org/10.1007/978-3-031-56471-0

AI agents Refer to both complex and simple algorithms used to make decisions.

AI chatbots Software applications used to conduct online chat conversations via text or text-to-speech. AI-based chatbots vary depending on the approaches employed, i.e., rule-based, ML-based, or hybrid AI.

AI governance Guardrails that ensure AI tools and systems are and remain safe and ethical.

AI system's life cycle Encompasses its development (including research, design, data provision, and limited trials), deployment (including implementation) and use phase.

AI personalisation Employing AI technologies such as machine learning and deep learning to create personalised experiences for users of a given product or service. AI personalisation is characterised with the ability of machine learning to ingest large amounts of data, analyse it and produce insights (see also personalisation).

AI user User of AI (tools) that offer speed up of processing (of information), enhanced performance and enriched experience.

AI powered user experience AI directly enhancing the user experience, equipping businesses with the tools to continually refine it through improved analytics

"Artificial" science Knowledge about artificial objects and phenomena.

Artificial Generative Intelligence (AGI) Have the ability to understand, learn, and perform any intellectual task that a human can do. It would be able to reason, have consciousness, and even possess emotional understanding.

Artificial Narrow Intelligence (ANI) Designed and trained to execute a specific task without possessing the general problem-solving abilities that a human has. It operates under a predefined set or context and does not possess consciousness, reasoning, or emotions.

Artificial Super Intelligence (ASI) Capable to enhance and refine human intelligence exponentially. It is the culmination of AI evolution, where machines might outthink, outlearn, and out-create humans.

Artificial neural networks (ANNs) Shortened to neural networks (NNs) or neural nets are a branch of machine learning models. ANN consists of nodes called artificial neurons connected by edges, modelling respectively the neurons and the synapses in a biological brain.

Attention-based networks Learn functions that provide a weighting over inputs or internal features to steer the information visible to other parts of a network.

Attitudes Beliefs about an object/person are evaluated (Expectancy value model), affecting the intention to behave and actual behaviour. Individual's feelings about the performed behaviour.

Attractiveness Associated with having a pleasant visual appearance. In the context of chatbots and AI systems, having an attractive voice and aesthetics have been also pointed out.

Automation Reflects the automatic operation and the process of making things automatic and is associated with the shift from manual to supervisory control. The human-computer interaction is characterised by different Levels of Automation, LOA.

Automatic rule extraction Approach for summarising decisions. It works on the neuron-level to extract rules to mimic the behaviour of individual unit.

Autonomy from the Greek word "autonomia"—which means independent and self-governing, where "auto" means self and "nomos" means law. In the context of engineering systems, it reflects their capability to make their own decisions about their actions while performing different tasks and this happens irrespective of external systems or supervision involvement.

Autonomous agents Computational systems that inhabit some complex dynamic environment, sense and act autonomously in this environment, and by doing so are capable to realise a set of goals/tasks for which they are designed.

Bayesian network A probabilistic graphical model that represents a set of variables and their conditional dependencies via a directed acyclic graph.

Benchmark Establishing metrics to quantify performance on standardised tasks. The act of running computer program(s), or other operations with the aim to assess the relative performance of an object, normally by enrolling a number of standard tests and trials against it.

Bias Inclination of prejudice towards or against a person, object, or position. A systematic error with respect to the ground truth, as opposed to a random error. Biases could have different causes and origins, e.g., algorithmic bias (appears as a result of the training process); human bias (replicating bias given the capacity of AI systems to generate decisions based on algorithms and models designed by humans); historically common bias (propagating stereotypes and problematic associations based on bias in original collective data).

Big data Refers to data sets that are too large or complex to be dealt with by traditional data-processing application software. Therefore, predictive analytics, user behaviour analytics, or other advanced data analytics methods are employed to extract value from big data.

Big Five factors of personality A taxonomy encompassing surgency, agreeableness, consciousness, emotional stability and intelligence as crucial personality traits (McCrae and Costa, 1987). According to Goldberg's (1990), the *Big Five* encompass neuroticism, extraversion, openness, agreeableness (vs. antagonism), and conscientiousness (vs. undirectedness).

Capsule networks Each layer is divided into many small groups of neurons called "capsules", i.e. a group of neurons whose activity vector represents the instantiation parameters of a specific type of entity such as an object or an object part (see also Neural network).

Computers as Social Actors (CASA) Assumes that users interact with computers applying social rules, although they are aware that computers are inanimate. Such behaviour is generated subconsciously as a natural response to social situations (see also Social Response Theory).

Causality controlled changes in the input due to a perturbation affect in the model behaviour.

Chatbot Software applications used to conduct online chat conversations via text or text-to-speech.

ChatGPT (Chat Generative Pre-trained Transformer) Chabot (designed by OpenAI organisation) based on a large language model. It aims at enabling users to refine and steer a conversation towards a desired length, format, style, level of detail, and language.

Competence Quality or state of being competent. It refers to having sufficient knowledge, judgment, skill, or strength for a particular duty or in a particular respect. Studied earliest in the context of Computer-Mediated Communication, logically it was investigated in the context of robot and chatbot applications.

Complexity The overall difficulty or effort required for a user to complete a task.

Compliance Functioning in line with all applicable laws and regulations.

Comprehensibility Ability of a learning algorithm to represent its learned knowledge in a human understandable fashion.

Computational social science A field emerging that leverages the capacity to collect and analyse data at a scale that may reveal patterns of individual and group behaviours.

Concept Activation Vectors (CAVs) A framework for interpretation of a neural nets representations by identifying and probing directions that align with human-interpretable concepts.

Confidence Trust that a model will act as intended when facing a given problem. Credibility that spans the hierarchy of representations. Output confidence reflects the reliability of the (model) decision and thus credibility.

Consumer Acceptance of Technology (CAT) CAT model postulates that attitudes, and thus adoption intentions depend on both, cognitive and affective components. A further extension of UTAUT (see also Unified Theory of Acceptance and Use of Technology).

Control People's perception of the ease or difficulty of performing the behaviour of interest. "WHO" human or system should perform "WHAT" task and "WHEN" is fundamental for assigning levels of control. To what extent the agent could be autonomous or controlled (see also Autonomy).

Conversion API (CAPI) Conversions application programming interface—a tool that allows advertisers to send web events from their servers directly to Facebook or Snap (see also API).

Conversational agent (CA) Natural language user interfaces that emulate human-to-human communication. Software agents that can engage in natural conversational interactions with humans, mimicking real people behaviour.

Convolutional Neural Network (CNN) A type of feed-forward neural network that is used to extract features from grid-like matrix datasets, such as images or videos. It learns feature engineering by itself via filters optimisation (see also Neural Network).

Credibility Reflects trustworthiness. Credibility of message, information and source are core aspects in user perception, and thus, adoption of technology. Credible AI systems are these assuring hierarchy of representations, trustworthy models, confidence in output and decision making.

Customer retention The ability of a company to keep its customers and prevent them from defecting to competitors.

Data mining The process of extracting and discovering patterns in large data sets involving methods at the intersection of machine learning, statistics, and database systems.

Deep learning (DL) Subset of machine learning methods based on artificial neural networks with representation learning. "Deep" reflects the use of multiple layers in the network, to progressively extract higher-level features from the raw input.

Decision tree A decision support hierarchical model that uses a tree-like model of decisions and their possible consequences.

Decision rule is any measurable function $d: R^p \rightarrow [0, 1]$, where $d(x)$ is interpreted as the probability that action $a1$ is taken for an individual with visible attributes x.

Decision support The use of information systems, computer programs, or evidence-based knowledge to assist in decision making with the aim to reduce errors and increase effectiveness. Decision support systems (DSS) help decision makers by providing information, rules, models, or predictions based on data and other inputs.

Deep Neural Network (DNN) A class of neural networks inspired by the structure and function of the human brain. DNN consists of multiple layers of artificial neurons that are interconnected.

Deep Reinforcement Learning (see also Reinforcement Learning) learning what to do—how to map situations to actions—so as to maximise a numerical reward signal. A learning system that wants something, that adapts its behaviour in order to maximise a special signal from its environment.

Descriptive analytics Using statistical techniques to describe or summarise a set of data. It is based on search and summary of historical data in order to identify patterns or meaning.

Diagnostic analytics Identify trends and behaviour pattern(s). A form of advanced analytics that examines data to determine the causes of trends and correlations between variables. It aims to understand the causes and factors that led to observed events or outcomes. Drill-down, data discovery, data mining, and correlations are among the techniques used in diagnostic analytics.

Dialogue design Common user interface design (patterns) allowing communication between computer and a human.

Diffusion of Innovation (DOI) Assumes for the rate of adoption to depend on the perceived attributes of innovation, type of innovation decision, communication channels, nature of the social system, extent of change and agent promotion effort (Roger, 1962). In the 1990s it was argued that tech innovations diffuse because of the cumulative decisions of individuals to adopt them.

Digital marketing Marketing that uses digital channels (internet and online-based digital technologies, e.g., websites, apps, mobile devices, social media and other digital platforms) to communicate with clients, to promote and sell products and services (see also Marketing).

Differential privacy based on the idea of "learning nothing about an individual while learning useful information about a population (see also Privacy).

Disruptive technology innovation that significantly alters the way that consumers, industries, or businesses operate.

Ease of use The degree of ease associated with the use of a system or effort expectancy. It is one of the core components of the Technology Acceptance Model (see also TAM).

Effort expectation (see also performance expectation) Fulfil the definition of one's desire to be in control and able to predict his or her surroundings.

Electronic Word of Mouth (eWOM) any positive or negative statement made by potential, actual, or former customers about a product or company, which is made available to a multitude of people and institutions via the Internet.

Embodied agents virtual, three-dimensional human characters that are displayed on computer screens, employing rendered, embodied interface and audible responses.

Empathy Reflects the capability to comprehend and react towards the feelings, thoughts, and experiences of others.

Empathic AI Ability of AI system to detect emotions and respond to them in an empathic way.

End user The ultimate human user of a software product. The term is used to distinguish people who only use the software from the developers of the system, who enhance the software for end users.

Engagement Reflects the degree of involvement and absorption by technology.

Enjoyment A core affect reflecting happiness. Linked to pleasurable experience. Interactional enjoyment is acknowledged to mediate the relationship between user satisfaction and intention to use a chatbot/AI system.

Experience A multidimensional construct that involves cognitive, emotional, behavioural, sensorial, social components.

Experiential journey The ongoing customer experience across the phases of a service cycle. The process a customer goes through, across all stages and touch points, that makes up the customer experience.

Exact matching of dynamic info (EDI) Classification involving categorisation of data based on its level of similarity and exactness when compared to other data. This classification helps in identifying which data records are exact matches, near matches, or unique records (see also Approximate matching of dynamic info, ADI).

Expectancy Theory of Motivation Postulates that motivation is a function of expectancy, instrumentality and valence. Individuals are motivated to select a specific behaviour over others, and thus, they will behave or act in a certain way, because of the expected result of that selected behaviour.

Explainability Ability to offer explainable models with high accuracy and performance; Enabling humans to understand, trust and to appropriately mange the AI.

Explainable AI (XAI) Reflects the ability of AI to offer explainable models (1) with high accuracy and performance; (2) by enabling humans to understand, to trust and to (3) appropriately mange the AI.

Explanation generation Deep networks generate their own human-understandable explanations as part of the explicit training of the system, both visual and textual.

FAT Fair, Accountable, and Transparent (FAT) algorithms.

FATML Fair, Accountable, and Transparent (FAT) algorithms and Interpretable Machine Learning (iML).

Fairness Presents model capacity to reach explainability without favouritism/discrimination.

Feedforward neural network (FNN) Is one of the two broad types of artificial neural network. It is characterised with a uni-directional flow. That means the information in the model flows in only one direction i.e. forward—from the input nodes, through the hidden nodes to the output nodes, without any cycles or loops (in contrast to recurrent neural networks, RNN).

Fidelity Reflects the capability of interpretable model in mimicking the behaviour of a black-box.

Filter bubble A state of intellectual isolation that can result from personalised searches, recommendation systems, and algorithmic curation.

Flexibility Reflects the possibility to accommodate complex and a wide variety of data in constructs of various formats and structures.

Flow theory Flow is experienced when perceived challenges and opportunities for action are in balance with the actor's skills. In the context of HCI experience, the flow incorporates the extent to which the user perceives (a) sense of control over the computer interaction, (b) attention focused on the interaction, (c) curiosity aroused during the interaction, and (d) the interaction is intrinsically interesting.

Foundation models (FM) Deep learning models trained on vast quantities of unstructured, unlabeled data that can be used for a wide range of tasks out of the box or adapted to specific tasks through fine-tuning. Examples of these models are GPT-4, PaLM, DALLE2, and Stable Diffusion.

Functionality Associated with a correct technical functioning, encompasses ease and usefulness of the system, functional and interface characteristics (see also Technology Acceptance Mosel, TAM).

Fuzzy logic Based on the observation that people make decisions based on imprecise and non-numerical information. It is employed to handle the concept of partial truth, where the truth value may range between completely true and completely false.

Generalisability Implementation of portable models that do not require special training regimes or restrictions. Generalisability provides transfer of the model through various application scenarios and the use of the same model with different data (see also Transferability).

Generative AI (GAI or GenAI) Artificial intelligence capable of generating text, images, or other data using generative models. GAI models learn the patterns and structure of their input training data and then generate new data that has similar characteristics.

Generative adversarial networks (GANs) A class of machine learning frameworks, consisting of the generator and the discriminator that compete with each other and are trained together simultaneously (see also InfoGAN).

Generative Pre-trained Transformer (GPT) A type of large language model (LLM), a prominent framework for generative artificial intelligence employed used in natural language processing tasks such as interpreting and producing language, recognising or creating images, and solving problems, in a way that mimics human performance (see ChatGPT).

Governing AI Range of policies, frameworks and practices implemented to ensure the responsible use of AI technologies.

Graphical user interface (GUI) A form of user interface that allows users to interact with electronic devices through graphical icons and visual indicators such as secondary notation.

Graphics processing units (GPUs) Computer chips that were originally developed for producing computer graphics (such as for video games) and are also useful for deep learning applications. In contrast, traditional machine learning and other analyses usually run on central processing units (CPUs), normally referred to as a computer's processor.

Gratification Theory Combines the social and psychological attributes of needs. In the mediated environment, individuals are assumed to be goal oriented and to select media that fit their needs (see also U&GT).

Human-Centric AI Human values are central to the way in which AI systems are developed, deployed, used and monitored. Respect for fundamental rights should also be ensured.

Informativeness Measures the quality of information. It was associated with the semantic success of the technology. The ability to extract information about the inner relations of a model. Model providing knowledge via outputs to human decision-makers.

InfoGAN Information-theoretic extension to the Generative Adversarial Network that is able to learn disentangled representations in a completely unsupervised manner (see also GAN).

Intelligent Assistance (IA) Software based agency that can perform a range of tasks or services for a user depending on user input such as commands or questions, including verbal ones.

Interactivity Emphasises the role of interaction between the user and the system. Reflecting the ability of a model/AI system to be interactive with the user. When individuals interact more easily with a technological system, they will perceive greater efficacy.

Internet of Things (IoT) Devices with sensors, processing ability, software and other technologies that connect and exchange data with other devices and systems over the Internet or other communications networks.

Interpretability The ability to explain or to provide the meaning in understandable terms to a human. This means that predictions, classifications, decision making, and recommendations for actions should be interpretable (see also Low Interpretability).

Interpretable CNNs Disentangling CNN features into human interpretable graphical representation (see also Convolutional Neural Network, CNN).

Hidden Markov Models (HMM) A statistical model that represents a system containing hidden states where the system evolves over time. As the state of the system is not directly visible to the observer, it is called "hidden". The observer can only see some output that depends on the state.

Large language model (LLM) A deep learning algorithm that can perform a variety of natural language processing (NLP). LLM operate using transformer models and employ massive/large datasets for being trained.

Levels of Automation (LOA) Refers to the degree to which a task is automated (see also Automation).

Linear proxy model A local linear model that serves as a simplified proxy for the full model in the neighbourhood of the input.

Low interpretability Associated with the passive properties of a learning model. Characterised by high discrimination power, deep neural networks still have low interpretability of their black-box representation (see also interpretability).

Machine learning (ML) A field of AI concerned with the development and study of statistical algorithms. It explores the problem of learning from data without being explicitly programmed. ML is split into three major areas: supervised, unsupervised and reinforcement learning.

Machine learning algorithms Consist of a set of tools for classification and prediction using structured and unstructured data (e.g., text, image, video, audio) in a variety of application domains. Employing several methods and tools they aim to reduce the complexity of data and search for hidden patterns among a huge quantity of clustered data.

Marketing The activity, set of institutions, and processes for creating, communicating, delivering, and exchanging offerings that have value for customers, clients, partners, and society at large.

Marketing research The function that links the consumer, customer, and public to the marketer through information.

Misinformation Related to incorrect data, fake data, false inputs, errors. Thus, fact checking and ML algorithms are enabled to detect and deal with misinformation.

Motivation to use Individuals are assumed to be goal oriented and to select system (product) that fit their needs.

Multilayer perceptron (MLP) Feedforward artificial neural network, consisting of fully connected neurons with a nonlinear kind of activation function, organised in at least three layers, notable for being able to distinguish data that is not linearly separable.

Natural language processing (NLP) Is primarily concerned with giving computers the ability to support and manipulate human language. Computers capable of "understanding" the contents of documents, are supposed to accurately extract information and insights contained in the documents as well as to categorise and organise documents themselves.

Neural network A computational learning system that uses a network of functions to understand and translate a data input of one form into a desired output. The concept of the artificial neural network was inspired by the way neurons of the human brain function (see also Convolutional Neural Network, CNN).

Normative social influence Social influence that leads to conformity, i.e., influence of other people that leads individual to conform in order to be liked and accepted by them (see also Subjective social norm).

Para-Social Relationship Accounts for the mediated interaction. It originates from media communication theories arguing for the illusion of face-to-face relationship with the performer. In the AI context, agent–human relationships are assumed when a media user engages with a media persona, in an illusionary mediated experience.

Pathways Language Model (PaLM) A large language model developed by Google AI. It aims to address the issue of long-term context modelling in natural language processing (NLP) tasks.

Performance expectation (see also Effort expectation) Fulfilling the definition of one's desire to be in control and able to predict his or her surroundings.

Performance deviation The failure of system to meet expectations in all aspects of performance, such as production, efficiency, quality, profitability, safety, or any other goal or standard against which are measured (see also Benchmark).

Personalisation Users are presented with recommendations or information feeds that are tailored to their tastes/preferences (see also AI personalisation).

Personal care Reflects the need for personal attention, understanding, and empathy.

Predictive analytics Aim to uncover relationships and patterns within large volumes of data that can be used to predict behaviour and events. Applying machine learning to generate a predictive model for certain business application (i.e. predict future outcomes, based on previous data).

Predictive power The demonstrated ability to be precise, accurate and to drive significant value. Concerning marketing, predictive power is associated with the capability of big data analytics to drive strategic value relative to the costs of data acquisition, management, integration, and real-time feature construction.

Prediction vector tampering Restriction of the output to the top k classes or predictions of a model.

Prescriptive analytics Providing personalised recommendations for intervention. Uses technology and large data sets to make better decision, suggesting optimisation of models and methods (see also Suggestive analytics).

Presence The degree to which the medium facilitates awareness of the other person, event, environment. A subjective experience of being in one place or environment and it could be achieved even when one is physically situated in another environment. Characterised with a submerge of the perceptual system of the user through a mediated environment (see also Social presence).

Programmatic Ads Automated bidding and placement of ads on a given platform. Characterised with advertiser-defined parameters to purchase digital ad inventory across the web, mobile, apps, video, and social media, it is real-time buying and selling of ad inventory through automated bidding system.

Privacy Reflects the protection of sensitive information, e.g., in the data, algorithms. It also concerns the control of how personal data are gathered, stored, processed, and disseminated.

Privacy leak Leak of data and model information, mainly due to the way the AI system is constructed.

Purchase intent Describes the extent to which customers are willing and inclined to buy a product or service from a company within a certain period of time.

Quality *R*eflects the (system) success. In the chatbot context, it was addressed as information and communication quality (measuring semantic success), system quality (measuring technical success), and service quality (measuring organisational impact and effectiveness success).

Recommendation The action of recommending, e.g., spreading positive word of mouth.

Recommender systems Machine learning systems widely used in eCommerce to provide tailored and personalised recommendations to customers based on their past behaviour and preferences.

Recurrent Neural Networks (RNN) Is one of the two broad types of artificial neural network. It is characterised with a bi-directional flow of information between its layers. That means to allow the output from some nodes to affect subsequent input to the same nodes (see also Feedforward neural network, FNN).

Reinforcement Learning Concerns itself with agents that make observations of the environment and use these to take actions with the goal of maximising a reward signal. In general, the set of actions is not predefined and the rewards are not necessarily immediate but can occur after a sequence of actions.

Reliability The ability to maintain certain levels of performance irrespective from small variations of the parameters or independently of the input data (see also Robustness).

Representation disentanglement Disentangled representations have individual dimensions that describe meaningful and independent factors of variation.

Risk Associated with a perceived threat to an individual's privacy. In the chatbot/AI context, it was acknowledged to reflect the increased level of information that technology gathers on individuals beyond their knowledge and sometimes control.

Robustness The ability to maintain certain levels of performance irrespective from small variations of the parameters or independently of the input data (see also Reliability).

Robust AI Robustness of an AI system encompasses both its technical robustness (appropriate in a given context, such as the application domain or life cycle phase) and as well as its robustness from a social perspective (ensuring that the AI system duly takes into account the context and environment in which the system operates).

Safety (see also security) System being protected from danger; safeguarding against potential risks.

Salience mapping DL approach where a network is repeatedly tested with portions of the input occluded to create a map showing which parts of the data actually have influence on the network output.

Satisfaction Occurs when customers find that products or services meet or exceed their positive expectations.

Scalability Opens opportunity to scale up to large input data with large input spaces.

Self-Determination Theory (SDT) Assumes that the basis for human self-motivation and personality integration is investigated in line with people's inherent growth tendencies and innate psychological needs, i.e., the needs for competence, relatedness and autonomy (see also Self-regulation theory).

Self-efficacy Individual's belief in their capacity to act in the ways necessary to accomplish a task, to reach specific goals. The theory of self-efficacy lies at the center of Bandura's Social Cognitive Theory (see also hereby), which emphasises the role of observational learning and social experience in the development of personality.

Self-regulation theory Postulates conscious, personal management that involves the process of guiding one's own thoughts, behaviours and feelings to reach goals. Four components of self-regulation were suggested, i.e., standards of desirable behaviour; motivation to meet standards; monitoring of situations; and willpower, internal strength to control urges (see also Self-Determination Theory).

Self-service technology (SST) Technological interfaces allowing customers to produce services independent of involvement of direct service employee. Replacing many face-to-face service interactions, SST aim at providing more accurate, convenient and faster services.

Search engine optimisation (SEO) The process of improving the quality and quantity of website traffic to a website or a web page from search engines.

Security (see also Safety) System being protected from danger; safeguarding against potential risks.

Service robots Autonomous and/or operated by built-in control systems that are supposed to assist humans and to performs useful tasks for them.

Social agent Agent demonstrating social behaviour. Increased number of human-like features attributed to an artificial agent leads to stronger human-like behaviour. Translating the social rules of human-to-human communication in the chatbot context, lead people to act as if they were in a conversation with another human, presumably due to the interpretation of the interaction as being social.

Social Agency Theory (SAT) Postulates that social cues in a multimedia message can prime the social conversation schema in the learner. Once the social conversation schema is activated, learners are highly likely to act as if they are in a conversation with another person. In the HCI context, social cues (e.g., modulated intonation and the human-like appearance of a computer) encourage people to interpret the interaction with a computer as being social in nature.

Social media Refers to new forms of media—interactive technologies that involve interactive participation, presumably in user-centric manner. It enables communal activity that facilitate the creation, sharing and aggregation of content, ideas, interests, and other forms of expression through virtual communities and networks.

Social media chatbots A software agent that communicates autonomously on social media. It may use artificial intelligence and machine learning to express messages in more natural human dialogue.

Social cognition Postulates a central role of cognitive processes in social interactions. It focuses on how people process, store, and apply information about other people and social situations.

Social Cognitive Theory (SCT) Accords a central role to cognitive, vicarious, self-reflective, and self-regulatory processes. People draw on their knowledge, cognitive and behavioural skills to produce desired results, by acting as agents in their environments (see also Social learning theory and Self-efficacy).

Social Learning Theory (SLT) Assumes that people learn by observing others in the context of their social interactions and experiences. Put differently, people's development is influenced by the environment, others' behaviour, and cognition.

Social influence Reflects the ways in which individuals adjust their behavior to meet the demands of a social environment. In the tech context, it was associated with the degree to which an individual perceives that important others believe that he or she should use the new system/technology.

Social Influence Theory (SIT) It accounts for three processes responsible for attitude change. These include compliance, internalisation, and identification. Introduced by Kelman (1958).

Social presence Sense of being with another in a mediated environment. It refers to the extent to which a medium is perceived as sociable, warm, sensitive, personal or intimate when it is used to interact with other people (see also Presence).

Social Presence Theory (SPT) Assumes that media outlets with a high degree of social presence are judged as warm, personal, sensitive and sociable. It encounters for awareness of and the representation of the other, the medium's capacity for social interaction and, the presence (or absence) of verbal or nonverbal cues in mediated communication.

Social Response Theory (SRT) Argues that humans apply social rules when they interact with machines and computers, assuming that computers are social actors. Although humans interact with computers mindlessly, they employ social rules similarly in what they do in human-human interaction such as politeness, self-disclosure, and trust.

Stickiness The intention of user to continue using system, product service.

Structured data Tabular data (for example, organised in tables, databases, or spreadsheets) that can be used to train some machine learning models effectively.

Subjective social norm Reflects the notion of subjective norm, i.e. what significant others might think of one's actions (see also Normative social influence).

Suggestive analytics Optimisation of models and methods, providing personalised recommendations for intervention (see also Prescriptive analytics).

Supervised Learning In supervised learning, a model f with parameters θ is a function between inputs x and the desired outputs $y = f(x; \theta)$, where x is a vector of attributes or features with dimensionality n. The data is known as training data D, and consists of a set of training examples. The output or label y can assume different dimensions depending on the learning task.

Support Vector Machines (SVMs) Where the support vectors are data points from the training dataset.

Swarm intelligence (SI) The collective behaviour of decentralised, self-organised systems, natural or artificial. The concept is employed in work on artificial intelligence.

Technology Acceptance Model (TAM) Addresses the ability to predict peoples' acceptance of technology, by measuring their intentions, and the ability to explain the intentions in terms of attitudes, subjective norms, perceived usefulness, and perceived ease of use (suggested by Davis et al., 1989).

Theory of Planned Behaviour (TPB) Assumes that intentions to perform behaviours of different kinds can be predicted with high accuracy from the following core components: attitudes towards the behaviour, subjective norms, and perceived behavioural control. An extension of the Theory of Reasoned Action, TRA (see also TRA).

Theory of Reasoned Action (TRA) Assumes that consumers' attitudes towards an object depend on the beliefs they have about several of its attributes. The core objective of TRA is to operationalise attitudes toward behaviour, i.e., attitudes toward the act (rather than just attitudes toward the object). It also recognises the role of normative belief, referred to as subjective norm, i.e., the power of other people to influence what an individual does.

Text mining The process of deriving high-quality information from text. Known also as Text data mining (TDM) or text analytics, it can automatically extract information from different written resources. Information extraction, data mining, and a knowledge discovery in databases have been acknowledged as three different perspectives of text mining.

Token Smaller text units like words, characters, or subwords.

Traceability Refers to the AI capability to keep track of the system's data, development and deployment processes, typically by means of documented recorded identification.

Transferability Provides transfer of the model through various application scenarios and the use of the same model with different data (see also Generalisability).

Transparency Human "seeing through" the AI decision and action. Human being in continuous and direct control of AI performance.

Trust The willingness to rely on exchange partners in whom one has confidence. Trust depends on social interaction and control. It plays central role in adoption of AI based technologies.

Trustworthy AI Having the confidence of human users that a model/system will perform well.

Uncanny Valley A hypothesised relation between an object's degree of resemblance to a human being and the emotional response to the object.

Uncanny Valley Theory Assumes that if a robot becomes more humanlike, observers' emotional response becomes increasingly positive and empathetic, until it reaches a point beyond which the response quickly turns in revulsion. In other words, if bots are made too humanlike, they are at risk of inducing an uncanny feeling in users. Uncanniness was associated with a sense of dislike, unease, and unpleasantness.

Understandability Functional understanding of the model, and what it predicts, without necessary to explain model internal structure or algorithmic functioning and data processing.

Unified Theory of Acceptance and Use of Technology (UTAUT) An extension of the Technology acceptance model, TAM. It encompasses four core determinants of intention and usage, and up to four moderators of key relationships. The direct determinants of user acceptance and usage behaviour are performance expectancy, effort expectancy, social influence, and facilitating conditions. The moderators were hypothesised in terms of attitudes toward using technology, self-efficacy, and anxiety.

Unique selling point (USP) The marketing strategy of informing customers about how one's own brand or product is superior to its competitors (in addition to its other values).

Unstructured data Lack a consistent format or structure (for example, text, images, and audio files) and typically require more advanced techniques to extract insights

Unsupervised Learning The training set D consists only of the inputs x_i. Unsupervised algorithms aim to find structure or patterns in the data without having access to labels (see also Supervised Learning)

Usability Extent to which a system, product or service can be used by specified users to achieve specified goals with effectiveness, efficiency and satisfaction in a specified context of use.

User A person who utilises a computer, network service, device.

User experience (UX) Looking at the individual's entire interaction with the system, product, as well as the thoughts, feelings, and perceptions that result from that interaction

Uses and Gratification Theory (U&GT) Combines the social and psychological attributes of needs. In particular, five categories of needs were recognised, i.e., cognitive, affective, personal integrative, social integrative, and tension-free needs (see also Gratification Theory)

Usefulness Derives from the word useful "capable of being used advantageously". Defined as the degree to which a person believes that using a particular system would enhance his or her job performance, it is a core component of the Technology Acceptance Model (see also TAM).

Variational autoencoders (VAEs) A probabilistic architecture consisting of two major aspects, the encoder, and the decoder network.

Versatility Reflects the variety of customer analytics initiatives and applications.

Virtual assistant Is a software agent that can perform various tasks or services for a user. It operates receiving commands or questions, including verbal ones by the user.

Voice assistance A voice assistant is a software application that can understand human language and perform a variety of tasks including answering questions, making calls, sending messages, etc. Such technologies often incorporate chatbot capabilities to simulate human conversation. After a question or command is addressed to the voice assistant, it is converted by Automatic Speech Recognition (ASR) to enable the device to recognise and translate it from speech to text. Once the text is generated, the voice assistant uses Natural Language Processing (NLP) to understand the meaning of the text and determine the appropriate response. By using Text-to-Speech (TTS) technology VA converts the response back into speech.

Author Index

Subject Index

Printed in the United States
by Baker & Taylor Publisher Services